# THE ESSENTIAL
# ROBERT FROST

First Warbler Press Edition 2025

*A Boy's Will* first published in 1913 by David Nutt, London, and by Holt, New York, in 1915; *North of Boston* first published in 1914 by David Nutt, London, and by Holt, New York, in 1914; *Mountain Interval* first published in 1916 by Holt, New York; *New Hampshire* first published in 1923 by Holt, New York.

Introduction and Notes © 2025 William E. Cain

"Robert Frost on Poetry" excerpted from Louis Mertins, *Robert Frost: Life and Talks-Walking*. Norman: University of Oklahoma Press, 1965. 197–198.

ISBN 978-1-965684-36-8 (paperback)
ISBN 978-1-965684-33-7(ebook)

Library of Congress Control Number: 2025931209

warblerpress.com
New York, NY

# THE ESSENTIAL ROBERT FROST

## COLLECTED POEMS
## 1913-1923

INTRODUCTION AND NOTES BY
### WILLIAM E. CAIN

warbler classics

# CONTENTS

## North of Boston

## Mountain Interval

### New Hampshire

One thing I care about, and wish young people could care about, is taking poetry as the first form of understanding. If poetry isn't understanding all, the whole world, then it isn't worth anything.

—Robert Frost

# INTRODUCTION

What I am interested in emphasizing is the sentence of
sound, because to me a sentence is not interesting merely
in conveying a meaning of words; it must do something
more; it must convey a meaning by sound.
                                           —Robert Frost, 1915

It's tone I'm in love with; that's what poetry is, tone.
                                           —Robert Frost, 1962

THIS INTRODUCTION HAS three parts. In Part 1, I talk about what
it's like to read Frost, especially for someone coming to him for
the first time. His poems engage us; they're accessible and enjoyable.
But when we reread and linger over them, we start to realize they
offer more, much more—that they are deep, complex, and mysteri-
ous. With the help of passages from Frost's letters, interviews, and
essays, I turn in Part 2 to a more detailed account of his approach to
poetry, and to his comments on his literary intentions, notably his
fondness for and commitment to sounds, to tones of voice. In Part 3,
I develop and review what we've learned, offering a few final tips for
responding to the work of this great poet.

## PART 1: READING FROST

When I was in grammar school and high school in the 1960s, we
were obliged to memorize many poems by the so-called American
"fireside poets": Henry Wadsworth Longfellow, William Cullen
Bryant, John Greenleaf Whittier, James Russell Lowell, and Oliver
Wendell Holmes Sr. Memorization isn't done much today: anything
we want to remember takes just a few taps on our cell phones. These
poets aren't studied in classrooms, and I wonder whether they're

being read at all. They seem long ago and far away, sentimental, too intent on making verse an occasion for moral betterment. But when I was young, they were popular, and my literature courses devoted ample time to them.

So, when one of my teachers in college said that Robert Frost's first book was titled *A Boy's Will*, I heard the echo of Longfellow's nostalgic poem about childhood, "My Lost Youth" (1855), with the haunting lines that he repeats to conclude each of his ten stanzas:

> A boy's will is the wind's will,
> And the thoughts of youth are long, long thoughts.

When Frost was a boy, growing up in San Francisco, California, then moving, at age eleven, to Massachusetts and next to New Hampshire, his mother often read to him poetry of all kinds, and he came to share her passion for it. In the late nineteenth century and into the early twentieth, Longfellow's poetry was everywhere in homes and schools and was highly esteemed. Frost knew it intimately and cherished it in his youth and throughout his life. Here, he is connecting himself to Longfellow and the tradition he was part of. Frost imitates and draws upon this venerable poet's styles and themes, and he adapts them, changes them, making them new in a conception of poetry that's uniquely Frost's own.

The first poem in *A Boy's Will* is titled "Into My Own." We see it's in first-person, but even more we should hear it's in first-person. Frost is interested in what we see on the page and in what we hear when we read his words and lines out loud. For him, what mattered about Longfellow and other poets he read was not only their sense, but their sound.

Let's look at and listen to the first stanza:

> One of my wishes is that those dark trees,
> So old and firm they scarcely show the breeze,
> Were not, as 'twere, the merest mask of gloom,
> But stretched away unto the edge of doom.

Can you hear the sound patterns? Frost is writing in iambic pentameter, ten syllables per line, the first unstressed, the second stressed, the third unstressed, and so on. He uses this meter, but not strictly.

INTRODUCTION

Sometimes he departs from it. There's rhyme: trees/breeze, gloom/
doom; elision of sound, "wishes is"; internal rhyme, were/'twere; and
alliteration, "merest mask."

Notice all the words are one or two syllables. The stanza has a nice
rhythm, which you and I can appreciate each time we read it out
loud or hear it resonating in our inner ear.

Frost makes his lines reassuring: he's using poetic devices to create
effects of sound that most of us are familiar with. His first readers,
coming to "Into My Own" from their experience of Longfellow and
poets like him, would have been well-acquainted with such sounds.

Something happens, however, when we pause for a moment,
glance back, and reflect on what we have read and heard, something
that's both interesting and perplexing.

Start with the title, a phrase many of us know, and from which we
proceed into the opening stanza. "Into My Own": when we give the
phrase a little thought, we see and hear how evocative it is. It refers
to reaching maturity, finding one's identity in the world. You and I
might say "into my own" to express a confidence we're developing
in ourselves, an independence. We're starting to reach our potential,
maybe achieving some recognition too.

It's a phrase that's used about writers, painters, and musicians, an
artist who formerly has been a student, an apprentice, and who is
moving into an authentic style. "She's coming into her own": that is,
she's making a place for herself, working capably, with distinction.

Frost's a poet we enjoy reading, and he's a poet we want and need
to reread. Look again, listen again, and we find his poems surprise
us. They're subtle and stimulating. There's more to them than we
realized.

I recall a passage in a letter Frost wrote to his friend Louis
Untermeyer, January 1, 1917:

You get more credit for thinking if you restate formulae or cite
cases that fall in easily under formulae, but all the fun is outside
saying things that suggest formulae that won't formulate—that
almost but don't quite formulate. I should like to be so subtle at
this game as to seem to the casual person altogether obvious.
The casual person would assume that I meant nothing or else I
came near enough meaning something he was familiar with to
mean it for all practical purposes.

Frost likes to look and sound obvious to a casual reader, and, in a way, it's fine with him if that's the response a reader wishes to have. But he seeks a deliberate reader, an attentive one who perceives his cleverness and ingenuity. He invokes formulas and common views, and then gives twists and turns to them. For Frost, that's where, as he often said, the "fun" is.

He made a related point two decades later, in an essay about the poet E. A. Robinson:

> The style is the man. Rather say the style is the way the man takes himself; and to be at all charming or even bearable, the way is almost rigidly prescribed. If it is with outer seriousness, it must be with inner humor. If it is with outer humor, it must be with inner seriousness. Neither one alone without the other under it will do.

Frost takes two attitudes toward his subjects and implies that readers of his work should do the same. If the poem seems serious, we should look at and listen for the humor that accompanies it; if the poem has humor on its surface, then we ought to expect there's a seriousness to it too. When we read a Frost poem, we should be aware he's giving more than first appears. He takes delight in doing this; he relishes being playful, making adroit use of wit and craft to give readers appealing experiences that turn out to reach far. Readers must know how and where to look for Frost's artfulness and what to listen for.

When Frost read his poems in public, he emphasized he wasn't "reciting" them; he was "saying" them. He wrote with care, precision, and delicacy, but he didn't want to give the impression he was reading from a script, lines of type sitting on the page. He was voicing words as though the lines were not in the printed text but, rather, in the person speaking out loud.

Let's return to "Into My Own." Line one begins, "One of my wishes," and this indicates to us the speaker has a single wish he will tell us about, among several wishes he has. "Those dark trees": the speaker is pointing to those trees over there, which he is seeing and we hear about from him, yet cannot see ourselves. They're visible to the speaker, not to us.

The trees are "dark," line one, and "old," line two. But it's not only that they're dark and old; they're "firm," able to resist the breeze. Though not entirely: Frost writes "scarcely show" and that's different from not at all. Nor does he use the word I just used: "resist." He says the trees do not "show" the breeze, as if it were something they were choosing not to display.

What is a "breeze"? The word derives from Old Spanish and Portuguese, *briza*, a northeast wind, gentle, light, refreshing, associated with pleasant weather conditions. Some readers might recall William Wordsworth's line about daffodils "fluttering and dancing in the breeze," and poems about breezes by John Keats and Percy Bysshe Shelley. Frost had lots of English and American poems in his memory, and these three poets were among his favorites. The associations are there for us if we know the poems and want to make comparisons. But Frost's poem doesn't depend on them, and we can be pleased and satisfied simply with the words he has given us.

The first two lines create an expectation about the trees—that they are something, that they mean or do something. What will this be? But the start of line three is a negative, "Were not," with the stress of the meter falling on "not" to accent it. And why, we might wonder, is Frost using the old-fashioned phrase "as 'twere"?

"The merest mask": this sounds almost like a put-down—that the trees are a mask, but not a formidable or threatening one. "The merest mask of gloom": "gloom" means partial or total darkness, a dim or dark place; it also means a state of depression or melancholy, lowness of spirit, despondency. Is this a feature and fact about the dark trees, or a projection of the speaker's mood upon them, the wish he touched on in line one?

Frost's speaker says he wishes the dark trees were not this mere mask, but "stretched away unto the edge of doom." He makes the distinction sharp by locating "But" at the beginning of line four, and he gets a keen effect, the feeling of something being extended, through the word "stretched," which is one syllable, yet which takes a moment to read, that is, to say, out loud.

There's a pickup in the pace that completes itself with the rhyme of "doom" with "gloom." Doom: this word originates from Old English *dōm*, "judgment" or "decree"; it means judgment, decree, law, fate, destiny; it connotes death, destruction, an impending or inevitable tragic end. In religious contexts, it refers to the Day of Judgment, the end of the world. Yet all this is not quite accurate, for Frost says he wishes the trees stretched to "the edge" of doom, not across and into it.

Readers have said they find Frost's poems charming, but I'm not sure that's the term I would use. To me, Frost is seductive, beguiling. His sounds attract us to the world of each poem; the plain language makes us feel welcome, not deterred, never intimidated, as we do when we read other modern poets whose work teems with abstruse words and recondite phrases, fragments from foreign languages, and allusions and references to figures from the past and historical events. When we make our way through Frost's poems, we feel we know where we are, enjoy what we hear, and understand what he's saying.

For many of us, that's what we think and feel when we read Frost, but there's another moment, the one when we notice a detail, wonder about an image, and start to ask questions. From there, we think about other details, in a form almost of a double-take. We pass into a second response and awareness, that there is more to the lines than we thought, that they are accessible yet enigmatic. We could saunter through one poem and amble to the next, but once we reflect on the poem we are reading, it becomes hard to release ourselves from it.

As I say this, I'm led to this poem below, which Frost first used in italics as an introduction to *North of Boston* and later, not italicized, as the poem that opened the *Collected Poems* he assembled in 1930 and again in his *Complete Poems*, 1949:

### The Pasture

I'm going out to clean the pasture spring;
I'll only stop to rake the leaves away
(And wait to watch the water clear, I may)
I sha'n't be gone long.—You come too.

I'm going out to fetch the little calf
That's standing by the mother. It's so young,
It totters when she licks it with her tongue.
I sha'n't be gone long.—You come too.

We know what a "pasture" is: land covered with grass and other low plants suitable for animals grazing in the daytime, especially cattle or sheep. This poem has simple settings, simple actions, not unsettling or provocative. There are two stanzas, each with three lines in iambic pentameter (ten syllables) and a fourth in iambic tetrameter (eight syllables). It has rhymes, basic vocabulary, nothing hard, no allusions or references we need to track down the meaning of.

Stanza one, there's the man's good cleaning, with a pun on "spring," a place where water wells up from an underground source, and the season between winter and summer when vegetation begins to appear. Stanza two is cute, sweet—the little calf and its mother. "Totters": from Middle Dutch *touteren*, "to swing," the original sense in English; to move in a feeble or unsteady way. A genial invitation comes from the speaker to the reader, from Frost to us: he'd like us to join him, "you come too." It seems and sounds familiar: we can visualize the scenes whether we've been on a farm in the countryside or not.

This short poem is pleasant and remains that way. But once we take it in and begin thinking about it, our attention caught by this detail or that one leading to others, "The Pasture" deepens. It feels alluring, and strange, quietly baffling, a little uncanny.

We might ask: Why did Frost choose to remove this poem from the first text of *North of Boston* and locate it at the outset of his *Collected Poems*? What might this decision, this poem, be saying to us about our movement into the books of poems that follow?

Who is this speaker? Is he a stand-in for the poet Frost? Or is there a speaker and Frost at a distance, offering a perspective on his speaker and on these settings and actions? Is the tone meant to be approving, or ironic?

The speaker is going to do something: clean the pasture spring. But no more than that, only raking away the leaves. He'll wait to watch the water become clear. No, that's not accurate, because as this parenthetical line ends, he says, "I may." He may; he may not. We might accompany him, since he will not be gone long. On the other hand: if he'll not be gone long, perhaps we should remain where we are.

What's the transition to the second stanza? There isn't one. Is the fetching of the little calf to occur next? Or has the speaker decided to fetch the calf instead of cleaning the spring? Why is he telling us about the calf and its mother? How does he intend for us to respond to this detail?

"Totters" is a tender word, the unsteady legs of this creature new to the world. But some of us might have to guard against a more disquieting meaning: to shake or sway as if about to collapse; insecure or about to fail. This will not happen, not now. But it could, and that's where all creation is headed over time, long-term. There's birth, the aging process, decay, death, like leaves falling from trees. The leaves come back: we do not.

How are we to hear the second "You come too?" The first time it's a friendly invitation. Is that the tone now? Or is it an injunction, even a command, as if the speaker were making an offer we dare not refuse?

At this juncture, we might recall that "pasture" also refers to a person's situation in life, as we know from everyday experience and from reading literature. "Pasture" evokes images of an idyllic rural landscape, pastoral care, harmony between human beings and nature. But there's also the phrase "being put out to pasture," in common currency by the late nineteenth century. It's to retire someone or something when they are considered too old or no longer useful for their previous role. This expression comes from the practice of putting old horses out to graze in a pasture, allowing them to live out their remaining years away from work, signifying retirement, but also obsolescence, out of date.

Once more, we're seeing and sensing that there are two approaches to reading Frost, two ways of thinking about what a Frost poem is and does. There's the poem at first encounter, the moment of impact. And there's the poem when we take our time with it, giving it a slow look and listen, living with it. We could say we then read it in slow motion, as an opportunity for contemplation. We perceive how it's organized, that it's gratifying and cryptic.

It's hard to explain, but I think we're aware of this on some level the first time through. We sense more is happening than we know, than we can put into words. Frost is writing with supreme skill and sensitivity, making adept use of meter, rhyme, and rhythm. The word choices, the lines and stanzas, the sentences he constructs: it's beautifully done. These are the feelings that come to us first, and that in many poems soothe and hearten us. But, again, this detail, or that one, catches our eyes and ears, something we notice, a word choice or image or sound. We reflect on why the poem affects us as it does, what might be within and underneath it that made us respond to it as we did. The poem gets hold of us. We remember lines and stanzas without even making the effort to do so.

Here's another poem from *A Boy's Will*, a sonnet titled "Mowing." The title is one word, an action, an ongoing one. In the table of contents for the first edition of *A Boy's Will*, Frost inserted sentences of summary for each poem, including this for "Mowing": "He takes up life simply with the small tasks." "Mowing" appears to express this dictum—that what counts is a life of simplicity that's grounded in duties and obligations. That's what's good, what we should strive for:

> There was never a sound beside the wood but one,
> And that was my long scythe whispering to the ground.
> What was it it whispered? I knew not well myself;
> Perhaps it was something about the heat of the sun,
> Something, perhaps, about the lack of sound—
> And that was why it whispered and did not speak.
> It was no dream of the gift of idle hours,
> Or easy gold at the hand of fay or elf:
> Anything more than the truth would have seemed too weak
> To the earnest love that laid the swale in rows,
> Not without feeble-pointed spikes of flowers
> (Pale orchises), and scared a bright green snake.
> The fact is the sweetest dream that labor knows.
> My long scythe whispered and left the hay to make.

Some of my students don't know what a "scythe" is. I tell them it's a tool for cutting crops such as grass or wheat, with a long, curved blade at the end of a long pole attached to which are one or two short handles. "Fay," I explain, is fairy. "Swale": a low or hollow place, a marshy depression between ridges. "Orchises": an orchid that's native to north temperate regions, characterized by a tuberous root and an erect fleshy stem bearing a spike of purple or pinkish flowers. But that's all I need to do. Frost has chosen words that are warm and supportive in their plainness.

When I read a poem like "Mowing," with its cordial idiom, I admire the beauty of the phrasing, the fineness (as I hear it) of the sentiment. Yet then, as so often, I hesitate: what is it that this line, and that one, and the next, mean? This poem is captivating, and puzzling as well. Each line is lucid, but also cagey, not quite graspable.

The sounds, the whispering scythe—lovely and enchanting. Then again, a scythe, a tool, doesn't whisper, though the person who swings it might. We might not notice this nuance when we first read and listen to the poem. That only comes later, when we return to the words and put some pressure on them.

The first six lines are a single sentence, as are the next six. Frost concludes with two sentences, each a line in length. The first sounds exactly right: "The fact is the sweetest dream that labor knows." The challenge is to understand it. The next and final sentence is both decisive and wistful, plaintive: "My long scythe whispered and left the hay to make." What's the meaning here, and why has Frost chosen this line to conclude the speaker's story?

Frost gives an adjective, "sweetest," to "dream," but not one to either "fact" or "labor." For the second time, he says the scythe is long. Is that significant? It must be, but in what way? When we think about mowing a field of hay, we may take for granted we would use a tool with length and weight that makes a wide cut as it's swung.

The speaker is a mower with his scythe. But he doesn't depict himself in the act of mowing. The most personalized element is the whispering scythe. "The fact is the sweetest dream that labor knows": I come back to this austere line. It sounds perfect. I wonder what it means.

In the final line, it's the scythe that whispers—nothing about the speaker, other than that this tool belongs to him. The final phrase, "and left the hay to make," creates an impression that's straightforward and profound. The syntax declares it's the scythe that does the leaving—leaving the hay to make…. To make what? To make how?

Frost is tantalizing, always somewhere beyond me, on the other side of my complete understanding. I've found that a close reading of Frost doesn't lead to a final statement about what his poems mean. I'm not certain we ever reach that point in our responses, yet this increases my pleasure in him. Reading Frost closely is an activity that the movement and tone of his lines, sentences, and stanzas intimate we don't really need to do, for, so it seems, the meanings are felicitously there for us to take in all along the way. But then we pause and read him more closely, and the poems become more powerful, intellectually and emotionally.

It's fascinating, almost eerie—and maybe this gets at why I enjoy Frost so much. The meanings of his poems are there for us to think and talk about, but, in my experience, I don't feel I reach the end of the process. I never get to the bottom of him. There's always more each time, something beyond my past summaries and descriptions. Frost's a poet who resists and evades close reading even as he beckons for and rewards it.

I'd like to invite you to turn to the poems on your own for a while, keeping in mind some of the thoughts about Frost I've described. Begin with *A Boy's Will*, and then move into and among the poems in the later three books: *North of Boston, Mountain Interval*, and *New Hampshire.* Perhaps you'll feel you've accepted Frost's summons to browse and roam in his pasture of poems. You'll see that some of them are long, three, four, or more pages. For now, you might pass them by, giving your attention instead to shorter poems that are easier to take in. We'll say more about the longer poems later. Read around, jot down some notes about the experience you're having. Give yourself time to begin knowing Frost, how he operates as a poet.

What makes this literary experience special? Which poems are your favorites and why? Are there some you like less than others? Anything that surprises you, that you didn't expect to find? In what ways is Frost speaking to you, one to one, personally?

## Part 2: Sentence-Sounds

Remember the phrase "edge of doom" from the poem "Into My Own"? It's succinct, three words, three syllables, linked by the "d" sounds. I liked the phrase for years—it's a classic Frost touch. But then one day I was reading Shakespeare's sonnets and noticed this phrase in one of them. Frost didn't invent it. He borrowed it from Shakespeare, Sonnet 116, which begins, "Let me not to the marriage of true minds / Admit impediments." Lines 11–12 are:

> Love alters not with his brief hours and weeks,
> But bears it out even to the edge of doom.

We think of Frost as an American poet, and he identified himself in these terms, stating his admiration for the poetry of his fellow Americans Longfellow, Ralph Waldo Emerson, and Emily Dickinson. "American" applies also to the characters, speakers, settings, and subjects of his literary work.

From 1900 to 1911, Frost and his family lived on a farm in Derry, New Hampshire, where he raised chickens and grew vegetables, and he taught at Pinkerton Academy, a secondary school nearby. In 1911, he took a position at Plymouth Normal School in Plymouth, New Hampshire. "Normal" comes from the French "école normale," which refers to schools that provide instruction in the norms or standards of teaching, training students in pedagogy for careers in the field of education. Frost was laboring on the land in a rural American region, and he was teaching in the classrooms of American schools. He wrote most of his first book, more than half of his second, and much of his third during this decade in Derry and Plymouth.

At the most significant juncture of Frost's career, however, he was not only an American poet, but also an Anglo-American one. I almost want to exaggerate and say he was in his heart and mind an English poet, and that's because in November 1911, Frost sold the Derry farm, resigned from his teaching position, and, with the benefit of some money he'd saved and inherited, made plans to journey with his family to England. He lived there until February 1915, becoming friends with poets, critics, and editors, including Ezra Pound, Ford Madox Ford, W. B. Yeats, and Edward Thomas.

Frost's first two books, *A Boy's Will* (1913) and *North of Boston* (1914), were published in England, and he benefited from the support, encouragement, praise, and promotion that his literary friends bestowed upon him. He returned to the United States with a reputation that had been established in England, and this led to the American publication of these books in 1915, with *North of Boston* appearing in February and *A Boy's Will* in April.

Frost's first two books emerged from his experiences of American life and literature, but also from his extensive study of English poetry, and his connections to and friendships with contemporary English poets and poets from elsewhere who were living in or visiting England while he was there.

Later in his career, in public readings and in college and university classrooms, Frost frequently was asked, "How does someone become a poet?" Nearly always he replied like this: "Read poems, lots of them—good ones, not cheap things—and read them enviously. See how it's done. I think they put it this way, 'don't miss any of the tricks.'"

Frost said we should start with poem A, which helps us to read poem B. From these two, we proceed to poems C, D, and so on. We respond to a poem and step by step perceive it in a tradition, in a structure of relationships. That's literary history, and it's the resource that gives poets their training and toolkit. A poet becomes original by learning about what others have done. These are the achievements, the possibilities: where do I fit in, how do I differentiate myself, what's the sound and sense of my voice?

One of Frost's most beloved books as a young man, a book he read to tatters over many years, was *The Golden Treasury of the Best Songs and Lyrical Poems in the English Language*. The poems in it were selected by the English critic and editor Francis Turner Palgrave (1824–1897), with advice from his friend, the poet Alfred Tennyson. The first edition was published in 1861, and it was revised and expanded in 1891.

Palgrave focused on lyric poetry and excluded works by poets who were alive at the time he made his choices. *The Golden Treasury* became one of the most popular and influential anthologies of all time, and its contents, including (in Frost's phrase) the "swing and sway" of its meters, rhymes, and rhythms, were in Frost's mind and imagination when he wrote. The 1861 edition is more than three hundred pages, and the 1891 edition is four hundred pages. All the poems are by English authors, and among the first is Shakespeare's Sonnet 116, with its soul-stirring reference to "the edge of doom."

Frost knew the voices of English poets, and this knowledge equipped him to hear and define his own. The question that interested him and propelled him forward was: How could he contribute to the tradition and make it new? He wanted to be an original voice, yet in another way a recognizable one, a writer working with and extending the literary line. From our reading and rereading, we get a feeling for Frost's voice, and it's very appealing, captivating. But we must go further, for Frost emphasized that his own "greatest exhilaration in writing" was "to see if I can make each poem sound different from all others I have written." It's the same voice in a general way, the same style, yet it's different in each poem, distinctive.

Frost began writing poems in earnest in the 1890s, which in turn enabled him to clarify his aims, and this spurred him to write more poems. This was the process, the theory and the practice arising together. He came to understand what he wanted to do, and he shaped forms and sounds and organizations of language that would give him the poems he aspired to, exemplifying his techniques and goals.

As an element of my response to Frost, my feeling for his intentions, I've benefited from letters he wrote to John Bartlett, whom he met in 1907 at Pinkerton Academy, where Frost was an instructor. Pinkerton was founded in 1815, its purpose "to promote piety and virtue and the education of youth in Science, Languages, and the Liberal Arts." Bartlett was one of Frost's prize pupils, as was another student, Margaret Abbott, whom Bartlett later married.

Frost was with Bartlett for many hours in classrooms, but even more noteworthy were their numerous talks and long walks together. In 1911, Bartlett was working for a newspaper in Vancouver, Canada, and Frost considered moving there with his family. But he decided to live in England instead, arriving in September 1912. He and Bartlett exchanged letters, and, in February 1913, Frost sent him an unbound copy of his first book, *A Boy's Will*. He trusted Bartlett, could tell him what he had been writing and what he believed he had accomplished.

In a letter dated "Fourth-of-July, 1913," Frost said to Bartlett: "To be perfectly frank with you I am one of the most notable craftsman of my time." He described the "principle of versification" he had embraced:

Both Swinburne and Tennyson aimed largely at effects in assonation. But they were on the wrong track or at any rate on a short track. They went the length of it. Anyone else who goes that way must go after them. And that's where most are going. I alone of English writers have consciously set myself to make music out of what I may call the sound of sense.

Frost connects this "sound of sense" to voices, not the words that the voices speak, but, rather, their sounds, the meanings in their sounds:

Now it is possible to have sense without the sound of sense (as in much prose that is supposed to pass muster but makes very dull reading) and the sound of sense without sense (as in Alice in Wonderland which makes anything but dull reading). The best place to get the abstract sound of sense is from voices behind a door that cuts off the words.

Frost urges Bartlett to imagine situations we all know, when we hear voices, but cannot apprehend the words. What we hear are the sounds, the tones:

Ask yourself how these sentences would sound without the words in which they are embodied:

*You mean to tell me you can't read? I said no such thing.*
*Well read then.*
*You're not my teacher.*

.　　.　　.

*He says it's too late.*
*Oh, say!*
*Damn an Ingersoll watch* [i.e., a widely available, inexpensive watch] *anyway.*

.　　.　　.

*One—two—three——go!*

Probably this has happened to you, when you are outside an office or in a room on the other side of a closed door. Can you hear the voices, the sounds? You don't know what is being said, yet then again you do. You know that someone is upset or happy, or that a man and a woman are having a heated argument. Frost knows these kinds of sounds, and he wants to get them into poems. There's sense in the phrases and sentences we speak—it's in the arrangements of the words. But there's also a sense in the sheer sounds.

He continues:

Those sounds are summoned by the audile imagination and they must be positive, strong, and definitely and unmistakably indicated by the context. The reader must be at no loss to give his voice the posture proper to the sentences.

Frost hears these sounds. He's not inventing them; he's recalling them, hearing them in his memory and locating them in his lines, sentences, and stanzas. He prompts us to hear and interpret them through the "context," the story, setting, and subject of each poem. There's more, Frost explains:

> But remember we are still talking merely of the raw material of poetry. An ear and an appetite for these sounds of sense is the first qualification of a writer, be it of prose or verse. But if one is to be a poet he must learn to get cadences by skillfully breaking the sounds of sense with all their irregularity of accent across the regular beat of the meter.

This might seem abstract and hard to comprehend, but I think I understand what Frost is saying. Consider how you sound, the sounds your voice makes, when you are in this or that situation. Your voice has highs and lows, pauses, it slows down, it picks up, hesitates, hurries forward. There's a tone to it, multiple tones.

Next, imagine these tones in a poem you've written in iambic pentameter, with its regular beat of unstressed/stressed syllables, ten to a line. The meter sets the pattern, and your voice, with its pace and rhythm and accent, is sometimes in accord with the meter and sometimes at odds with it. The motion and play of the voice collaborate with the metrical pattern and are in tension with it.

When I was a student and young teacher, I paid minimal attention to sound, rhyme, and meter. I was intent on a poem's meaning, and I wasn't aware how important these tools for poets were. My view changed year by year as I taught Shakespeare, spoke with actors, and invited them to do workshops in my classes. They talked about Shakespeare's use of iambic pentameter, and the dramatic effects he achieved from adhering to the meter and, also, reordering it through the movement of the speaking voice, where its emphases wanted to be.

I remember discovering this interplay of sound and sense, the sound of sense, in Hamlet's soliloquy:

> To be, or not to be, that is the question:
> Whether 'tis nobler in the mind to suffer
> The slings and arrows of outrageous fortune,
> Or to take arms against a sea of troubles
> And by opposing end them.

Say these lines out aloud in keeping with the meter. You'll hear a stress on "be," and on "not," and on "be." There's a stress on "is," too. But perhaps there isn't, because your voice moving across the line may want to stress the word "that."

Listen to this: "To **be**, or **not** to **be**, that **is** the **question**." It's tricky, and interesting, the sort of thing Frost is keen on and experiments with. The meter tells you to put a stress on "is," but your voice is indicating that you should stress "that." If you were on the stage, this is where you'd want the emphasis, on "that," so you could highlight the significance of the question. **That's** the question.

And "question": it's a two-syllable word, but if you speak it with two syllables, you'll have a line with eleven syllables, one more than the ten that an iambic pentameter line should have. Saying the word with two syllables sounds awkward, so you should do it as one.

Now, listen to the fourth line when you speak it, "Or to take arms…." The iambic pattern coaxes you to stress the word "to." But that sounds wrong. As you move from line three to four, your voice impels you to stress the first word, with its single syllable, "Or."

I hope you're still with me. We refer to "reading poetry," but that's misleading, especially for Frost. He's "saying" his poems, and, when we read them, we should be hearing his creative work with sounds. In a way, we should be reading/hearing, looking/listening. That's how good poets write, hearing the words, and this is the case with Frost. It's part of the fun of reading him, making the interested effort to take note of the voice, detect the meter, and catch hold of the tone and rhythm.

Here's a passage from another letter Frost wrote to Bartlett, December 8, 1913, about the new book he was working on:

> In *North of Boston* you are to see me performing in a language absolutely unliterary. What I would like is to get so I would never use a word or combination of words that I hadn't heard used in running speech. I bar words and expressions I have merely seen. You do it on your ear. Of course I allow expressions I make myself. War on clichés.

Frost rejects what he merely sees. He embraces what he hears: "you do it on your ear." He's a poet who is making explicit the approach he takes to writing poems, supplying advice about how he is to be read and understood, with a new form of attentiveness.

I sense Frost's excitement about his discoveries, in, for example, this letter to Bartlett, February 22, 1914:

> I give you a new definition of a sentence: A sentence is a sound in itself on which other sounds called words may be strung.
>
> You may string words together without a sentence-sound to string them on just as you may tie clothes together by the sleeves and stretch them without a clothesline between two trees, but—it is bad for the clothes.
>
> The number of words you may string on one sentence-sound is not fixed but there is always danger of overloading.
>
> The sentence-sounds are very definite entities. (This is no literary mysticism I am preaching.) They are as definite as words. It is not impossible that they could be collected in a book or dictionary though I don't at present see on what system they would be catalogued.

Frost takes sound, voice, and tone seriously, and speaks about them with curiosity and joy. About these "sentence-sounds," he says:

> They are apprehended by the ear. They are gathered by the ear from the vernacular and brought into books. Many of them are already familiar to us in books. I think no writer invents them. The most original writer only catches them fresh from talk, where they grow spontaneously.
>
> A man is a writer if all his words are strung on definite recognizable sentence-sounds. The voice of the imagination, the speaking voice must know certainly how to behave how to posture in every sentence he offers.

We know plenty of sentence-sounds through reading books. But that's not what Frost is pursuing. He listens to how the people around him talk, the sentences they speak, the sounds they make. That's fresh material, and Frost aims to work with it. It's a complicated process: there are the words, the sentence-sounds, and the meter. He likes the challenge, the intensity and thrill of the performance. As he noted in an interview, November 1921: "I try to make each word serve two purposes; in addition to its own meaning, it serves as a guide to the voice in reading preceding and succeeding words. If this is not always true of each word, it is true of each phrase or line."

For Frost, there's leeway and liberty to be found within boundaries and constraints. That's why he frequently said he didn't like "free verse," poems written without a metrical pattern and structure. He declared that to him this was like "playing tennis with the net down."

Frost composes simple seeming and simple sounding poems that win our contented response right away, but that, as we reread them, dwelling among them, stimulate us with complex effects. There's more to the poems than we thought, depths of feeling about life and death, choice, self-knowledge, relationship, vocation, and more. Frost asks questions in his poems that all of us can relate to, essential questions that are hard to answer.

## PART 3: REMINDERS

By now, many of you will be primed to read, inhabit, and study Frost's work and world on your own. You might not need any more from me, and if that's the case, that's fine. Please read and enjoy the poems.

For some of you, however, a final review and summing up might be helpful, along with a few suggestions for reading Frost's longer poems. He's a superb writer, an original one, but, as we've seen, he's not easy. Not because he requires troves of background knowledge, but because he's shrewd, sly, and subtle. We must be on the alert and observant when we read him, the short poems and the longer ones.

Here's the first stanza of one of Frost's best-known poems, the short lyric "Stopping by Woods on a Snowy Evening":

> Whose woods these are I think I know.
> His house is in the village though;
> He will not see me stopping here
> To watch his woods fill up with snow.

Listen to the lines, feel the beat of the meter. This is Frost at his most regular, sticking to the unstressed/stressed pattern of iambic tetrameter, eight syllables in each line:

Whose **woods** these **are** I **think** I **know.**
His **house** is **in** the **village though;**
He **will** not **see** me **stop**ping **here**
To **watch** his **woods** fill **up** with **snow.**

Eight syllables per line, as here, or ten syllables: we should know the pattern, so we can hear and sense the changes Frost performs when he complicates it through sentence-sounds, through the movement of the speaking voice.

Now the first stanza of another famous short poem, "The Road Not Taken":

Two roads diverged in a yellow wood,
And sorry I could not travel both
And be one traveler, long I stood
And looked down one as far as I could
To where it bent in the undergrowth;

These lines, also in iambic tetrameter, are harder to get through. That's deliberate, that's what Frost wants. When I say the first words out loud, I know the stress should fall on "roads." Perhaps it does. But my voice wants a stress on both "two" and "roads." It sounds awkward to accent "roads" alone. I'm tempted to say that the meter of these first two words is and isn't regular.

In the third line, how should we say "traveler"? It has three syllables, but if we say all three, we'll end up with nine syllables in the line. We might want to voice "traveler" as if it were a two-syllable word: "trav-ler."

I'm not sure about the fourth line. Could you try speaking it out loud? Where is the meter telling you to locate the stresses? What is your voice telling you about where the stresses do and do not belong?

I remember posing this question to myself in one of my first readings of this stanza. I began to wonder about the syllables and stresses in other lines. I sensed that while the lines seemed smooth and clear and resonant, supported by the meter and vowel sounds and rhymes, they weren't really, not quite. I wasn't certain how to speak them, that is, how to hear them. I struggled, speaking the lines in various ways. The stanza was feeling rough and irregular to me, and I realized that's the effect Frost is aiming for. He has written a poem about a speaker who is reflecting on decisions about how to live, brooding about them, mulling over what's wrong and right, what he might regret.

It's the poems that are only a page or so in length that many of Frost's readers value most of all. But there are readers who prefer the expansive poems, where we encounter a narrator and one or more speakers, characters in conversation. Early in his career, Frost tried his hand at writing a novel, but he set it aside. He realized that wasn't where his talent and inclination were. His instinct, imagination, life history, and skill made him know he was a poet, not a writer of fictional prose. But the long poems he wrote are akin to short stories, and a few even have the potential to be enlarged into novels.

Another way to make this point is to say that sometimes Frost wrote dramatic poems. They resemble short stories, yet we could also view and hear them in theatrical terms. "The Death of the Hired Man," "The Mountain," "A Hundred Collars," "Home Burial," and other lengthy poems that present the voices of speakers in addition to the voice of the narrator who introduces, frames, and comments on the action: we could define these poems as dramas, visualize them being transferred to the stage.

I've experienced some of these poems at literary readings when actors on a stage or at the front of a room portray the speakers. They "acted out" the poems, paying attention to facial expressions, gestures, movement and spacing, sometimes with choices of clothes and props. This helped me to perceive how entertaining Frost is, that his poems are performances, that he takes pleasure in putting on a good dramatic show for us.

We might think about the opening of "The Death of the Hired Man":

> Mary sat musing on the lamp-flame at the table
> Waiting for Warren. When she heard his step,
> She ran on tip-toe down the darkened passage
> To meet him in the doorway with the news
> And put him on his guard. "Silas is back."
> She pushed him outward with her through the door
> And shut it after her. "Be kind," she said.
> She took the market things from Warren's arms
> And set them on the porch, then drew him down
> To sit beside her on the wooden steps.

When you read this passage, do your best to hear it, or, better still, speak it out loud. It takes some concentration, but it's fun, it's rewarding. Keep to a natural speech rhythm, not too fast or slow. Heed the length of the lines, and the punctuation. Some have no punctuation at the end, but don't hurry the transition to the next line. Give a slight pause, so you seem not to be reciting the poem, but, rather, saying it, as though it were coming into existence at each moment.

All the words are one or two syllables, and, as you articulate them in your natural voice, you'll feel them in relation to the meter. This passage is unrhymed, blank verse. It's iambic pentameter, but this pattern includes changes, shifts, surprises, variations. The verse isn't monotonous, not sing-song. Take in the vowels and consonants. This is carefully organized language—it's artfully written speech—that engages and sustains our interest.

You'll pick up the sentence-sounds and the movements of the meter functioning together. It's there as early as the first word, "Mary," a two-syllable name that should have a stress on the second syllable. But that wouldn't sound right. It's not how we pronounce this name. Perhaps we should say the name as if it were a single syllable, which would prompt us then to stress "sat." I suspect we want a stress on the first syllable of "musing." Now, look at and speak this first line again. Ten syllables? Eleven? Could it even have twelve?

The second line: the stress should be on the second syllable of "Waiting," but, again, that wouldn't have a good sound: my voice puts the stress on the first syllable.

Moving down the lines, the iambic stress falls on *ran, meet, put, pushed, shut, took, set, and sit*: Frost is foregrounding the verbs.

Frost gives us Mary's voice, and he teaches us how to hear it through the context. What's Mary doing? How does she react when she hears Warren's step? What's the nature of their encounter at the doorway? And why at the doorway? "Pushed him" and "shut it" are deliberate, forceful actions. Mary is doing a lot: she takes the things from the market that Warren is carrying; she sets them on the porch; she leads him to sit with her—and she is making him do this whether he wants to or not.

We assume Mary and Warren are wife and husband, but we don't know that for sure. It's important to her, and she knows it will be important to him, that "Silas is back." Who is he, and why is his return disquieting? Frost implies that Warren has been hard on Silas in the past, for Mary enjoins him to "be kind." She knows Warren might not be. She's acting as a mediator, which could be in keeping with her name, the name of the mother of Jesus, who intercedes between her son and humankind. There's a history to their relationship with Silas, and tension and conflict between Mary and Warren about how he has been treated.

Could Silas be the "hired man" of the title? Will this poem be telling the story of his death? It's a silent scene as it begins. Mary is at the table; she is pensive, absorbed in the flame of the lamp. She's waiting, expectant. It's noteworthy that she "runs," and down a "darkened passage," which is ominous, the dark she enters in contrast to the lamp's light and warmth. Is she fearful, apprehensive, about the response of her husband to the news she'll be delivering to him?

Mary is decisive: she intercepts Warren before he comes into the house. Maybe that's too strong. Perhaps it's more of a gentle control. She runs, she acts; she is thoughtful, patient.

This opening is suspenseful, emotionally charged, probing in its characterizations. You and I might differ in our interpretation, and we might modify and adjust our first impressions. That's a tribute to what Frost has done, the complexity of his narrative.

Warren responds sharply:

> "When was I ever anything but kind to him?
> But I'll not have the fellow back," he said.
> "I told him so last haying, didn't I?
> If he left then, I said, that ended it.
> What good is he? Who else will harbor him
> At his age for the little he can do?
> What help he is there's no depending on.
> Off he goes always when I need him most.
> He thinks he ought to earn a little pay,
> Enough at least to buy tobacco with,
> So he won't have to beg and be beholden...."

Warren takes Mary's injunction to be "kind" as a criticism, as an accusation. He's on the defensive, full of self-justification. As he sees it, the wrong is on Silas's side. There's frustration and implied disagreement, and it's expressed in the clear, direct informality of conversational speech that's true to the people we are coming to know.

Listen once more to these two lines, two sentences:

> What help he is there's no depending on.
> Off he goes always when I need him most.

Warren isn't comfortable with his behavior toward Silas, though he believes he should be because he has been tolerant and fair. He needed help with the haying; he gave work to Silas, who let him down. Warren and Mary are not poor, but they are not well off, either. Silas has dignity; he should work and make money, at least enough to buy tobacco. He sounds like someone who has no home of his own. He moves around, seeking a job, doing it for a time, but not responsibly.

Warren continues—we need to be aware that Mary is next to him, listening, and we might imagine the expressions on her face, steady yet changing as she hears Warren's words and tones of voice:

> "All right," I say, "I can't afford to pay
> Any fixed wages, though I wish I could."
> "Someone else can." "Then someone else will have to."
> I shouldn't mind his bettering himself
> If that was what it was. You can be certain,
> When he begins like that, there's someone at him
> Trying to coax him off with pocket-money,—
> In haying time, when any help is scarce.
> In winter he comes back to us. I'm done.

So far, we have the speaker/narrator's voice, and Mary's and Warren's voices. I'm not certain, but we now may have Silas's voice, recalled and uttered by Warren, a voice within a voice. What happened on this past occasion was that Warren offered to hire Silas but couldn't pay fixed wages. He wishes he could, but he doesn't have that kind of money. "Someone else can": is this Warren remembering what Silas said to him? "Then someone else will have to": that's Warren's reply.

Warren says he's not severe; he understands, he's sympathetic. If Silas could get a better deal for himself, that's acceptable to Warren. But he's suspicious. He thinks that someone was trying to draw away Silas at "haying time" when it's tough to get help. Warren is irritated by Silas's disloyalty; he takes advantage of the good will of Warren and Mary. He knows they'll take him back even though he wasn't a reliable worker for them.

"I'm done" sounds resolute and determined, but we perceive it's not. There's too much unease, and self-reproach, which Warren is attempting to overcome. He's over-insistent about his own rightness, and next to him, he has Mary, urging him to be kind.

I understand why some readers lean toward Frost's narrative poems, which frequently include this rendering of and interplay of voices—the tones and sentence-sounds of multiple speakers. We're reading poems that give us the insight and depth of drama or prose fiction. These are narratives recounting a good story, with a plot, a well-designed beginning, middle, and end. Frost belongs with Shakespeare and the Russian playwright and short-story writer Anton Chekhov, creators of voices and characters in all-too-human plights and predicaments, with distinctive idioms and perspectives.

Frost remarked to a friend: "Even poets forget that words exist in the mouth, not in books." To another, he said it was "talking with people" that pushed him to bring voices into poems: "I didn't know until then what I was after. I was after poetry that talked. If my poems were talking poems—if to read one of them you heard a voice—that would be to my liking!" It thus was lofty praise for Frost to say to his friend E. A. Robinson in a letter in 1915: "It is good writing, or better than that, good speaking caught alive—every sentence of it."

"I hear everything I write," Frost told an interviewer in 1916: "All poetry is to me first a matter of sound. I hear my things spoken." He made the same point in a letter to a friend the following year: "I can't keep up any interest in sentences that don't SHAPE on *some speaking tone* of voice."

Frost is writing speech, attentive to sounds, tones, and rhythms, and he's thinking all the time about us as his readers. Frost loved the pleasure and challenge of being a poet, of selecting and arranging words and organizing them in metrical patterns and sentence-sounds. But he emphasized he didn't write for "my own pleasure": "A poet is never without the sense of an audience; he has something to say to somebody and that is why he writes it." As you read and reflect on the poems in this collection, think about what Frost is saying to you.

# NOTE ON THE TEXT

M Y GOAL IS to give you the experience of Robert Frost at his best, in his first four books. These books made his reputation, winning attention and admiration from reviewers, critics, and other poets, and gaining for him an appreciative and enthusiastic audience.

This edition includes:

*A Boy's Will* (1913)
*North of Boston* (1914)
*Mountain Interval* (1916)
*New Hampshire* (1923)

There are a few minor differences between the first editions of these four books and the reprinting of them in Frost's *Complete Poems,* published in 1949. Where these differences arise, I have abided by the choices he made for the 1949 volume, his final intentions.

Frost's later books include very good poems, and I've listed some of them below. You can find these poems online, and even more in the books I've listed in Further Reading. But for readers coming to Frost for the first time, or who have some familiarity with him and seek to know him more deeply, it's a special experience to turn to his first four books.

We enjoy Frost for the connections he makes to our literary and personal lives today even as we look backward to imagine and reflect on the responses of readers to his poetry, and to his voice, on the literary scene of the 1910s into the 1920s. Readers were drawn to and curious about Frost's style; they were trying to understand his strategies and themes; and they were observing the development from book to book of his literary project. What was he doing in each one that made him special, and where and how did he move forward from it to the next? Each of Frost's first four books is a chapter, an installment, in an unfolding story that you and I can study all at once, in its entirety.

From later in Frost's career, I'd recommend:

*West-Running Brook* (1928)
"Once by the Pacific"
"Acquainted with the Night"

*A Further Range* (1936)
"Neither Out Far Nor in Deep"
"Design"

*A Witness Tree* (1942)
"The Silken Tent"
"The Most of It"
"The Gift Outright"

*Steeple Bush* (1947)
"Directive"

*In the Clearing* (1962)
"The Draft Horse"

I've provided annotations for many words and references. I'm aware, as I have done so, that Frost would have resisted such aids to reading his work: he believed his poetry stood on its own. Commentaries, footnotes, annotations: to Frost, these would have seemed distractions, interferences. But for readers in the twenty-first century, Frost's poems benefit from, and may even require, this interpretive assistance. I say this in part from my experience teaching Frost to students at Wellesley College, many of whom come to English as their second or third language. I've located this material at the back, where you can keep a bookmark, for you to consult as much or as little as you'd like.

## THE PASTURE

I'm going out to clean the pasture spring;
I'll only stop to rake the leaves away
(And wait to watch the water clear, I may)
I sha'n't be gone long.—You come too.

I'm going out to fetch the little calf
That's standing by the mother. It's so young,
It totters when she licks it with her tongue.
I sha'n't be gone long.—You come too.

# A BOY'S WILL

# INTO MY OWN

One of my wishes is that those dark trees,
So old and firm they scarcely show the breeze,
Were not, as 'twere, the merest mask of gloom,
But stretched away unto the edge of doom.

I should not be withheld but that some day
Into their vastness I should steal away,
Fearless of ever finding open land,
Or highway where the slow wheel pours the sand.

I do not see why I should e'er turn back,
Or those should not set forth upon my track
To overtake me, who should miss me here
And long to know if still I held them dear.

They would not find me changed from him they knew—
Only more sure of all I thought was true.

# GHOST HOUSE

I dwell in a lonely house I know
That vanished many a summer ago,
   And left no trace but the cellar walls,
   And a cellar in which the daylight falls,
And the purple-stemmed wild raspberries grow.

O'er ruined fences the grapevines shield
The woods come back to the mowing field;
   The orchard tree has grown one copse
   Of new wood and old where the woodpecker chops;
The footpath down to the well is healed.

I dwell with a strangely aching heart
In that vanished abode there far apart
   On that disused and forgotten road
   That has no dust-bath now for the toad.
Night comes; the black bats tumble and dart;

The whippoorwill is coming to shout
And hush and cluck and flutter about:
   I hear him begin far enough away
   Full many a time to say his say
Before he arrives to say it out.

It is under the small, dim, summer star.
I know not who these mute folk are
   Who share the unlit place with me—
   Those stones out under the low-limbed tree
Doubtless bear names that the mosses mar.

They are tireless folk, but slow and sad,
Though two, close-keeping, are lass and lad,—
   With none among them that ever sings,
   And yet, in view of how many things,
As sweet companions as might be had.

# MY NOVEMBER GUEST

My Sorrow, when she's here with me,
  Thinks these dark days of autumn rain
Are beautiful as days can be;
She loves the bare, the withered tree;
  She walks the sodden pasture lane.

Her pleasure will not let me stay.
  She talks and I am fain to list:
She's glad the birds are gone away,
She's glad her simple worsted gray
  Is silver now with clinging mist.

The desolate, deserted trees,
  The faded earth, the heavy sky,
The beauties she so truly sees,
She thinks I have no eye for these,
  And vexes me for reason why.

Not yesterday I learned to know
  The love of bare November days
Before the coming of the snow,
But it were vain to tell her so,
  And they are better for her praise.

# LOVE AND A QUESTION

A Stranger came to the door at eve,
  And he spoke the bridegroom fair.
He bore a green-white stick in his hand,
  And, for all burden, care.
He asked with the eyes more than the lips
  For a shelter for the night,
And he turned and looked at the road afar
  Without a window light.

The bridegroom came forth into the porch
  With "Let us look at the sky,
And question what of the night to be,
  Stranger, you and I."
The woodbine leaves littered the yard,
  The woodbine berries were blue,
Autumn, yes, winter was in the wind;
  "Stranger, I wish I knew."

Within, the bride in the dusk alone
  Bent over the open fire,
Her face rose-red with the glowing coal
  And the thought of the heart's desire.
The bridegroom looked at the weary road,
  Yet saw but her within,
And wished her heart in a case of gold
  And pinned with a silver pin.

The bridegroom thought it little to give
  A dole of bread, a purse,
A heartfelt prayer for the poor of God,
  Or for the rich a curse;
But whether or not a man was asked
  To mar the love of two
By harboring woe in the bridal house,
  The bridegroom wished he knew.

# A LATE WALK

When I go up through the mowing field,
  The headless aftermath,
Smooth-laid like thatch with the heavy dew,
  Half closes the garden path.

And when I come to the garden ground,
  The whir of sober birds
Up from the tangle of withered weeds
  Is sadder than any words.

A tree beside the wall stands bare,
  But a leaf that lingered brown,
Disturbed, I doubt not, by my thought,
  Comes softly rattling down.

I end not far from my going forth
  By picking the faded blue
Of the last remaining aster flower
  To carry again to you.

# STARS

How countlessly they congregate
    O'er our tumultuous snow,
Which flows in shapes as tall as trees
    When wintry winds do blow!—

As if with keenness for our fate,
    Our faltering few steps on
To white rest, and a place of rest
    Invisible at dawn,—

And yet with neither love nor hate,
    Those stars like some snow-white
Minerva's snow-white marble eyes
    Without the gift of sight.

# STORM FEAR

When the wind works against us in the dark,
And pelts with snow
The lowest chamber window on the east,
And whispers with a sort of stifled bark,
The beast,
"Come out! Come out!"—
It costs no inward struggle not to go,
Ah, no!
I count our strength,
Two and a child,
Those of us not asleep subdued to mark
How the cold creeps as the fire dies at length,—
How drifts are piled,
Dooryard and road ungraded,
Till even the comforting barn grows far away,
And my heart owns a doubt
Whether 'tis in us to arise with day
And save ourselves unaided.

# WIND AND WINDOW FLOWER

Lovers, forget your love,
  And list to the love of these,
She a window flower,
  And he a winter breeze.

When the frosty window veil
  Was melted down at noon,
And the cagèd yellow bird
  Hung over her in tune,

He marked her through the pane
  He could not help but mark,
And only passed her by,
  To come again at dark.

He was a winter wind,
  Concerned with ice and snow,
Dead weeds and unmated birds,
  And little of love could know.

But he sighed upon the sill,
  He gave the sash a shake,
As witness all within
  Who lay that night awake.

Perchance he half prevailed
  To win her for the flight
From the firelit looking-glass
  And warm stove-window light.

But the flower leaned aside
  And thought of naught to say,
And morning found the breeze
  A hundred miles away.

# TO THE THAWING WIND

Come with rain, O loud Southwester!
Bring the singer, bring the nester;
Give the buried flower a dream;
Make the settled snowbank steam;
Find the brown beneath the white;
But whate'er you do tonight,
Bathe my window, make it flow,
Melt it as the ice will go;
Melt the glass and leave the sticks
Like a hermit's crucifix;
Burst into my narrow stall;
Swing the picture on the wall;
Run the rattling pages o'er;
Scatter poems on the floor;
Turn the poet out of door.

# A PRAYER IN SPRING

Oh, give us pleasure in the flowers today;
And give us not to think so far away
As the uncertain harvest; keep us here
All simply in the springing of the year.

Oh, give us pleasure in the orchard white,
Like nothing else by day, like ghosts by night;
And make us happy in the happy bees,
The swarm dilating round the perfect trees.

And make us happy in the darting bird
That suddenly above the bees is heard,
The meteor that thrusts in with needle bill,
And off a blossom in mid air stands still.

For this is love and nothing else is love,
The which it is reserved for God above
To sanctify to what far ends He will,
But which it only needs that we fulfill.

## FLOWER-GATHERING

I left you in the morning,
And in the morning glow,
You walked a way beside me
To make me sad to go.
Do you know me in the gloaming,
Gaunt and dusty gray with roaming?
Are you dumb because you know me not,
Or dumb because you know?

All for me? And not a question
For the faded flowers gay
That could take me from beside you
For the ages of a day?
They are yours, and be the measure
Of their worth for you to treasure,
The measure of the little while
That I've been long away.

# ROSE POGONIAS

A saturated meadow,
    Sun-shaped and jewel-small,
A circle scarcely wider
    Than the trees around were tall;
Where winds were quite excluded,
    And the air was stifling sweet
With the breath of many flowers,—
    A temple of the heat.

There we bowed us in the burning,
    As the sun's right worship is,
To pick where none could miss them
    A thousand orchises;
For though the grass was scattered,
    Yet every second spear
Seemed tipped with wings of color,
    That tinged the atmosphere.

We raised a simple prayer
    Before we left the spot,
That in the general mowing
    That place might be forgot;
Or if not all so favored,
    Obtain such grace of hours,
That none should mow the grass there
    While so confused with flowers.

# WAITING
## Afield at Dusk

What things for dream there are when specter-like,
Moving along tall haycocks lightly piled,
I enter alone upon the stubble field,
From which the laborers' voices late have died,
And in the antiphony of afterglow
And rising full moon, sit me down
Upon the full moon's side of the first haycock
And lose myself amid so many alike.

I dream upon the opposing lights of the hour,
Preventing shadow until the moon prevail;
I dream upon the nighthawks peopling heaven,
Each circling each with vague unearthly cry,
Or plunging headlong with fierce twang afar;
And on the bat's mute antics, who would seem
Dimly to have made out my secret place,
Only to lose it when he pirouettes,
And seek it endlessly with purblind haste;
On the last swallow's sweep; and on the rasp
In the abyss of odor and rustle at my back,
That, silenced by my advent, finds once more,
After an interval, his instrument,
And tries once—twice—and thrice if I be there;
And on the worn book of old-golden song
I brought not here to read, it seems, but hold
And freshen in this air of withering sweetness;
But on the memory of one absent most,
For whom these lines when they shall greet her eye.

# IN A VALE

When I was young, we dwelt in a vale
  By a misty fen that rang all night,
And thus it was the maidens pale
I knew so well, whose garments trail
  Across the reeds to a window light.

The fen had every kind of bloom,
  And for every kind there was a face,
And a voice that has sounded in my room
Across the sill from the outer gloom.
  Each came singly unto her place,

But all came every night with the mist;
  And often they brought so much to say
Of things of moment to which, they wist,
One so lonely was fain to list,
  That the stars were almost faded away

Before the last went, heavy with dew,
  Back to the place from which she came—
Where the bird was before it flew,
Where the flower was before it grew,
  Where bird and flower were one and the same.

And thus it is I know so well
  Why the flower has odor, the bird has song.
You have only to ask me, and I can tell.
No, not vainly there did I dwell,
  Nor vainly listen all the night long.

# A DREAM PANG

I had withdrawn in forest, and my song
Was swallowed up in leaves that blew alway;
And to the forest edge you came one day
(This was my dream) and looked and pondered long,
But did not enter, though the wish was strong:
You shook your pensive head as who should say,
"I dare not—too far in his footsteps stray—
He must seek me would he undo the wrong."

Not far, but near, I stood and saw it all
Behind low boughs the trees let down outside;
And the sweet pang it cost me not to call
And tell you that I saw does still abide.
But 'tis not true that thus I dwelt aloof,
For the wood wakes, and you are here for proof.

# IN NEGLECT

They leave us so to the way we took,
   As two in whom they were proved mistaken,
That we sit sometimes in the wayside nook,
With mischievous, vagrant, seraphic look,
   And *try* if we cannot feel forsaken.

## THE VANTAGE POINT

If tired of trees I seek again mankind,
   Well I know where to hie me—in the dawn,
   To a slope where the cattle keep the lawn.
There amid lolling juniper reclined,
Myself unseen, I see in white defined
   Far off the homes of men, and farther still,
   The graves of men on an opposing hill,
Living or dead, whichever are to mind.

And if by noon I have too much of these,
   I have but to turn on my arm, and lo,
   The sun-burned hillside sets my face aglow,
My breathing shakes the bluet like a breeze,
   I smell the earth, I smell the bruisèd plant,
   I look into the crater of the ant.

# MOWING

There was never a sound beside the wood but one,
And that was my long scythe whispering to the ground.
What was it it whispered? I knew not well myself;
Perhaps it was something about the heat of the sun,
Something, perhaps, about the lack of sound—
And that was why it whispered and did not speak.
It was no dream of the gift of idle hours,
Or easy gold at the hand of fay or elf:
Anything more than the truth would have seemed too weak
To the earnest love that laid the swale in rows,
Not without feeble-pointed spikes of flowers
(Pale orchises), and scared a bright green snake.
The fact is the sweetest dream that labor knows.
My long scythe whispered and left the hay to make.

# GOING FOR WATER

The well was dry beside the door,
   And so we went with pail and can
Across the fields behind the house
   To seek the brook if still it ran;

Not loth to have excuse to go,
   Because the autumn eve was fair
(Though chill), because the fields were ours,
   And by the brook our woods were there.

We ran as if to meet the moon
   That slowly dawned behind the trees,
The barren boughs without the leaves,
   Without the birds, without the breeze.

But once within the wood, we paused
   Like gnomes that hid us from the moon,
Ready to run to hiding new
   With laughter when she found us soon.

Each laid on other a staying hand
   To listen ere we dared to look,
And in the hush we joined to make
   We heard, we knew we heard the brook.

A note as from a single place,
   A slender tinkling fall that made
Now drops that floated on the pool
   Like pearls, and now a silver blade.

# REVELATION

We make ourselves a place apart
  Behind light words that tease and flout,
But oh, the agitated heart
  Till someone really find us out.

'Tis pity if the case require
  (Or so we say) that in the end
We speak the literal to inspire
  The understanding of a friend.

But so with all, from babes that play
  At hide-and-seek to God afar,
So all who hide too well away
  Must speak and tell us where they are.

## THE TRIAL BY EXISTENCE

Even the bravest that are slain
   Shall not dissemble their surprise
On waking to find valor reign,
   Even as on earth, in paradise;
And where they sought without the sword
   Wide fields of asphodel fore'er,
To find that the utmost reward
   Of daring should be still to dare.

The light of heaven falls whole and white
   And is not shattered into dyes,
The light forever is morning light;
   The hills are verdured pasture-wise;
The angel hosts with freshness go,
   And seek with laughter what to brave;—
And binding all is the hushed snow
   Of the far-distant breaking wave.

And from a cliff-top is proclaimed
   The gathering of the souls for birth,
The trial by existence named,
   The obscuration upon earth.
And the slant spirits trooping by
   In streams and cross- and counter-streams
Can but give ear to that sweet cry
   For its suggestion of what dreams!

And the more loitering are turned
   To view once more the sacrifice
Of those who for some good discerned
   Will gladly give up paradise.
And a white shimmering concourse rolls
   Toward the throne to witness there
The speeding of devoted souls
   Which God makes his especial care.

And none are taken but who will,
  Having first heard the life read out
That opens earthward, good and ill,
  Beyond the shadow of a doubt;
And very beautifully God limns,
  And tenderly, life's little dream,
But naught extenuates or dims,
  Setting the thing that is supreme.

Nor is there wanting in the press
  Some spirit to stand simply forth,
Heroic in its nakedness,
  Against the uttermost of earth.
The tale of earth's unhonored things
  Sounds nobler there than 'neath the sun;
And the mind whirls and the heart sings,
  And a shout greets the daring one.

But always God speaks at the end:
  "One thought in agony of strife
The bravest would have by for friend,
  The memory that he chose the life;
But the pure fate to which you go
  Admits no memory of choice,
Or the woe were not earthly woe
  To which you give the assenting voice."

And so the choice must be again,
  But the last choice is still the same;
And the awe passes wonder then,
  And a hush falls for all acclaim.
And God has taken a flower of gold
  And broken it, and used therefrom
The mystic link to bind and hold
  Spirit to matter till death come.

'Tis of the essence of life here,
  Though we choose greatly, still to lack
The lasting memory at all clear,

That life has for us on the wrack
Nothing but what we somehow chose;
    Thus are we wholly stripped of pride
In the pain that has but one close,
    Bearing it crushed and mystified.

# THE TUFT OF FLOWERS

I went to turn the grass once after one
Who mowed it in the dew before the sun.

The dew was gone that made his blade so keen
Before I came to view the leveled scene.

I looked for him behind an isle of trees;
I listened for his whetstone on the breeze.

But he had gone his way, the grass all mown,
And I must be, as he had been,—alone,

"As all must be," I said within my heart,
"Whether they work together or apart."

But as I said it, swift there passed me by
On noiseless wing a bewildered butterfly,

Seeking with memories grown dim o'er night
Some resting flower of yesterday's delight.

And once I marked his flight go round and round,
As where some flower lay withering on the ground.

And then he flew as far as eye could see,
And then on tremulous wing came back to me.

I thought of questions that have no reply,
And would have turned to toss the grass to dry;

But he turned first, and led my eye to look
At a tall tuft of flowers beside a brook,

A leaping tongue of bloom the scythe had spared
Beside a reedy brook the scythe had bared.

The mower in the dew had loved them thus,
By leaving them to flourish, not for us,

Nor yet to draw one thought of ours to him,
But from sheer morning gladness at the brim.

The butterfly and I had lit upon,
Nevertheless, a message from the dawn,

That made me hear the wakening birds around,
And hear his long scythe whispering to the ground,

And feel a spirit kindred to my own;
So that henceforth I worked no more alone;

But glad with him, I worked as with his aid,
And weary, sought at noon with him the shade;

And dreaming, as it were, held brotherly speech
With one whose thought I had not hoped to reach.

"Men work together," I told him from the heart,
"Whether they work together or apart."

# PAN WITH US

Pan came out of the woods one day,—
His skin and his hair and his eyes were gray,
The gray of the moss of walls were they,—
    And stood in the sun and looked his fill
    At wooded valley and wooded hill.

He stood in the zephyr, pipes in hand,
On a height of naked pasture land;
In all the country he did command
    He saw no smoke and he saw no roof.
    That was well! and he stamped a hoof.

His heart knew peace, for none came here
To this lean feeding save once a year
Someone to salt the half-wild steer,
    Or homespun children with clicking pails
    Who see no little they tell no tales.

He tossed his pipes, too hard to teach
A new-world song, far out of reach,
For a sylvan sign that the blue jay's screech
    And the whimper of hawks beside the sun
    Were music enough for him, for one.

Times were changed from what they were:
Such pipes kept less of power to stir
The fruited bough of the juniper
    And the fragile bluets clustered there
    Than the merest aimless breath of air.

They were pipes of pagan mirth,
And the world had found new terms of worth.
He laid him down on the sun-burned earth
    And raveled a flower and looked away—
    Play? Play?—What should he play?

# THE DEMIURGE'S LAUGH

It was far in the sameness of the wood;
   I was running with joy on the Demon's trail,
Though I knew what I hunted was no true god.
   It was just as the light was beginning to fail
That I suddenly heard—all I needed to hear:
It has lasted me many and many a year.

The sound was behind me instead of before,
   A sleepy sound, but mocking half,
As of one who utterly couldn't care.
   The Demon arose from his wallow to laugh,
Brushing the dirt from his eye as he went;
And well I knew what the Demon meant.

I shall not forget how his laugh rang out.
   I felt as a fool to have been so caught,
And checked my steps to make pretense
   It was something among the leaves I sought
(Though doubtful whether he stayed to see).
Thereafter I sat me against a tree.

## NOW CLOSE THE WINDOWS

Now close the windows and hush all the fields:
   If the trees must, let them silently toss;
No bird is singing now, and if there is,
   Be it my loss.

It will be long ere the marshes resume,
   It will be long ere the earliest bird:
So close the windows and not hear the wind,
   But see all wind-stirred.

# IN HARDWOOD GROVES

The same leaves over and over again!
They fall from giving shade above
To make one texture of faded brown
And fit the earth like a leather glove.

Before the leaves can mount again
To fill the trees with another shade,
They must go down past things coming up.
They must go down into the dark decayed.

They *must* be pierced by flowers and put
Beneath the feet of dancing flowers.
However it is in some other world
I know that this is the way in ours.

# A LINE-STORM SONG

The line-storm clouds fly tattered and swift.
　　The road is forlorn all day,
Where a myriad snowy quartz stones lift,
　　And the hoof-prints vanish away.
The roadside flowers, too wet for the bee,
　　Expend their bloom in vain.
Come over the hills and far with me,
　　And be my love in the rain.

The birds have less to say for themselves
　　In the wood-world's torn despair
Than now these numberless years the elves,
　　Although they are no less there:
All song of the woods is crushed like some
　　Wild, easily shattered rose.
Come, be my love in the wet woods, come,
　　Where the boughs rain when it blows.

There is the gale to urge behind
　　And bruit our singing down,
And the shallow waters aflutter with wind
　　From which to gather your gown.
What matter if we go clear to the west,
　　And come not through dry-shod?
For wilding brooch shall wet your breast
　　The rain-fresh goldenrod.

Oh, never this whelming east wind swells
　　But it seems like the sea's return
To the ancient lands where it left the shells
　　Before the age of the fern;
And it seems like the time when after doubt
　　Our love came back amain.
Oh, come forth into the storm and rout
　　And be my love in the rain.

# OCTOBER

O hushed October morning mild,
Thy leaves have ripened to the fall;
Tomorrow's wind, if it be wild,
Should waste them all.
The crows above the forest call;
Tomorrow they may form and go.
O hushed October morning mild,
Begin the hours of this day slow.
Make the day seem to us less brief.
Hearts not averse to being beguiled,
Beguile us in the way you know.
Release one leaf at break of day;
At noon release another leaf;
One from our trees, one far away.
Retard the sun with gentle mist;
Enchant the land with amethyst.
Slow, slow!
For the grapes' sake, if they were all,
Whose leaves already are burnt with frost,
Whose clustered fruit must else be lost—
For the grapes' sake along the wall.

# MY BUTTERFLY

Thine emulous fond flowers are dead, too,
And the daft sun-assaulter, he
That frighted thee so oft, is fled or dead:
Save only me
(Nor is it sad to thee!)
Save only me
There is none left to mourn thee in the fields.

The gray grass is scarce dappled with the snow;
Its two banks have not shut upon the river;
But it is long ago—
It seems forever—
Since first I saw thee glance,
With all thy dazzling other ones,
In airy dalliance,
Precipitate in love,
Tossed, tangled, whirled and whirled above,
Like a limp rose-wreath in a fairy dance.

When that was, the soft mist
Of my regret hung not on all the land,
And I was glad for thee,
And glad for me, I wist.

Thou didst not know, who tottered, wandering on high,
That fate had made thee for the pleasure of the wind,
With those great careless wings,
Nor yet did I.

And there were other things:
It seemed God let thee flutter from his gentle clasp:
Then fearful he had let thee win
Too far beyond him to be gathered in,
Snatched thee, o'ereager, with ungentle grasp.

Ah! I remember me
How once conspiracy was rife

Against my life—
The languor of it and the dreaming fond;
Surging, the grasses dizzied me of thought,
The breeze three odors brought,
And a gem-flower waved in a wand!

Then when I was distraught
And could not speak,
Sidelong, full on my cheek,
What should that reckless zephyr fling
But the wild touch of thy dye-dusty wing!

I found that wing broken today!
For thou art dead, I said,
And the strange birds say.
I found it with the withered leaves
Under the eaves.

# RELUCTANCE

Out through the fields and the woods
   And over the walls I have wended;
I have climbed the hills of view
   And looked at the world, and descended;
I have come by the highway home,
   And lo, it is ended.

The leaves are all dead on the ground,
   Save those that the oak is keeping
To ravel them one by one
   And let them go scraping and creeping
Out over the crusted snow,
   When others are sleeping.

And the dead leaves lie huddled and still,
   No longer blown hither and thither;
The last lone aster is gone;
   The flowers of the witch-hazel wither;
The heart is still aching to seek,
   But the feet question "Whither?"

Ah, when to the heart of man
   Was it ever less than a treason
To go with the drift of things,
   To yield with a grace to reason,
And bow and accept the end
   Of a love or a season?

# NORTH OF BOSTON

# MENDING WALL

Something there is that doesn't love a wall,
That sends the frozen-ground-swell under it,
And spills the upper boulders in the sun;
And makes gaps even two can pass abreast.
The work of hunters is another thing:
I have come after them and made repair
Where they have left not one stone on a stone,
But they would have the rabbit out of hiding,
To please the yelping dogs. The gaps I mean,
No one has seen them made or heard them made,
But at spring mending-time we find them there.
I let my neighbor know beyond the hill;
And on a day we meet to walk the line
And set the wall between us once again.
We keep the wall between us as we go.
To each the boulders that have fallen to each.
And some are loaves and some so nearly balls
We have to use a spell to make them balance:
"Stay where you are until our backs are turned!"
We wear our fingers rough with handling them.
Oh, just another kind of outdoor game,
One on a side. It comes to little more:
There where it is we do not need the wall:
He is all pine and I am apple orchard.
My apple trees will never get across
And eat the cones under his pines, I tell him.
He only says, "Good fences make good neighbors."
Spring is the mischief in me, and I wonder
If I could put a notion in his head:
"*Why* do they make good neighbors? Isn't it
Where there are cows? But here there are no cows.
Before I built a wall I'd ask to know
What I was walling in or walling out,
And to whom I was like to give offense.
Something there is that doesn't love a wall,
That wants it down." I could say "Elves" to him,
But it's not elves exactly, and I'd rather

He said it for himself. I see him there
Bringing a stone grasped firmly by the top
In each hand, like an old-stone savage armed.
He moves in darkness as it seems to me,
Not of woods only and the shade of trees
He will not go behind his father's saying,
And he likes having thought of it so well
He says again, "Good fences make good neighbors."

# THE DEATH OF THE HIRED MAN

Mary sat musing on the lamp-flame at the table
Waiting for Warren. When she heard his step,
She ran on tip-toe down the darkened passage
To meet him in the doorway with the news
And put him on his guard. "Silas is back."
She pushed him outward with her through the door
And shut it after her. "Be kind," she said.
She took the market things from Warren's arms
And set them on the porch, then drew him down
To sit beside her on the wooden steps.

"When was I ever anything but kind to him?
But I'll not have the fellow back," he said.
"I told him so last haying, didn't I?
If he left then, I said, that ended it.
What good is he? Who else will harbor him
At his age for the little he can do?
What help he is there's no depending on.
Off he goes always when I need him most.
He thinks he ought to earn a little pay,
Enough at least to buy tobacco with,
So he won't have to beg and be beholden.
'All right,' I say, 'I can't afford to pay
Any fixed wages, though I wish I could.'
'Someone else can.' 'Then someone else will have to.'
I shouldn't mind his bettering himself
If that was what it was. You can be certain,
When he begins like that, there's someone at him
Trying to coax him off with pocket-money,—
In haying time, when any help is scarce.
In winter he comes back to us. I'm done."

"Sh! not so loud: he'll hear you," Mary said.

"I want him to: he'll have to soon or late."

"He's worn out. He's asleep beside the stove.
When I came up from Rowe's I found him here,
Huddled against the barn-door fast asleep,
A miserable sight, and frightening, too—
You needn't smile—I didn't recognize him—
I wasn't looking for him—and he's changed.
Wait till you see."

                    "Where did you say he'd been?"

"He didn't say. I dragged him to the house,
And gave him tea and tried to make him smoke.
I tried to make him talk about his travels.
Nothing would do: he just kept nodding off."

"What did he say? Did he say anything?"

"But little."

                    "Anything? Mary, confess
He said he'd come to ditch the meadow for me."

"Warren!"

                    "But did he? I just want to know."

"Of course he did. What would you have him say?
Surely you wouldn't grudge the poor old man
Some humble way to save his self-respect.
He added, if you really care to know,
He meant to clear the upper pasture, too.
That sounds like something you have heard before?
Warren, I wish you could have heard the way
He jumbled everything. I stopped to look
Two or three times—he made me feel so queer—
To see if he was talking in his sleep.
He ran on Harold Wilson—you remember—
The boy you had in haying four years since.
He's finished school, and teaching in his college.

Silas declares you'll have to get him back.
He says they two will make a team for work:
Between them they will lay this farm as smooth!
The way he mixed that in with other things.
He thinks young Wilson a likely lad, though daft
On education—you know how they fought
All through July under the blazing sun,
Silas up on the cart to build the load,
Harold along beside to pitch it on."

"Yes, I took care to keep well out of earshot."

"Well, those days trouble Silas like a dream.
You wouldn't think they would. How some things linger!
Harold's young college boy's assurance piqued him.
After so many years he still keeps finding
Good arguments he sees he might have used.
I sympathize. I know just how it feels
To think of the right thing to say too late.
Harold's associated in his mind with Latin.
He asked me what I thought of Harold's saying
He studied Latin like the violin
Because he liked it—that an argument!
He said he couldn't make the boy believe
He could find water with a hazel prong—
Which showed how much good school had ever done him.
He wanted to go over that. But most of all
He thinks if he could have another chance
To teach him how to build a load of hay—"

"I know, that's Silas' one accomplishment.
He bundles every forkful in its place,
And tags and numbers it for future reference,
So he can find and easily dislodge it
In the unloading. Silas does that well.
He takes it out in bunches like big birds' nests.
You never see him standing on the hay
He's trying to lift, straining to lift himself."

"He thinks if he could teach him that, he'd be
Some good perhaps to someone in the world.
He hates to see a boy the fool of books.
Poor Silas, so concerned for other folk,
And nothing to look backward to with pride,
And nothing to look forward to with hope,
So now and never any different."

Part of a moon was falling down the west,
Dragging the whole sky with it to the hills.
Its light poured softly in her lap. She saw
And spread her apron to it. She put out her hand
Among the harp-like morning-glory strings,
Taut with the dew from garden bed to eaves,
As if she played unheard some tenderness
That wrought on him beside her in the night.
"Warren," she said, "he has come home to die:
You needn't be afraid he'll leave you this time."

"Home," he mocked gently.

                              "Yes, what else but home?
It all depends on what you mean by home.
Of course he's nothing to us, any more
Than was the hound that came a stranger to us
Out of the woods, worn out upon the trail."

"Home is the place where, when you have to go there,
They have to take you in."

                              "I should have called it
Something you somehow haven't to deserve."

Warren leaned out and took a step or two,
Picked up a little stick, and brought it back
And broke it in his hand and tossed it by.
"Silas has better claim on us you think
Than on his brother? Thirteen little miles
As the road winds would bring him to his door.

Silas has walked that far no doubt today.
Why doesn't he go there? His brother's rich,
A somebody—director in the bank."

"He never told us that."

                    "We know it though."

"I think his brother ought to help, of course.
I'll see to that if there is need. He ought of right
To take him in, and might be willing to—
He may be better than appearances.
But have some pity on Silas. Do you think
If he had any pride in claiming kin
Or anything he looked for from his brother,
He'd keep so still about him all this time?"

"I wonder what's between them."

                              "I can tell you.
Silas is what he is—we wouldn't mind him—
But just the kind that kinsfolk can't abide.
He never did a thing so very bad.
He don't know why he isn't quite as good
As anybody. Worthless though he is,
He won't be made ashamed to please his brother."

"*I* can't think Si ever hurt anyone."

"No, but he hurt my heart the way he lay
And rolled his old head on that sharp-edged chair-back.
He wouldn't let me put him on the lounge.
You must go in and see what you can do.
I made the bed up for him there tonight.
You'll be surprised at him—how much he's broken.
His working days are done; I'm sure of it."

"I'd not be in a hurry to say that."

47

"I haven't been. Go, look, see for yourself.
But, Warren, please remember how it is:
He's come to help you ditch the meadow.
He has a plan. You mustn't laugh at him.
He may not speak of it, and then he may.
I'll sit and see if that small sailing cloud
Will hit or miss the moon."

                              It hit the moon.
Then there were three there, making a dim row,
The moon, the little silver cloud, and she.

Warren returned—too soon, it seemed to her,
Slipped to her side, caught up her hand and waited.

"Warren?" she questioned.

                               "Dead," was all he answered.

# THE MOUNTAIN

The mountain held the town as in a shadow.
I saw so much before I slept there once:
I noticed that I missed stars in the west,
Where its black body cut into the sky.
Near me it seemed: I felt it like a wall
Behind which I was sheltered from a wind.
And yet between the town and it I found,
When I walked forth at dawn to see new things,
Were fields, a river, and beyond, more fields.
The river at the time was fallen away,
And made a widespread brawl on cobblestones;
But the signs showed what it had done in spring:
Good grassland gullied out, and in the grass
Ridges of sand, and driftwood stripped of bark.
I crossed the river and swung round the mountain.
And there I met a man who moved so slow
With white-faced oxen in a heavy cart,
It seemed no harm to stop him altogether.

"What town is this?" I asked.

                    "This? Lunenburg."

Then I was wrong: the town of my sojourn,
Beyond the bridge, was not that of the mountain,
But only felt at night its shadowy presence.
"Where is your village? Very far from here?"

"There is no village—only scattered farms.
We were but sixty voters last election.
We can't in nature grow to many more:
That thing takes all the room!" He moved his goad.
The mountain stood there to be pointed at.
Pasture ran up the side a little way,
And then there was a wall of trees with trunks;
After that only tops of trees, and cliffs
Imperfectly concealed among the leaves.

A dry ravine emerged from under boughs
Into the pasture.

            "That looks like a path.
Is that the way to reach the top from here?—
Not for this morning, but some other time:
I must be getting back to breakfast now."

"I don't advise your trying from this side.
There is no proper path, but those that *have*
Been up, I understand, have climbed from Ladd's.
That's five miles back. You can't mistake the place:
They logged it there last winter some way up.
I'd take you, but I'm bound the other way."

"You've never climbed it?"

                      "I've been on the sides,
Deer-hunting and trout-fishing. There's a brook
That starts up on it somewhere—I've heard say
Right on the top, tip-top—a curious thing.
But what would interest you about the brook,
It's always cold in summer, warm in winter.
One of the great sights going is to see
It steam in winter like an ox's breath,
Until the bushes all along its banks
Are inch-deep with the frosty spines and bristles—
You know the kind. Then let the sun shine on it!"

"There ought to be a view around the world
From such a mountain—if it isn't wooded
Clear to the top." I saw through leafy screens
Great granite terraces in sun and shadow,
Shelves one could rest a knee on getting up—
With depths behind him sheer a hundred feet.
Or turn and sit on and look out and down,
With little ferns in crevices at his elbow.

"As to that I can't say. But there's the spring,

Right on the summit, almost like a fountain.
That ought to be worth seeing."

                              "If it's there.
You never saw it?"

                              "I guess there's no doubt
About its being there. I never saw it.
It may not be right on the very top:
It wouldn't have to be a long way down
To have some head of water from above,
And a *good distance* down might not be noticed
By anyone who'd come a long way up.
One time I asked a fellow climbing it
To look and tell me later how it was."

"What did he say?"

                              "He said there was a lake
Somewhere in Ireland on a mountain top."

"But a lake's different. What about the spring?"

"He never got up high enough to see.
That's why I don't advise your trying this side.
He tried this side. I've always meant to go
And look myself, but you know how it is:
It doesn't seem so much to climb a mountain
You've worked around the foot of all your life.
What would I do? Go in my overalls,
With a big stick, the same as when the cows
Haven't come down to the bars at milking time?
Or with a shotgun for a stray black bear?
'Twouldn't seem real to climb for climbing it."

"I shouldn't climb it if I didn't want to—
Not for the sake of climbing. What's its name?"

"We call it Hor: I don't know if that's right."

"Can one walk around it? Would it be too far?"

"You can drive round and keep in Lunenburg,
But it's as much as ever you can do,
The boundary lines keep in so close to it.
Hor is the township, and the township's Hor—
*And* a few houses sprinkled round the foot,
Like boulders broken off the upper cliff,
Rolled out a little farther than the rest."

"Warm in December, cold in June, you say?"

"I don't suppose the water's changed at all.
You and I know enough to know it's warm
Compared with cold, and cold compared with warm
But all the fun's in how you say a thing."

"You've lived here all your life?"

              "Ever since Hor
Was no bigger than a—" What, I did not hear.
He drew the oxen toward him with light touches
Of his slim goad on nose and offside flank,
Gave them their marching orders and was moving.

# A HUNDRED COLLARS

Lancaster bore him—such a little town,
Such a great man. It doesn't see him often
Of late years, though he keeps the old homestead
And sends the children down there with their mother
To run wild in the summer—a little wild.
Sometimes he joins them for a day or two
And sees old friends he somehow can't get near.
They meet him in the general store at night,
Preoccupied with formidable mail,
Rifling a printed letter as he talks.
They seem afraid. He wouldn't have it so:
Though a great scholar, he's a democrat,
If not at heart, at least on principle.
Lately when coming up to Lancaster,
His train being late, he missed another train
And had four hours to wait at Woodsville Junction
After eleven o'clock at night. Too tired
To think of sitting such an ordeal out,
He turned to the hotel to find a bed.

"No room," the night clerk said. "Unless—"

Woodsville's a place of shrieks and wandering lamps
And cars that shock and rattle—and *one* hotel.

"You say 'unless.'"

                    "Unless you wouldn't mind
Sharing a room with someone else."

                              "Who is it?"

"A man."

          "So I should hope. What kind of man?"

"I know him: he's all right. A man's a man.

Separate beds, of course, you understand."
The night clerk blinked his eyes and dared him on.

"Who's that man sleeping in the office chair?
Has he had the refusal of my chance?"

"He was afraid of being robbed or murdered.
What do you say?"

        "I'll have to have a bed."

The night clerk led him up three flights of stairs
And down a narrow passage full of doors,
At the last one of which he knocked and entered.
"Lafe, here's a fellow wants to share your room."

"Show him this way. I'm not afraid of him.
I'm not so drunk I can't take care of myself."

The night clerk clapped a bedstead on the foot.
"This will be yours. Good-night," he said, and went.

"Lafe was the name, I think?"

        "Yes, *Lay*fayette.
You got it the first time. And yours?"

        "Magoon.
Doctor Magoon."

    "A Doctor?"

        "Well, a teacher."

"Professor Square-the-circle-till-you're-tired?
Hold on, there's something I don't think of now
That I had on my mind to ask the first
Man that knew anything I happened in with.
I'll ask you later—don't let me forget it."

The Doctor looked at Lafe and looked away.
A man? A brute. Naked above the waist,
He sat there creased and shining in the light,
Fumbling the buttons in a well-starched shirt.
"I'm moving into a size-larger shirt.
I've felt mean lately; mean's no name for it.
I just found what the matter was tonight:
I've been a-choking like a nursery tree
When it outgrows the wire band of its name tag.
I blamed it on the hot spell we've been having.
'Twas nothing but my foolish hanging back,
Not liking to own up I'd grown a size.
Number eighteen this is. What size do you wear?"

The Doctor caught his throat convulsively.
"Oh—ah—fourteen—fourteen."

                    "Fourteen! You say so!
I can remember when I wore fourteen.
And come to think I must have back at home
More than a hundred collars, size fourteen.
Too bad to waste them all. You ought to have them.
They're yours and welcome; let me send them to you.
What makes you stand there on one leg like that?
You're not much furtherer than where Kike left you.
You act as if you wished you hadn't come.
Sit down or lie down, friend; you make me nervous."

The Doctor made a subdued dash for it,
And propped himself at bay against a pillow.

"Not that way, with your shoes on Kike's white bed.
You can't rest that way. Let me pull your shoes off."

"Don't touch me, please—I say, don't touch me, please.
I'll not be put to bed by you, my man."

"Just as you say. Have it your own way then.
'My man' is it? You talk like a professor.

Speaking of who's afraid of who, however,
I'm thinking I have more to lose than you
If anything should happen to be wrong.
Who wants to cut your number fourteen throat!
Let's have a showdown as an evidence
Of good faith. There is ninety dollars.
Come, if you're not afraid."

                    "I'm not afraid.
There's five: that's all I carry."

                         "I can search you?
Where are you moving over to? Stay still.
You'd better tuck your money under you
And sleep on it the way I always do
When I'm with people I don't trust at night."

"Will you believe me if I put it there
Right on the counterpane—that I do trust you?"

"You'd say so, Mister Man.—I'm a collector.
My ninety isn't mine—you won't think that.
I pick it up a dollar at a time
All round the country for the *Weekly News*,
Published in Bow. You know the *Weekly News?*"

"Known it since I was young."

                         "Then you know me.
Now we are getting on together—talking.
I'm sort of Something for it at the front.
My business is to find what people want:
They pay for it, and so they ought to have it.
Fairbanks, he says to me—he's editor—
'Feel out the public sentiment'—he says.
A good deal comes on me when all is said.
The only trouble is we disagree
In politics: I'm Vermont Democrat—
You know what that is, sort of double-dyed;

56

The *News* has always been Republican.
Fairbanks, he says to me, 'Help us this year,'
Meaning by us their ticket. 'No,' I says,
'I can't and won't. You've been in long enough:
It's time you turned around and boosted us.
You'll have to pay me more than ten a week
If I'm expected to elect Bill Taft.
I doubt if I could do it anyway.'"

"You seem to shape the paper's policy."

"You see I'm in with everybody, know 'em all.
I almost know their farms as well as they do."

"You drive around? It must be pleasant work."

"It's business, but I can't say it's not fun.
What I like best's the lay of different farms,
Coming out on them from a stretch of woods,
Or over a hill or round a sudden corner.
I like to find folks getting out in spring,
Raking the dooryard, working near the house.
Later they get out further in the fields.
Everything's shut sometimes except the barn;
The family's all away in some back meadow.
There's a hay load a-coming—when it comes.
And later still they all get driven in:
The fields are stripped to lawn, the garden patches
Stripped to bare ground, the maple trees
To whips and poles. There's nobody about.
The chimney, though, keeps up a good brisk smoking.
And I lie back and ride. I take the reins
Only when someone's coming, and the mare
Stops when she likes: I tell her when to go.
I've spoiled Jemima in more ways than one.
She's got so she turns in at every house
As if she had some sort of curvature,
No matter if I have no errand there.
She thinks I'm sociable. I maybe am.

It's seldom I get down except for meals, though.
Folks entertain me from the kitchen doorstep,
All in a family row down to the youngest."

"One would suppose they might not be as glad
To see you as you are to see them."

                                   "Oh,
Because I want their dollar? I don't want
Anything they've not got. I never dun.
I'm there, and they can pay me if they like.
I go nowhere on purpose: I happen by.
Sorry there is no cup to give you a drink.
I drink out of the bottle—not your style.
Mayn't I offer you—?"

                                "No, no, no, thank you."

"Just as you say. Here's looking at you then.—
And now I'm leaving you a little while.
You'll rest easier when I'm gone, perhaps—
Lie down—let yourself go and get some sleep.
But first—let's see—what was I going to ask you?
Those collars—who shall I address them to,
Suppose you aren't awake when I come back?"

"Really, friend, I can't let you. You—may need them."

"Not till I shrink, when they'll be out of style."

"But really I—I have so many collars."

"I don't know who I rather would have have them.
They're only turning yellow where they are.
But you're the doctor as the saying is.
I'll put the light out. Don't you wait for me:
I've just begun the night. You get some sleep.
I'll knock so-fashion and peep round the door
When I come back so you'll know who it is.

There's nothing I'm afraid of like scared people.
I don't want you should shoot me in the head.
What am I doing carrying off this bottle?
There now, you get some sleep."

                                        He shut the door.
The Doctor slid a little down the pillow.

# HOME BURIAL

He saw her from the bottom of the stairs
Before she saw him. She was starting down,
Looking back over her shoulder at some fear.
She took a doubtful step and then undid it
To raise herself and look again. He spoke
Advancing toward her. "What is it you see
From up there always—for I want to know."
She turned and sank upon her skirts at that,
And her face changed from terrified to dull.
He said to gain time: "What is it you see,"
Mounting until she cowered under him.
"I will find out now—you must tell me, dear."
She, in her place, refused him any help
With the least stiffening of her neck and silence.
She let him look, sure that he wouldn't see,
Blind creature; and awhile he didn't see.
But at last he murmured, "Oh," and again, "Oh."

"What is it—what?" she said.

                    "Just that I see."

"You don't," she challenged. "Tell me what it is."

"The wonder is I didn't see at once.
I never noticed it from here before.
I must be wonted to it—that's the reason.
The little graveyard where my people are!
So small the window frames the whole of it.
Not so much larger than a bedroom, is it?
There are three stones of slate and one of marble,
Broad-shouldered little slabs there in the sunlight
On the sidehill. We haven't to mind *those*.
But I understand: it is not the stones,
But the child's mound—"

          "Don't, don't, don't, don't," she cried.

She withdrew shrinking from beneath his arm
That rested on the banister, and slid downstairs;
And turned on him with such a daunting look,
He said twice over before he knew himself:
"Can't a man speak of his own child he's lost?"

"Not you! Oh, where's my hat? Oh, I don't need it!
I must get out of here. I must get air.
I don't know rightly whether any man can."

"Amy! Don't go to someone else this time.
Listen to me. I won't come down the stairs."
He sat and fixed his chin between his fists.
"There's something I should like to ask you, dear."

"You don't know how to ask it."

                                    "Help me, then."

Her fingers moved the latch for all reply.

"My words are nearly always an offense.
I don't know how to speak of anything
So as to please you. But I might be taught
I should suppose. I can't say I see how.
A man must partly give up being a man
With women-folk. We could have some arrangement
By which I'd bind myself to keep hands off
Anything special you're a-mind to name.
Though I don't like such things 'twixt those that love.
Two that don't love can't live together without them.
But two that do can't live together with them."
She moved the latch a little. "Don't—don't go.
Don't carry it to someone else this time.
Tell me about it if it's something human.
Let me into your grief. I'm not so much
Unlike other folks as your standing there
Apart would make me out. Give me my chance.
I do think, though, you overdo it a little.

What was it brought you up to think it the thing
To take your mother-loss of a first child
So inconsolably—in the face of love.
You'd think his memory might be satisfied—"

"There you go sneering now!"

                              "I'm not, I'm not!
You make me angry. I'll come down to you.
God, what a woman! And it's come to this,
A man can't speak of his own child that's dead."

"You can't because you don't know how to speak.
If you had any feelings, you that dug
With your own hand—how could you?—his little grave;
I saw you from that very window there,
Making the gravel leap and leap in air,
Leap up, like that, like that, and land so lightly
And roll back down the mound beside the hole.
I thought, Who is that man? I didn't know you.
And I crept down the stairs and up the stairs
To look again, and still your spade kept lifting.
Then you came in. I heard your rumbling voice
Out in the kitchen, and I don't know why,
But I went near to see with my own eyes.
You could sit there with the stains on your shoes
Of the fresh earth from your own baby's grave
And talk about your everyday concerns.
You had stood the spade up against the wall
Outside there in the entry, for I saw it."

"I shall laugh the worst laugh I ever laughed.
I'm cursed. God, if I don't believe I'm cursed."

"I can repeat the very words you were saying.
'Three foggy mornings and one rainy day
Will rot the best birch fence a man can build.'
Think of it, talk like that at such a time!
What had how long it takes a birch to rot

To do with what was in the darkened parlor.
You *couldn't* care! The nearest friends can go
With anyone to death, comes so far short
They might as well not try to go at all.
No, from the time when one is sick to death,
One is alone, and he dies more alone.
Friends make pretense of following to the grave,
But before one is in it, their minds are turned
And making the best of their way back to life
And living people, and things they understand.
But the world's evil. I won't have grief so
If I can change it. Oh, I won't, I won't!"

"There, you have said it all and you feel better.
You won't go now. You're crying. Close the door.
The heart's gone out of it: why keep it up.
Amy! There's someone coming down the road!"

"*You*—oh, you think the talk is all. I must go—
Somewhere out of this house. How can I make you—"

"If—you—do!" She was opening the door wider.
"Where do you mean to go? First tell me that.
I'll follow and bring you back by force. I *will!*—"

# THE BLACK COTTAGE

We chanced in passing by that afternoon
To catch it in a sort of special picture
Among tar-banded ancient cherry trees,
Set well back from the road in rank lodged grass,
The little cottage we were speaking of,
A front with just a door between two windows,
Fresh painted by the shower a velvet black.
We paused, the minister and I, to look.
He made as if to hold it at arm's length
Or put the leaves aside that framed it in.
"Pretty," he said. "Come in. No one will care."
The path was a vague parting in the grass
That led us to a weathered window-sill.
We pressed our faces to the pane. "You see," he said,
"Everything's as she left it when she died.
Her sons won't sell the house or the things in it.
They say they mean to come and summer here
Where they were boys. They haven't come this year.
They live so far away—one is out west—
It will be hard for them to keep their word.
Anyway they won't have the place disturbed."
A buttoned hair-cloth lounge spread scrolling arms
Under a crayon portrait on the wall,
Done sadly from an old daguerreotype.
"That was the father as he went to war.
She always, when she talked about the war,
Sooner or later came and leaned, half knelt
Against the lounge beside it, though I doubt
If such unlifelike lines kept power to stir
Anything in her after all the years.
He fell at Gettysburg or Fredericksburg,
I ought to know—it makes a difference which:
Fredericksburg wasn't Gettysburg, of course.
But what I'm getting to is how forsaken
A little cottage this has always seemed;
Since she went more than ever, but before—
I don't mean altogether by the lives

That had gone out of it, the father first,
Then the two sons, till she was left alone.
(Nothing could draw her after those two sons.
She valued the considerate neglect
She had at some cost taught them after years.)
I mean by the world's having passed it by—
As we almost got by this afternoon.
It always seems to me a sort of mark
To measure how far fifty years have brought us.
Why not sit down if you are in no haste?
These doorsteps seldom have a visitor.
The warping boards pull out their own old nails
With none to tread and put them in their place.
She had her own idea of things, the old lady.
And she liked talk. She had seen Garrison
And Whittier, and had her story of them.
One wasn't long in learning that she thought
Whatever else the Civil War was for
It wasn't just to keep the States together,
Nor just to free the slaves, though it did both.
She wouldn't have believed those ends enough
To have given outright for them all she gave.
Her giving somehow touched the principle
That all men are created free and equal.
And to hear her quaint phrases—so removed
From the world's view today of all those things.
That's a hard mystery of Jefferson's.
What did he mean? Of course the easy way
Is to decide it simply isn't true.
It may not be. I heard a fellow say so.
But never mind, the Welshman got it planted
Where it will trouble us a thousand years.
Each age will have to reconsider it.
You couldn't tell her what the West was saying,
And what the South to her serene belief.
She had some art of hearing and yet not
Hearing the latter wisdom of the world.
White was the only race she ever knew.
Black she had scarcely seen, and yellow never.

But how could they be made so very unlike
By the same hand working in the same stuff?
She had supposed the war decided that.
What are you going to do with such a person?
Strange how such innocence gets its own way.
I shouldn't be surprised if in this world
It were the force that would at last prevail.
Do you know but for her there was a time
When to please younger members of the church,
Or rather say non-members in the church,
Whom we all have to think of nowadays,
I would have changed the Creed a very little?
Not that she ever had to ask me not to;
It never got so far as that; but the bare thought
Of her old tremulous bonnet in the pew,
And of her half asleep was too much for me.
Why, I might wake her up and startle her.
It was the words 'descended into Hades'
That seemed too pagan to our liberal youth.
You know they suffered from a general onslaught.
And well, if they weren't true why keep right on
Saying them like the heathen? We could drop them.
Only—there was the bonnet in the pew.
Such a phrase couldn't have meant much to her.
But suppose she had missed it from the Creed
As a child misses the unsaid Good-night,
And falls asleep with heartache—how should I feel?
I'm just as glad she made me keep hands off,
For, dear me, why abandon a belief
Merely because it ceases to be true.
Cling to it long enough, and not a doubt
It will turn true again, for so it goes.
Most of the change we think we see in life
Is due to truths being in and out of favor.
As I sit here, and oftentimes, I wish
I could be monarch of a desert land
I could devote and dedicate forever
To the truths we keep coming back and back to.
So desert it would have to be, so walled

By mountain ranges half in summer snow,
No one would covet it or think it worth
The pains of conquering to force change on.
Scattered oases where men dwelt, but mostly
Sand dunes held loosely in tamarisk
Blown over and over themselves in idleness.
Sand grains should sugar in the natal dew
The babe born to the desert, the sand storm
Retard mid-waste my cowering caravans—
There are bees in this wall." He struck the clapboards,
Fierce heads looked out; small bodies pivoted.
We rose to go. Sunset blazed on the windows.

# BLUEBERRIES

"You ought to have seen what I saw on my way
To the village, through Patterson's pasture today:
Blueberries as big as the end of your thumb,
Real sky-blue, and heavy, and ready to drum
In the cavernous pail of the first one to come!
And all ripe together, not some of them green
And some of them ripe! You ought to have seen!"

"I don't know what part of the pasture you mean."

"You know where they cut off the woods—let me see—
It was two years ago—or no!—can it be
No longer than that?—and the following fall
The fire ran and burned it all up but the wall."

"Why, there hasn't been time for the bushes to grow.
That's always the way with the blueberries, though:
There may not have been the ghost of a sign
Of them anywhere under the shade of the pine,
But get the pine out of the way, you may burn
The pasture all over until not a fern
Or grass-blade is left, not to mention a stick,
And presto, they're up all around you as thick
And hard to explain as a conjuror's trick."

"It must be on charcoal they fatten their fruit.
I taste in them sometimes the flavor of soot.
And after all really they're ebony skinned:
The blue's but a mist from the breath of the wind,
A tarnish that goes at a touch of the hand,
And less than the tan with which pickers are tanned."

"Does Patterson know what he has, do you think?"

"He may and not care and so leave the chewink
To gather them for him—you know what he is.
He won't make the fact that they're rightfully his

An excuse for keeping us other folk out."

"I wonder you didn't see Loren about."

"The best of it was that I did. Do you know,
I was just getting through what the field had to show
And over the wall and into the road,
When who should come by, with a democrat-load
Of all the young chattering Lorens alive,
But Loren, the fatherly, out for a drive."

"He saw you, then? What did he do? Did he frown?"

"He just kept nodding his head up and down.
You know how politely he always goes by.
But he thought a big thought—I could tell by his eye—
Which being expressed, might be this in effect:
'I have left those there berries, I shrewdly suspect,
To ripen too long. I am greatly to blame.'"

"He's a thriftier person than some I could name."

"He seems to be thrifty; and hasn't he need,
With the mouths of all those young Lorens to feed?
He has brought them all up on wild berries, they say,
Like birds. They store a great many away.
They eat them the year round, and those they don't eat
They sell in the store and buy shoes for their feet."

"Who cares what they say? It's a nice way to live,
Just taking what Nature is willing to give,
Not forcing her hand with harrow and plow."

"I wish you had seen his perpetual bow—
And the air of the youngsters! No one of them turned,
And they looked so solemn-absurdly concerned."

"I wish I knew half what the flock of them know
Of where all the berries and other things grow,

Cranberries in bogs and raspberries on top
Of the boulder-strewn mountain, and when they will crop.
I met them one day and each had a flower
Stuck into his berries as fresh as a shower;
Some strange kind—they told me it hadn't a name."

"I've told you how once not long after we came,
I almost provoked poor Loren to mirth
By going to him of all people on earth
To ask if he knew any fruit to be had
For the picking. The rascal, he said he'd be glad
To tell if he knew. But the year had been bad.
There *had* been some berries—but those were all gone.
He didn't say where they had been. He went on:
'I'm sure—I'm sure'—as polite as could be.
He spoke to his wife in the door, 'Let me see,
Mame, *we* don't know any good berrying place?'
It was all he could do to keep a straight face."

"If he thinks all the fruit that grows wild is for him,
He'll find he's mistaken. See here, for a whim,
We'll pick in the Pattersons' pasture this year.
We'll go in the morning, that is, if it's clear,
And the sun shines out warm: the vines must be wet.
It's so long since I picked I almost forget
How we used to pick berries: we took one look round,
Then sank out of sight like trolls underground,
And saw nothing more of each other, or heard,
Unless when you said I was keeping a bird
Away from its nest, and I said it was you.
'Well, one of us is.' For complaining it flew
Around and around us. And then for a while
We picked, till I feared you had wandered a mile,
And I thought I had lost you. I lifted a shout
Too loud for the distance you were, it turned out,
For when you made answer, your voice was as low
As talking—you stood up beside me, you know."

"We sha'n't have the place to ourselves to enjoy—

Not likely, when all the young Lorens deploy.
They'll be there tomorrow, or even tonight.
They won't be too friendly—they may be polite—
To people they look on as having no right
To pick where they're picking. But we won't complain.
You ought to have seen how it looked in the rain,
The fruit mixed with water in layers of leaves,
Like two kinds of jewels, a vision for thieves."

# A SERVANT TO SERVANTS

I didn't make you know how glad I was
To have you come and camp here on our land.
I promised myself to get down some day
And see the way you lived, but I don't know!
With a houseful of hungry men to feed
I guess you'd find....It seems to me
I can't express my feelings any more
Than I can raise my voice or want to lift
My hand (oh, I can lift it when I have to).
Did ever you feel so? I hope you never.
It's got so I don't even know for sure
Whether I *am* glad, sorry, or anything.
There's nothing but a voice-like left inside
That seems to tell me how I ought to feel,
And would feel if I wasn't all gone wrong.
You take the lake. I look and look at it.
I see it's a fair, pretty sheet of water.
I stand and make myself repeat out loud
The advantages it has, so long and narrow,
Like a deep piece of some old running river
Cut short off at both ends. It lies five miles
Straight away through the mountain notch
From the sink window where I wash the plates,
And all our storms come up toward the house,
Drawing the slow waves whiter and whiter and whiter.
It took my mind off doughnuts and soda biscuit
To step outdoors and take the water dazzle
A sunny morning, or take the rising wind
About my face and body and through my wrapper,
When a storm threatened from the Dragon's Den,
And a cold chill shivered across the lake.
I see it's a fair, pretty sheet of water,
Our Willoughby! How did you hear of it?
I expect, though, everyone's heard of it.
In a book about ferns? Listen to that!
You let things more like feathers regulate
Your going and coming. And you like it here?

I can see how you might. But I don't know!
It would be different if more people came,
For then there would be business. As it is,
The cottages Len built, sometimes we rent them,
Sometimes we don't. We've a good piece of shore
That ought to be worth something, and may yet.
But I don't count on it as much as Len.
He looks on the bright side of everything,
Including me. He thinks I'll be all right
With doctoring. But it's not medicine—
Lowe is the only doctor's dared to say so—
It's rest I want—there, I have said it out—
From cooking meals for hungry hired men
And washing dishes after them—from doing
Things over and over that just won't stay done.
By good rights I ought not to have so much
Put on me, but there seems no other way.
Len says one steady pull more ought to do it.
He says the best way out is always through.
And I agree to that, or in so far
As that I can see no way out but through—
Leastways for me—and then they'll be convinced.
It's not that Len don't want the best for me.
It was his plan our moving over in
Beside the lake from where that day I showed you
We used to live—ten miles from anywhere.
We didn't change without some sacrifice,
But Len went at it to make up the loss.
His work's a man's, of course, from sun to sun,
But he works when he works as hard as I do—
Though there's small profit in comparisons.
(Women and men will make them all the same.)
But work ain't all. Len undertakes too much.
He's into everything in town. This year
It's highways, and he's got too many men
Around him to look after that make waste.
They take advantage of him shamefully,
And proud, too, of themselves for doing so.
We have four here to board, great good-for-nothings,

Sprawling about the kitchen with their talk
While I fry their bacon. Much they care!
No more put out in what they do or say
Than if I wasn't in the room at all.
Coming and going all the time, they are:
I don't learn what their names are, let alone
Their characters, or whether they are safe
To have inside the house with doors unlocked.
I'm not afraid of them, though, if they're not
Afraid of me. There's two can play at that.
I have my fancies: it runs in the family.
My father's brother wasn't right. They kept him
Locked up for years back there at the old farm.
I've been away once—yes, I've been away.
The State Asylum. I was prejudiced;
I wouldn't have sent anyone of mine there;
You know the old idea—the only asylum
Was the poorhouse, and those who could afford,
Rather than send their folks to such a place,
Kept them at home; and it does seem more human.
But it's not so: the place is the asylum.
There they have every means proper to do with,
And you aren't darkening other people's lives—
Worse than no good to them, and they no good
To you in your condition; you can't know
Affection or the want of it in that state.
I've heard too much of the old-fashioned way.
My father's brother, he went mad quite young.
Some thought he had been bitten by a dog,
Because his violence took on the form
Of carrying his pillow in his teeth;
But it's more likely he was crossed in love,
Or so the story goes. It was some girl.
Anyway all he talked about was love.
They soon saw he would do someone a mischief
If he wa'n't kept strict watch of, and it ended
In father's building him a sort of cage,
Or room within a room, of hickory poles,
Like stanchions in the barn, from floor to ceiling,—

A narrow passage all the way around.
Anything they put in for furniture
He'd tear to pieces, even a bed to lie on.
So they made the place comfortable with straw,
Like a beast's stall, to ease their consciences.
Of course they had to feed him without dishes.
They tried to keep him clothed, but he paraded
With his clothes on his arm—all of his clothes.
Cruel—it sounds. I s'pose they did the best
They knew. And just when he was at the height,
Father and mother married, and mother came,
A bride, to help take care of such a creature,
And accommodate her young life to his.
That was what marrying father meant to her.
She had to lie and hear love things made dreadful
By his shouts in the night. He'd shout and shout
Until the strength was shouted out of him,
And his voice died down slowly from exhaustion.
He'd pull his bars apart like bow and bowstring,
And let them go and make them twang until
His hands had worn them smooth as any oxbow.
And then he'd crow as if he thought that child's play—
The only fun he had. I've heard them say, though,
They found a way to put a stop to it.
He was before my time—I never saw him;
But the pen stayed exactly as it was
There in the upper chamber in the ell,
A sort of catch-all full of attic clutter.
I often think of the smooth hickory bars.
It got so I would say—you know, half fooling—
"It's time I took my turn upstairs in jail"—
Just as you will till it becomes a habit.
No wonder I was glad to get away.
Mind you, I waited till Len said the word.
I didn't want the blame if things went wrong.
I was glad though, no end, when we moved out,
And I looked to be happy, and I was,
As I said, for a while—but I don't know!
Somehow the change wore out like a prescription.

And there's more to it than just window-views
And living by a lake. I'm past such help—
Unless Len took the notion, which he won't,
And I won't ask him—it's not sure enough.
I s'pose I've got to go the road I'm going:
Other folks have to, and why shouldn't I?
I almost think if I could do like you,
Drop everything and live out on the ground—
But it might be, come night, I shouldn't like it,
Or a long rain. I should soon get enough,
And be glad of a good roof overhead.
I've lain awake thinking of you, I'll warrant,
More than you have yourself, some of these nights.
The wonder was the tents weren't snatched away
From over you as you lay in your beds.
I haven't courage for a risk like that.
Bless you, of course, you're keeping me from work,
But the thing of it is, I need to *be* kept.
There's work enough to do—there's always that;
But behind's behind. The worst that you can do
Is set me back a little more behind.
I sha'n't catch up in this world, anyway.
I'd *rather* you'd not go unless you must.

# AFTER APPLE-PICKING

My long two-pointed ladder's sticking through a tree
Toward heaven still,
And there's a barrel that I didn't fill
Beside it, and there may be two or three
Apples I didn't pick upon some bough.
But I am done with apple-picking now.
Essence of winter sleep is on the night,
The scent of apples: I am drowsing off.
I cannot rub the strangeness from my sight
I got from looking through a pane of glass
I skimmed this morning from the drinking trough
And held against the world of hoary grass.
It melted, and I let it fall and break.
But I was well
Upon my way to sleep before it fell,
And I could tell
What form my dreaming was about to take.
Magnified apples appear and disappear,
Stem end and blossom end,
And every fleck of russet showing clear.
My instep arch not only keeps the ache,
It keeps the pressure of a ladder-round.
I feel the ladder sway as the boughs bend.
And I keep hearing from the cellar bin
The rumbling sound
Of load on load of apples coming in.
For I have had too much
Of apple-picking: I am overtired
Of the great harvest I myself desired.
There were ten thousand thousand fruit to touch,
Cherish in hand, lift down, and not let fall.
For all
That struck the earth,
No matter if not bruised or spiked with stubble,
Went surely to the cider-apple heap
As of no worth.
One can see what will trouble

This sleep of mine, whatever sleep it is.
Were he not gone,
The woodchuck could say whether it's like his
Long sleep, as I describe its coming on,
Or just some human sleep.

# THE CODE

There were three in the meadow by the brook
Gathering up windrows, piling cocks of hay,
With an eye always lifted toward the west
Where an irregular sun-bordered cloud
Darkly advanced with a perpetual dagger
Flickering across its bosom. Suddenly
One helper, thrusting pitchfork in the ground,
Marched himself off the field and home. One stayed.
The town-bred farmer failed to understand.

"What is there wrong?"

                              "Something you just now said."

"What did I say?"

                    "About our taking pains."

"To cock the hay?—because it's going to shower?
I said that more than half an hour ago.
I said it to myself as much as you."

"You didn't know. But James is one big fool.
He thought you meant to find fault with his work.
That's what the average farmer would have meant.
James would take time, of course, to chew it over
Before he acted: he's just got round to act."

"He is a fool if that's the way he takes me."

"Don't let it bother you. You've found out something.
The hand that knows his business won't be told
To do work better or faster—those two things.
I'm as particular as anyone:
Most likely I'd have served you just the same.
But I know you don't understand our ways.
You were just talking what was in your mind,

What was in all our minds, and you weren't hinting.
Tell you a story of what happened once:
I was up here in Salem at a man's
Named Sanders with a gang of four or five
Doing the haying. No one liked the boss.
He was one of the kind sports call a spider,
All wiry arms and legs that spread out wavy
From a humped body nigh as big's a biscuit.
But work! that man could work, especially
If by so doing he could get more work
Out of his hired help. I'm not denying
He was hard on himself. I couldn't find
That he kept any hours—not for himself.
Daylight and lantern-light were one to him:
I've heard him pounding in the barn all night.
But what he liked was someone to encourage.
Them that he couldn't lead he'd get behind
And drive, the way you can, you know, in mowing—
Keep at their heels and threaten to mow their legs off.
I'd seen about enough of his bulling tricks
(We call that bulling). I'd been watching him.
So when he paired off with me in the hayfield
To load the load, thinks I, Look out for trouble.
I built the load and topped it off; old Sanders
Combed it down with a rake and says, 'O.K.'
Everything went well till we reached the barn
With a big jag to empty in a bay.
You understand that meant the easy job
For the man up on top of throwing *down*
The hay and rolling it off wholesale,
Where on a mow it would have been slow lifting.
You wouldn't think a fellow'd need much urging
Under those circumstances, would you now?
But the old fool seizes his fork in both hands,
And looking up bewhiskered out of the pit,
Shouts like an army captain, 'Let her come!'
Thinks I, D'ye mean it? 'What was that you said?'
I asked out loud, so's there'd be no mistake,
'Did you say, Let her come?' 'Yes, let her come.'

He said it over, but he said it softer.
Never you say a thing like that to a man,
Not if he values what he is. God, I'd as soon
Murdered him as left out his middle name.
I'd built the load and knew right where to find it.
Two or three forkfuls I picked lightly round for
Like meditating, and then I just dug in
And dumped the rackful on him in ten lots.
I looked over the side once in the dust
And caught sight of him treading-water-like,
Keeping his head above. 'Damn ye,' I says,
'That gets ye!' He squeaked like a squeezed rat.
That was the last I saw or heard of him.
I cleaned the rack and drove out to cool off.
As I sat mopping hayseed from my neck,
And sort of waiting to be asked about it,
One of the boys sings out, 'Where's the old man?'
'I left him in the barn under the hay.
If ye want him, ye can go and dig him out.'
They realized from the way I swabbed my neck
More than was needed something must be up.
They headed for the barn; I stayed where I was.
They told me afterward. First they forked hay,
A lot of it, out into the barn floor.
Nothing! They listened for him. Not a rustle.
I guess they thought I'd spiked him in the temple
Before I buried him, or I couldn't have managed.
They excavated more. 'Go keep his wife
Out of the barn.' Someone looked in a window,
And curse me if he wasn't in the kitchen
Slumped way down in a chair, with both his feet
Against the stove, the hottest day that summer.
He looked so clean disgusted from behind
There was no one that dared to stir him up,
Or let him know that he was being looked at.
Apparently I hadn't buried him
(I may have knocked him down); but my just trying
To bury him had hurt his dignity.
He had gone to the house so's not to meet me.

He kept away from us all afternoon.
We tended to his hay. We saw him out
After a while picking peas in his garden:
He couldn't keep away from doing something."

"Weren't you relieved to find he wasn't dead?"

"No! and yet I don't know—it's hard to say.
I went about to kill him fair enough."

"You took an awkward way. Did he discharge you?"

"Discharge me? No! He knew I did just right."

# THE GENERATIONS OF MEN

A governor it was proclaimed this time,
When all who would come seeking in New Hampshire
Ancestral memories might come together.
And those of the name Stark gathered in Bow,
A rock-strewn town where farming has fallen off,
And sprout-lands flourish where the ax has gone.
Someone had literally run to earth
In an old cellar hole in a by-road
The origin of all the family there.
Thence they were sprung, so numerous a tribe
That now not all the houses left in town
Made shift to shelter them without the help
Of here and there a tent in grove and orchard.
They were at Bow, but that was not enough:
Nothing would do but they must fix a day
To stand together on the crater's verge
That turned them on the world, and try to fathom
The past and get some strangeness out of it.
But rain spoiled all. The day began uncertain,
With clouds low trailing and moments of rain that misted.
The young folk held some hope out to each other
Till well toward noon when the storm settled down
With a swish in the grass. "What if the others
Are there," they said. "It isn't going to rain."
Only one from a farm not far away
Strolled thither, not expecting he would find
Anyone else, but out of idleness.
One, and one other, yes, for there were two.
The second round the curving hillside road
Was a girl; and she halted some way off
To reconnoiter, and then made up her mind
At least to pass by and see who he was,
And perhaps hear some word about the weather.
This was some Stark she didn't know. He nodded.
"No fête today," he said.

                    "It looks that way."

She swept the heavens, turning on her heel.
"I only idled down."

        "I idled down."

Provision there had been for just such meeting
Of stranger cousins, in a family tree
Drawn on a sort of passport with the branch
Of the one bearing it done in detail—
Some zealous one's laborious device.
She made a sudden movement toward her bodice,
As one who clasps her heart. They laughed together.
"Stark?" he inquired. "No matter for the proof."

"Yes, Stark. And you?"

                "I'm Stark." He drew his passport.

"You know we might not be and still be cousins:
The town is full of Chases, Lowes, and Baileys,
All claiming some priority in Starkness.
My mother was a Lane, yet might have married
Anyone upon earth and still her children
Would have been Starks, and doubtless here today."

"You riddle with your genealogy
Like a Viola. I don't follow you."

"I only mean my mother was a Stark
Several times over, and by marrying father
No more than brought us back into the name."

"One ought not to be thrown into confusion
By a plain statement of relationship,
But I own what you say makes my head spin.
You take my card—you seem so good at such things—
And see if you can reckon our cousinship.
Why not take seats here on the cellar wall
And dangle feet among the raspberry vines?"

"Under the shelter of the family tree."

"Just so—that ought to be enough protection."

"Not from the rain. I think it's going to rain."

"It's raining."

> "No, it's misting; let's be fair.
Does the rain seem to you to cool the eyes?"

The situation was like this: the road
Bowed outward on the mountain halfway up,
And disappeared and ended not far off.
No one went home that way. The only house
Beyond where they were was a shattered seedpod.
And below roared a brook hidden in trees,
The sound of which was silence for the place.
This he sat listening to till she gave judgment.

"On father's side, it seems, we're—let me see—"

"Don't be too technical.—You have three cards."

"Four cards, one yours, three mine, one for each branch
Of the Stark family I'm a member of."

"D'you know a person so related to herself
Is supposed to be mad."

> "I may be mad."

"You look so, sitting out here in the rain
Studying genealogy with me
You never saw before. What will we come to
With all this pride of ancestry, we Yankees?
I think we're all mad. Tell me why we're here
Drawn into town about this cellar hole
Like wild geese on a lake before a storm?

85

What do we see in such a hole, I wonder."

"The Indians had a myth of Chicamoztoc,
Which means The Seven Caves that We Came out of.
This is the pit from which we Starks were digged."

"You must be learned. That's what you see in it?"

"And what do you see?"

                    "Yes, what *do* I see?
First let me look. I see raspberry vines—"

"Oh, if you're going to use your eyes, just hear
What *I* see. It's a little, little boy,
As pale and dim as a match flame in the sun;
He's groping in the cellar after jam,
He thinks it's dark and it's flooded with daylight."

"He's nothing. Listen. When I lean like this
I can make out old Grandsir Stark distinctly,—
With his pipe in his mouth and his brown jug—
Bless you, it isn't Grandsir Stark, it's Granny,
But the pipe's there and smoking and the jug.
She's after cider, the old girl, she's thirsty;
Here's hoping she gets her drink and gets out safely."

"Tell me about her. Does she look like me?"

"She should, shouldn't she, you're so many times
Over descended from her. I believe
She does look like you. Stay the way you are.
The nose is just the same, and so's the chin—
Making allowance, making due allowance."

"You poor, dear, great, great, great, great Granny!"

"See that you get her greatness right. Don't stint her."

"Yes, it's important, though you think it isn't.
I won't be teased. But see how wet I am."

"Yes, you must go; we can't stay here for ever.
But wait until I give you a hand up.
A bead of silver water more or less
Strung on your hair won't hurt your summer looks.
I wanted to try something with the noise
That the brook raises in the empty valley.
We have seen visions—now consult the voices.
Something I must have learned riding in trains
When I was young. I used to use the roar
To set the voices speaking out of it,
Speaking or singing, and the band-music playing.
Perhaps you have the art of what I mean.
I've never listened in among the sounds
That a brook makes in such a wild descent.
It ought to give a purer oracle."

"It's as you throw a picture on a screen:
The meaning of it all is out of you;
The voices give you what you wish to hear."

"Strangely, it's anything they wish to give."

"Then I don't know. It must be strange enough.
I wonder if it's not your make-believe.
What do you think you're like to hear today?"

"From the sense of our having been together—
But why take time for what I'm like to hear?
I'll tell you what the voices really say.
You will do very well right where you are
A little longer. I mustn't feel too hurried,
Or I can't give myself to hear the voices."

"Is this some trance you are withdrawing into?"

"You must be very still; you mustn't talk."

"I'll hardly breathe."

　　　　"The voices seem to say—"

"I'm waiting."

　　　　"Don't! The voices seem to say:
Call her Nausicaä, the unafraid
Of an acquaintance made adventurously."

"I let you say that—on consideration."

"I don't see very well how you can help it.
You want the truth. I speak but by the voices.
You see they know I haven't had your name,
Though what a name should matter between us—"

"I shall suspect—"

　　　　"Be good. The voices say:
Call her Nausicaä, and take a timber
That you shall find lies in the cellar charred
Among the raspberries, and hew and shape it
For a door-sill or other corner piece
In a new cottage on the ancient spot.
The life is not yet all gone out of it.
And come and make your summer dwelling here,
And perhaps she will come, still unafraid,
And sit before you in the open door
With flowers in her lap until they fade,
But not come in across the sacred sill—"

"I wonder where your oracle is tending.
You can see that there's something wrong with it,
Or it would speak in dialect. Whose voice
Does it purport to speak in? Not old Grandsir's
Nor Granny's, surely. Call up one of them.
They have best right to be heard in this place."

"You seem so partial to our great-grandmother
(Nine times removed. Correct me if I err.)
You will be likely to regard as sacred
Anything she may say. But let me warn you,
Folks in her day were given to plain speaking.
You think you'd best tempt her at such a time?"

"It rests with us always to cut her off."

"Well then, it's Granny speaking: 'I dunnow!
Mebbe I'm wrong to take it as I do.
There ain't no names quite like the old ones though,
Nor never will be to my way of thinking.
One mustn't bear too hard on the newcomers,
But there's a dite too many of them for comfort.
I should feel easier if I could see
More of the salt wherewith they're to be salted.
Son, you do as you're told! You take the timber—
It's as sound as the day when it was cut—
And begin over—' There, she'd better stop.
You can see what is troubling Granny, though.
But don't you think we sometimes make too much
Of the old stock? What counts is the ideals,
And those will bear some keeping still about."

"I can see we are going to be good friends."

"I like your 'going to be.' You said just now
It's going to rain."

      "I know, and it was raining.
I let you say all that. But I must go now."

"You let me say it? on consideration?
How shall we say good-by in such a case?"

"How shall we?"

      "Will you leave the way to me?"

"No, I don't trust your eyes. You've said enough.
Now give me your hand up.—Pick me that flower."

"Where shall we meet again?"

                         "Nowhere but here
Once more before we meet elsewhere."

                                "In rain?"

"It ought to be in rain. Sometime in rain.
In rain tomorrow, shall we, if it rains?
But if we must, in sunshine." So she went.

# THE HOUSEKEEPER

I let myself in at the kitchen door.

"It's you," she said. "I can't get up. Forgive me
Not answering your knock. I can no more
Let people in than I can keep them out.
I'm getting too old for my size, I tell them.
My fingers are about all I've the use of
So's to take any comfort. I can sew:
I help out with this beadwork what I can."

"That's a smart pair of pumps you're beading there.
Who are they for?"

           "You mean?—oh, for some miss.
I can't keep track of other people's daughters.
Lord, if I were to dream of everyone
Whose shoes I primped to dance in!"

                    "And where's John?"

"Haven't you seen him? Strange what set you off
To come to his house when he's gone to yours.
You can't have passed each other. I know what:
He must have changed his mind and gone to Garland's.
He won't be long in that case. You can wait.
Though what good you can be, or anyone—
It's gone so far. You've heard? Estelle's run off."

"Yes, what's it all about? When did she go?"

"Two weeks since."

             "She's in earnest, it appears."

"I'm sure she won't come back. She's hiding somewhere.
I don't know where myself. John thinks I do.
He thinks I only have to say the word,

And she'll come back. But, bless you, I'm her mother—
I can't talk to her, and, Lord, if I could!"

"It will go hard with John. What will he do?
He can't find anyone to take her place."

"Oh, if you ask me that, what *will* he do?
He gets some sort of bakeshop meals together,
With me to sit and tell him everything,
What's wanted and how much and where it is.
But when I'm gone—of course I can't stay here:
Estelle's to take me when she's settled down.
He and I only hinder one another.
I tell them they can't get me through the door, though:
I've been built in here like a big church organ.
We've been here fifteen years."

                              "That's a long time
To live together and then pull apart.
How do you see him living when you're gone?
Two of you out will leave an empty house."

"I don't just see him living many years,
Left here with nothing but the furniture.
I hate to think of the old place when we're gone,
With the brook going by below the yard,
And no one here but hens blowing about.
If he could sell the place, but then, he can't:
No one will ever live on it again.
It's too run down. This is the last of it.
What I think he will do, is let things smash.
He'll sort of swear the time away. He's awful!
I never saw a man let family troubles
Make so much difference in his man's affairs.
He's just dropped everything. He's like a child.
I blame his being brought up by his mother.
He's got hay down that's been rained on three times.
He hoed a little yesterday for me:
I thought the growing things would do him good."

Something went wrong. I saw him throw the hoe
Sky-high with both hands. I can see it now—
Come here—I'll show you—in that apple tree.
That's no way for a man to do at his age:
He's fifty-five, you know, if he's a day."

"Aren't you afraid of him? What's that gun for?"

"Oh, that's been there for hawks since chicken-time.
John Hall touch me! Not if he knows his friends.
I'll say that for him, John's no threatener
Like some menfolk. No one's afraid of him;
All is, he's made up his mind not to stand
What he has got to stand."

              "Where is Estelle?
Couldn't one talk to her? What does she say?
You say you don't know where she is."

                       "Nor want to!
She thinks if it was bad to live with him,
It must be right to leave him."

                  "Which is wrong!"

"Yes, but he should have married her."

                     "I know."

"The strain's been too much for her all these years:
I can't explain it any other way.
It's different with a man, at least with John:
He knows he's kinder than the run of men.
Better than married ought to be as good
As married—that's what he has always said.
I know the way he's felt—but all the same!"

"I wonder why he doesn't marry her
And end it."

93

"Too late now: she wouldn't have him.
He's given her time to think of something else.
That's his mistake. The dear knows my interest
Has been to keep the thing from breaking up.
This is a good home: I don't ask for better.
But when I've said, 'Why shouldn't they be married,'
He'd say, 'Why should they?' no more words than that."

"And after all why should they? John's been fair
I take it. What was his was always hers.
There was no quarrel about property."

"Reason enough, there was no property.
A friend or two as good as own the farm,
Such as it is. It isn't worth the mortgage."

"I mean Estelle has always held the purse."

"The rights of that are harder to get at.
I guess Estelle and I have filled the purse.
'Twas we let him have money, not he us.
John's a bad farmer. I'm not blaming him.
Take it year in, year out, he doesn't make much.
We came here for a home for me, you know,
Estelle to do the housework for the board
Of both of us. But look how it turns out:
She seems to have the housework, and besides
Half of the outdoor work, though as for that,
He'd say she does it more because she likes it.
You see our pretty things are all outdoors.
Our hens and cows and pigs are always better
Than folks like us have any business with.
Farmers around twice as well off as we
Haven't as good. They don't go with the farm.
One thing you can't help liking about John,
He's fond of nice things—too fond, some would say.
But Estelle don't complain: she's like him there.
She wants our hens to be the best there are.
You never saw this room before a show,

Full of lank, shivery, half-drowned birds
In separate coops, having their plumage done.
The smell of the wet feathers in the heat!
You spoke of John's not being safe to stay with.
You don't know what a gentle lot we are:
We wouldn't hurt a hen! You ought to see us
Moving a flock of hens from place to place.
We're not allowed to take them upside down,
All we can hold together by the legs.
Two at a time's the rule, one on each arm,
No matter how far and how many times
We have to go."

       "You mean that's John's idea."

"And we live up to it; or I don't know
What childishness he wouldn't give way to.
He manages to keep the upper hand
On his own farm. He's boss. But as to hens:
We fence our flowers in and the hens range.
Nothing's too good for them. We say it pays.
John likes to tell the offers he has had,
Twenty for this cock, twenty-five for that.
He never takes the money. If they're worth
That much to sell, they're worth as much to keep.
Bless you, it's all expense, though. Reach me down
The little tin box on the cupboard shelf,
The upper shelf, the tin box. That's the one.
I'll show you. Here you are."

       "What's this?"

       "A bill—
For fifty dollars for one Langshang cock—
Receipted. And the cock is in the yard."

"Not in a glass case, then?"

       "He'd need a tall one:

He can eat off a barrel from the ground.
He's been in a glass case, as you may say,
The Crystal Palace, London. He's imported.
John bought him, and we paid the bill with beads—
Wampum, I call it. Mind, we don't complain.
But you see, don't you, we take care of him."

"And like it, too. It makes it all the worse."

"It seems as if. And that's not all: he's helpless
In ways that I can hardly tell you of.
Sometimes he gets possessed to keep accounts
To see where all the money goes so fast.
You know how men will be ridiculous.
But it's just fun the way he gets bedeviled—
If he's untidy now, what will he be—?"

"It makes it all the worse. You must be blind."

"Estelle's the one. You needn't talk to me."

"Can't you and I get to the root of it?
What's the real trouble? What will satisfy her?"

"It's as I say: she's turned from him, that's all."

"But why, when she's well off? Is it the neighbors,
Being cut off from friends?"

                    "We have our friends.
That isn't it. Folks aren't afraid of us."

"She's let it worry her. You stood the strain,
And you're her mother."

                    "But I didn't always.
I didn't relish it along at first.
But I got wonted to it. And besides—
John said I was too old to have grandchildren.

But what's the use of talking when it's done?
She won't come back—it's worse than that—she can't."

"Why do you speak like that? What do you know?
What do you mean?—she's done harm to herself?"

"I mean she's married—married someone else."

"Oho, oho!"

    "You don't believe me."

                  "Yes, I do,
Only too well. I knew there must be something!
So that was what was back. She's bad, that's all!"

"Bad to get married when she had the chance?"

"Nonsense! See what she's done! But who, but who—"

"Who'd marry her straight out of such a mess?
Say it right out—no matter for her mother.
The man was found. I'd better name no names.
John himself won't imagine who he is."

"Then it's all up. I think I'll get away.
You'll be expecting John. I pity Estelle;
I suppose she deserves some pity, too.
You ought to have the kitchen to yourself
To break it to him. You may have the job."

"You needn't think you're going to get away.
John's almost here. I've had my eye on someone
Coming down Ryan's Hill. I thought 'twas him.
Here he is now. This box! Put it away.
And this bill."

       "What's the hurry? He'll unhitch."

"No, he won't, either. He'll just drop the reins
And turn Doll out to pasture, rig and all.
She won't get far before the wheels hang up
On something—there's no harm. See, there he is!
My, but he looks as if he must have heard!"

John threw the door wide but he didn't enter.
"How are you, neighbor? Just the man I'm after.
Isn't it Hell," he said. "I want to know.
Come out here if you want to hear me talk.
I'll talk to you, old woman, afterward.
I've got some news that maybe isn't news.
What are they trying to do to me, these two?"

"Do go along with him and stop his shouting."
She raised her voice against the closing door:
"Who wants to hear your news, you—dreadful fool?"

# THE FEAR

A lantern light from deeper in the barn
Shone on a man and woman in the door
And threw their lurching shadows on a house
Nearby, all dark in every glossy window.
A horse's hoof pawed once the hollow floor,
And the back of the gig they stood beside
Moved in a little. The man grasped a wheel,
The woman spoke out sharply, "Whoa, stand still!
I saw it just as plain as a white plate,"
She said, "as the light on the dashboard ran
Along the bushes at the roadside—a man's face,
You *must* have seen it too."

                    "I didn't see it.

Are you sure—"

            "Yes, I'm sure!"

                        "—it was a face?"

"Joel, I'll have to look. I can't go in,
I can't, and leave a thing like that unsettled.
Doors locked and curtains drawn will make no difference.
I always have felt strange when we came home
To the dark house after so long an absence,
And the key rattled loudly into place
Seemed to warn someone to be getting out
At one door as we entered at another.
What if I'm right, and someone all the time—
Don't hold my arm!"

                "I say it's someone passing."

"You speak as if this were a traveled road.
You forget where we are. What is beyond
That he'd be going to or coming from

At such an hour of night, and on foot too?
What was he standing still for in the bushes?"

"It's not so very late—it's only dark.
There's more in it than you're inclined to say.
Did he look like—?"

     "He looked like anyone.
I'll never rest tonight unless I know.
Give me the lantern."

      "You don't want the lantern."

She pushed past him and got it for herself.

"You're not to come," she said. "This is my business
If the time's come to face it, I'm the one
To put it the right way. He'd never dare—
Listen! He kicked a stone. Hear that, hear that!
He's coming towards us. Joel, *go* in—please.
Hark!—I don't hear him now. But please go in."

"In the first place you can't make me believe it's—"

"It is—or someone else he's sent to watch.
And now's the time to have it out with him
While we know definitely where he is.
Let him get off and he'll be everywhere
Around us, looking out of trees and bushes
Till I sha'n't dare to set a foot outdoors.
And I can't stand it. Joel, let me go!"

"But it's nonsense to think he'd care enough."

"You mean you couldn't understand his caring.
Oh, but you see he hadn't had enough—
Joel, I won't—I won't—I promise you.
We mustn't say hard things. You mustn't either."

"I'll be the one, if anybody goes!
But you give him the advantage with this light.
What couldn't he do to us standing here!
And if to see was what he wanted, why,
He has seen all there was to see and gone."

He appeared to forget to keep his hold,
But advanced with her as she crossed the grass.

"What do you want?" she cried to all the dark.
She stretched up tall to overlook the light
That hung in both hands hot against her skirt.

"There's no one; so you're wrong," he said.

                                    "There is.—
What do you want?" she cried, and then herself
Was startled when an answer really came.

"Nothing." It came from well along the road.

She reached a hand to Joel for support:
The smell of scorching woolen made her faint.
"What are you doing round this house at night?"

"Nothing." A pause: there seemed no more to say.

And then the voice again: "You seem afraid.
I saw by the way you whipped up the horse.
I'll just come forward in the lantern light
And let you see."

                    "Yes, do.—Joel, go back!"

She stood her ground against the noisy steps
That came on, but her body rocked a little.

"You see," the voice said.

"Oh." She looked and looked.

"You don't see—I've a child here by the hand.
A robber wouldn't have his family with him."

"What's a child doing at this time of night—?"

"Out walking. Every child should have the memory
Of at least one long-after-bedtime walk.
What, son?"

"Then I should think you'd try to find
Somewhere to walk—"

                    "The highway, as it happens—
We're stopping for the fortnight down at Dean's."

"But if that's all—Joel—you realize—
You won't think anything. You understand?
You understand that we have to be careful.
This is a very, very lonely place.
Joel!" She spoke as if she couldn't turn.
The swinging lantern lengthened to the ground,
It touched, it struck, it clattered and went out.

# THE SELF-SEEKER

"Willis, I didn't want you here today:
The lawyer's coming for the company.
I'm going to sell my soul, or, rather, feet.
Five hundred dollars for the pair, you know."

"With you the feet have nearly been the soul;
And if you're going to sell them to the devil,
I want to see you do it. When's he coming?"

"I half suspect you knew, and came on purpose
To try to help me drive a better bargain."

"Well, if it's true! Yours are no common feet.
The lawyer don't know what it is he's buying:
So many miles you might have walked you won't walk.
You haven't run your forty orchids down.
What does he think?—How *are* the blessed feet?
The doctor's sure you're going to walk again?"

"He thinks I'll hobble. It's both legs and feet."

"They must be terrible—I mean to look at."

"I haven't dared to look at them uncovered.
Through the bed blankets I remind myself
Of a starfish laid out with rigid points."

"The wonder is it hadn't been your head."

"It's hard to tell you how I managed it.
When I saw the shaft had me by the coat,
I didn't try too long to pull away,
Or fumble for my knife to cut away,
I just embraced the shaft and rode it out—
Till Weiss shut off the water in the wheel-pit.
That's how I think I didn't lose my head.
But my legs got their knocks against the ceiling."

"Awful. Why didn't they throw off the belt
Instead of going clear down in the wheel-pit?"

"They say some time was wasted on the belt—
Old streak of leather—doesn't love me much
Because I make him spit fire at my knuckles,
The way Ben Franklin used to make the kite-string.
That must be it. Some days he won't stay on.
That day a woman couldn't coax him off.
He's on his rounds now with his tail in his mouth
Snatched right and left across the silver pulleys.
Everything goes the same without me there.
You can hear the small buzz saws whine, the big saw
Caterwaul to the hills around the village
As they both bite the wood. It's all our music.
One ought as a good villager to like it.
No doubt it has a sort of prosperous sound,
And it's our life."

       "Yes, when it's not our death."

"You make that sound as if it wasn't so
With everything. What we live by we die by.
I wonder where my lawyer is. His train's in.
I want this over with; I'm hot and tired."

"You're getting ready to do something foolish."

"Watch for him, will you, Will? You let him in.
I'd rather Mrs. Corbin didn't know;
I've boarded here so long, she thinks she owns me.
You're bad enough to manage without her."

"I'm going to be worse instead of better.
You've got to tell me how far this is gone:
Have you agreed to any price?"

       "Five hundred.
Five hundred—five—five! One, two, three, four, five.

You needn't look at me."

                    "I don't believe you."

"I told you, Willis, when you first came in.
Don't you be hard on me. I have to take
What I can get. You see they have the feet,
Which gives them the advantage in the trade.
I can't get back the feet in any case."

"But your flowers, man, you're selling out your flowers."

"Yes, that's one way to put it—all the flowers
Of every kind everywhere in this region
For the next forty summers—call it forty.
But I'm not selling those, I'm giving them,
They never earned me so much as one cent:
Money can't pay me for the loss of them.
No, the five hundred was the sum they named
To pay the doctor's bill and tide me over.
It's that or fight, and I don't want to fight—
I just want to get settled in my life,
Such as it's going to be, and know the worst,
Or best—it may not be so bad. The firm
Promise me all the shooks I want to nail."

"But what about your flora of the valley?"

"You have me there. But that—you didn't think
That was worth money to me? Still I own
It goes against me not to finish it
For the friends it might bring me. By the way,
I had a letter from Burroughs—did I tell you?—
About my *Cyprepedium reginæ*;
He says it's not reported so far north.
There! there's the bell. He's rung. But you go down
And bring him up, and don't let Mrs. Corbin.—
Oh, well, we'll soon be through with it. I'm tired."

Willis brought up besides the Boston lawyer
A little barefoot girl who in the noise
Of heavy footsteps in the old frame house,
And baritone importance of the lawyer,
Stood for a while unnoticed with her hands
Shyly behind her.

        "Well, and how is Mister—"

The lawyer was already in his satchel
As if for papers that might bear the name
He hadn't at command. "You must excuse me,
I dropped in at the mill and was detained."

"Looking round, I suppose," said Willis.

                  "Yes,
Well, yes."

     "Hear anything that might prove useful?"

The Broken One saw Anne. "Why, here is Anne.
What do you want, dear? Come, stand by the bed;
Tell me what is it?" Anne just wagged her dress
With both hands held behind her. "Guess," she said.

"Oh, guess which hand? My, my! Once on a time
I knew a lovely way to tell for certain
By looking in the ears. But I forget it.
Er, let me see. I think I'll take the right.
That's sure to be right even if it's wrong.
Come, hold it out. Don't change.—A Ram's Horn orchid!
A Ram's Horn! What would I have got, I wonder,
If I had chosen left. Hold out the left.
Another Ram's Horn! Where did you find those,
Under what beech tree, on what woodchuck's knoll?"

Anne looked at the large lawyer at her side,
And thought she wouldn't venture on so much.

"Were there no others?"

"There were four or five.
I knew you wouldn't let me pick them all."

"I wouldn't—so I wouldn't. You're the girl!
You see Anne has her lesson learned by heart."

"I wanted there should be some there next year."

"Of course you did. You left the rest for seed,
And for the backwoods woodchuck. You're the girl!
A Ram's Horn orchid seedpod for a woodchuck
Sounds something like. Better than farmer's beans
To a discriminating appetite,
Though the Ram's Horn is seldom to be had
In bushel lots—doesn't come on the market.
But, Anne, I'm troubled; have you told me all?
You're hiding something. That's as bad as lying.
You ask this lawyer man. And it's not safe
With a lawyer at hand to find you out.
Nothing is hidden from some people, Anne.
You don't tell me that where you found a Ram's Horn
You didn't find a Yellow Lady's Slipper.
What did I tell you? What? I'd blush, I would.
Don't you defend yourself. If it was there,
Where is it now, the Yellow Lady's Slipper?"

"Well, wait—it's common—it's too *common*."

"Common?
The Purple Lady's Slipper's commoner."

"I didn't bring a Purple Lady's Slipper
To *You*—to you I mean—they're both too common."

The lawyer gave a laugh among his papers
As if with some idea that she had scored.

"I've broken Anne of gathering bouquets.
It's not fair to the child. It can't be helped though:
Pressed into service means pressed out of shape.
Somehow I'll make it right with her—she'll see.
She's going to do my scouting in the field,
Over stone walls and all along a wood
And by a river bank for water flowers,
The floating Heart, with small leaf like a heart,
And at the *sinus* under water a fist
Of little fingers all kept down but one,
And that thrust up to blossom in the sun
As if to say, 'You! You're the Heart's desire.'
Anne has a way with flowers to take the place
Of that she's lost: she goes down on one knee
And lifts their faces by the chin to hers
And says their names, and leaves them where they are."

The lawyer wore a watch the case of which
Was cunningly devised to make a noise
Like a small pistol when he snapped it shut
At such a time as this. He snapped it now.

"Well, Anne, go, dearie. Our affair will wait.
The lawyer man is thinking of his train.
He wants to give me lots and lots of money
Before he goes, because I hurt myself,
And it may take him I don't know how long.
But put our flowers in water first. Will, help her:
The pitcher's too full for her. There's no cup?
Just hook them on the inside of the pitcher.
Now run.—Get out your documents! You see
I have to keep on the good side of Anne.
I'm a great boy to think of number one.
And you can't blame me in the place I'm in.
Who will take care of my necessities
Unless I do?"

                    "A pretty interlude,"
The lawyer said. "I'm sorry, but my train—

Luckily terms are all agreed upon.
You only have to sign your name. Right—there."

"You, Will, stop making faces. Come round here
Where you can't make them. What is it you want?
I'll put you out with Anne. Be good or go."

"You don't mean you will sign that thing unread?"

"Make yourself useful then, and read it for me.
Isn't it something I have seen before?"

"You'll find it is. Let your friend look at it."

"Yes, but all that takes time, and I'm as much
In haste to get it over with as you.
But read it, read it. That's right, draw the curtain:
Half the time I don't know what's troubling me.—
What do you say, Will? Don't you be a fool,
You, crumpling folk's legal documents.
Out with it if you've any real objection."

"Five hundred dollars!"

                    "What would you think right?"

"A thousand wouldn't be a cent too much;
You know it, Mr. Lawyer. The sin is
Accepting anything before he knows
Whether he's ever going to walk again.
It smells to me like a dishonest trick."

"I think—I think—from what I heard today—
And saw myself—he would be ill-advised—"

"What did you hear, for instance?" Willis said.

"Now the place where the accident occurred—"

The Broken One was twisted in his bed.
"This is between you two apparently.
Where I come in is what I want to know.
You stand up to it like a pair of cocks.
Go outdoors if you want to fight. Spare me.
When you come back, I'll have the papers signed.
Will pencil do? Then, please, your fountain pen.
One of you hold my head up from the pillow."

Willis flung off the bed. "I wash my hands—
I'm no match—no, and don't pretend to be—"

The lawyer gravely capped his fountain pen.
"You're doing the wise thing: you won't regret it.
We're very sorry for you."

                              Willis sneered:
"Who's *we?*—some stockholders in Boston?
I'll go outdoors, by gad, and won't come back."

"Willis, bring Anne back with you when you come.
Yes. Thanks for caring. Don't mind Will: he's savage.
He thinks you ought to pay me for my flowers.
You don't know what I mean about the flowers.
Don't stop to try to now. You'll miss your train.
Good-by." He flung his arms around his face.

# THE WOOD-PILE

Out walking in the frozen swamp one gray day,
I paused and said, "I will turn back from here.
No, I will go on farther—and we shall see."
The hard snow held me, save where now and then
One foot went through. The view was all in lines
Straight up and down of tall slim trees
Too much alike to mark or name a place by
So as to say for certain I was here
Or somewhere else: I was just far from home.
A small bird flew before me. He was careful
To put a tree between us when he lighted,
And say no word to tell me who he was
Who was so foolish as to think what *he* thought.
He thought that I was after him for a feather—
The white one in his tail; like one who takes
Everything said as personal to himself.
One flight out sideways would have undeceived him.
And then there was a pile of wood for which
I forgot him and let his little fear
Carry him off the way I might have gone,
Without so much as wishing him good-night.
He went behind it to make his last stand.
It was a cord of maple, cut and split
And piled—and measured, four by four by eight.
And not another like it could I see.
No runner tracks in this year's snow looped near it.
And it was older sure than this year's cutting,
Or even last year's or the year's before.
The wood was gray and the bark warping off it
And the pile somewhat sunken. Clematis
Had wound strings round and round it like a bundle.
What held it though on one side was a tree
Still growing, and on one a stake and prop,
These latter about to fall. I thought that only
Someone who lived in turning to fresh tasks
Could so forget his handiwork on which
He spent himself, the labor of his ax,

And leave it there far from a useful fireplace
To warm the frozen swamp as best it could
With the slow smokeless burning of decay.

# GOOD HOURS

I had for my winter evening walk—
No one at all with whom to talk,
But I had the cottages in a row
Up to their shining eyes in snow.

And I thought I had the folk within:
I had the sound of a violin;
I had a glimpse through curtain laces
Of youthful forms and youthful faces.

I had such company outward bound.
I went till there were no cottages found.
I turned and repented, but coming back
I saw no window but that was black.

Over the snow my creaking feet
Disturbed the slumbering village street
Like profanation, by your leave,
At ten o'clock of a winter eve.

# MOUNTAIN INTERVAL

# THE ROAD NOT TAKEN

Two roads diverged in a yellow wood,
And sorry I could not travel both
And be one traveler, long I stood
And looked down one as far as I could
To where it bent in the undergrowth;

Then took the other, as just as fair,
And having perhaps the better claim,
Because it was grassy and wanted wear;
Though as for that the passing there
Had worn them really about the same,

And both that morning equally lay
In leaves no step had trodden black.
Oh, I kept the first for another day!
Yet knowing how way leads on to way,
I doubted if I should ever come back.

I shall be telling this with a sigh
Somewhere ages and ages hence:
Two roads diverged in a wood, and I—
I took the one less traveled by,
And that has made all the difference.

# CHRISTMAS TREES
## A Christmas Circular Letter

The city had withdrawn into itself
And left at last the country to the country;
When between whirls of snow not come to lie
And whirls of foliage not yet laid, there drove
A stranger to our yard, who looked the city,
Yet did in country fashion in that there
He sat and waited till he drew us out
A-buttoning coats to ask him who he was.
He proved to be the city come again
To look for something it had left behind
And could not do without and keep its Christmas.
He asked if I would sell my Christmas trees;
My woods—the young fir balsams like a place
Where houses all are churches and have spires.
I hadn't thought of them as Christmas trees.
I doubt if I was tempted for a moment
To sell them off their feet to go in cars
And leave the slope behind the house all bare,
Where the sun shines now no warmer than the moon.
I'd hate to have them know it if I was.
Yet more I'd hate to hold my trees except
As others hold theirs or refuse for them,
Beyond the time of profitable growth,
The trial by market everything must come to.
I dallied so much with the thought of selling.
Then whether from mistaken courtesy
And fear of seeming short of speech, or whether
From hope of hearing good of what was mine,
I said, "There aren't enough to be worth while."

"I could soon tell how many they would cut,
You let me look them over."

                              "You could look.
But don't expect I'm going to let you have them."
Pasture they spring in, some in clumps too close

That lop each other of boughs, but not a few
Quite solitary and having equal boughs
All round and round. The latter he nodded "Yes" to,
Or paused to say beneath some lovelier one,
With a buyer's moderation, "That would do."
I thought so too, but wasn't there to say so.
We climbed the pasture on the south, crossed over,
And came down on the north.

                              He said, "A thousand."

"A thousand Christmas trees!—at what apiece?"

He felt some need of softening that to me:
"A thousand trees would come to thirty dollars."

Then I was certain I had never meant
To let him have them. Never show surprise!
But thirty dollars seemed so small beside
The extent of pasture I should strip, three cents
(For that was all they figured out apiece),
Three cents so small beside the dollar friends
I should be writing to within the hour
Would pay in cities for good trees like those,
Regular vestry trees whole Sunday Schools
Could hang enough on to pick off enough.
A thousand Christmas trees I didn't know I had!
Worth three cents more to give away than sell,
As may be shown by a simple calculation.
Too bad I couldn't lay one in a letter.
I can't help wishing I could send you one
In wishing you herewith a Merry Christmas.

# AN OLD MAN'S WINTER NIGHT

All out-of-doors looked darkly in at him
Through the thin frost, almost in separate stars,
That gathers on the pane in empty rooms.
What kept his eyes from giving back the gaze
Was the lamp tilted near them in his hand.
What kept him from remembering what it was
That brought him to that creaking room was age.
He stood with barrels round him—at a loss.
And having scared the cellar under him
In clomping here, he scared it once again
In clomping off;—and scared the outer night,
Which has its sounds, familiar, like the roar
Of trees and crack of branches, common things,
But nothing so like beating on a box.
A light he was to no one but himself
Where now he sat, concerned with he knew what,
A quiet light, and then not even that.
He consigned to the moon, such as she was,
So late-arising, to the broken moon
As better than the sun in any case
For such a charge, his snow upon the roof,
His icicles along the wall to keep;
And slept. The log that shifted with a jolt
Once in the stove, disturbed him and he shifted,
And eased his heavy breathing, but still slept.
One aged man—one man—can't keep a house,
A farm, a countryside, or if he can,
It's thus he does it of a winter night.

# THE EXPOSED NEST

You were forever finding some new play.
So when I saw you down on hands and knees
In the meadow, busy with the new-cut hay,
Trying, I thought, to set it up on end,
I went to show you how to make it stay,
If that was your idea, against the breeze,
And, if you asked me, even help pretend
To make it root again and grow afresh.
But 'twas no make-believe with you today,
Nor was the grass itself your real concern,
Though I found your hand full of wilted fern,
Steel-bright June-grass, and blackening heads of clover.
'Twas a nest full of young birds on the ground
The cutter-bar had just gone champing over
(Miraculously without tasting flesh)
And left defenseless to the heat and light.
You wanted to restore them to their right
Of something interposed between their sight
And too much world at once—could means be found.
The way the nest-full every time we stirred
Stood up to us as to a mother-bird
Whose coming home has been too long deferred,
Made me ask would the mother-bird return
And care for them in such a change of scene
And might our meddling make her more afraid.
That was a thing we could not wait to learn.
We saw the risk we took in doing good,
But dared not spare to do the best we could
Though harm should come of it; so built the screen
You had begun, and gave them back their shade.
All this to prove we cared. Why is there then
No more to tell? We turned to other things.
I haven't any memory—have you?—
Of ever coming to the place again
To see if the birds lived the first night through,
And so at last to learn to use their wings.

# A PATCH OF OLD SNOW

There's a patch of old snow in a corner
   That I should have guessed
Was a blow-away paper the rain
   Had brought to rest.

It is speckled with grime as if
   Small print overspread it,
The news of a day I've forgotten—
   If I ever read it.

# IN THE HOME STRETCH

She stood against the kitchen sink, and looked
Over the sink out through a dusty window
At weeds the water from the sink made tall.
She wore her cape; her hat was in her hand.
Behind her was confusion in the room,
Of chairs turned upside down to sit like people
In other chairs, and something, come to look,
For every room a house has—parlor, bedroom,
And dining room—thrown pell-mell in the kitchen.
And now and then a smudged, infernal face
Looked in a door behind her and addressed
Her back. She always answered without turning.

"Where will I put this walnut bureau, lady?"

"Put it on top of something that's on top
Of something else," she laughed. "Oh, put it where
You can tonight, and go. It's almost dark;
You must be getting started back to town."

Another blackened face thrust in and looked
And smiled, and when she did not turn, spoke gently,
"What are you seeing out the window, *lady?*"

"Never was I beladied so before.
Would evidence of having been called lady
More than so many times make me a lady
In common law, I wonder."

                              "But I ask,
What are you seeing out the window, lady?"

"What I'll be seeing more of in the years
To come as here I stand and go the round
Of many plates with towels many times."

"And what is that? You only put me off."

"Rank weeds that love the water from the dishpan
More than some women like the dishpan, Joe;
A little stretch of mowing-field for you;
Not much of that until I come to woods
That end all. And it's scarce enough to call
A view."

"And yet you think you like it, dear?"

"That's what you're so concerned to know! You hope
I like it. Bang goes something big away
Off there upstairs. The very tread of men
As great as those is shattering to the frame
Of such a little house. Once left alone,
You and I, dear, will go with softer steps
Up and down stairs and through the rooms, and none
But sudden winds that snatch them from our hands
Will ever slam the doors."

"I think you see
More than you like to own to out that window."

"No; for besides the things I tell you of,
I only see the years. They come and go
In alternation with the weeds, the field,
The wood."

"What kind of years?"

"Why, latter years—
Different from early years."

"I see them, too.
You didn't count them?"

"No, the further off
So ran together that I didn't try to.
It can scarce be that they would be in number
We'd care to know, for we are not young now.

And bang goes something else away off there.
It sounds as if it were the men went down,
And every crash meant one less to return
To lighted city streets we, too, have known,
But now are giving up for country darkness."

"Come from that window where you see too much,
And take a livelier view of things from here.
They're going. Watch this husky swarming up
Over the wheel into the sky-high seat,
Lighting his pipe now, squinting down his nose
At the flame burning downward as he sucks it."

"See how it makes his nose-side bright, a proof
How dark it's getting. Can you tell what time
It is by that? Or by the moon? The new moon!
What shoulder did I see her over? Neither.
A wire she is of silver, as new as we
To everything. Her light won't last us long.
It's something, though, to know we're going to have her
Night after night and stronger every night
To see us through our first two weeks. But, Joe,
The stove! Before they go! Knock on the window;
Ask them to help you get it on its feet.
We stand here dreaming. Hurry! Call them back!"

"They're not gone yet."

                    "We've got to have the stove,
Whatever else we want for. And a light.
Have we a piece of candle if the lamp
And oil are buried out of reach?"

                              Again
The house was full of tramping, and the dark,
Door-filling men burst in and seized the stove.
A cannon-mouth-like hole was in the wall,
To which they set it true by eye; and then
Came up the jointed stovepipe in their hands,

So much too light and airy for their strength
It almost seemed to come ballooning up,
Slipping from clumsy clutches toward the ceiling.
"A fit!" said one, and banged a stovepipe shoulder.
"It's good luck when you move in to begin
With good luck with your stovepipe. Never mind,
It's not so bad in the country, settled down,
When people're getting on in life. You'll like it."
Joe said: "You big boys ought to find a farm,
And make good farmers, and leave other fellows
The city work to do. There's not enough
For everybody as it is in there."
"God!" one said wildly, and, when no one spoke:
"Say that to Jimmy here. He needs a farm."
But Jimmy only made his jaw recede
Fool-like, and rolled his eyes as if to say
He saw himself a farmer. Then there was a French boy
Who said with seriousness that made them laugh,
"Ma friend, you ain't know what it is you're ask."
He doffed his cap and held it with both hands
Across his chest to make as 'twere a bow:
"We're giving you our chances on de farm."
And then they all turned to with deafening boots
And put each other bodily out of the house.
"Good-by to them! We puzzle them. They think—
I don't know what they think we see in what
They leave us to: that pasture slope that seems
The back some farm presents us; and your woods
To northward from your window at the sink,
Waiting to steal a step on us whenever
We drop our eyes or turn to other things,
As in the game 'Ten-step' the children play."

"Good boys they seemed, and let them love the city.
All they could say was 'God!' when you proposed
Their coming out and making useful farmers."

"Did they make something lonesome go through you?
It would take more than them to sicken you—

126

Us of our bargain. But they left us so
As to our fate, like fools past reasoning with.
They almost shook *me*."

        "It's all so much
What we have always wanted, I confess
It's seeming bad for a moment makes it seem
Even worse still, and so on down, down, down.
It's nothing; it's their leaving us at dusk.
I never bore it well when people went.
The first night after guests have gone, the house
Seems haunted or exposed. I always take
A personal interest in the locking up
At bedtime; but the strangeness soon wears off."
He fetched a dingy lantern from behind
A door. "There's that we didn't lose! And these!"—
Some matches he unpocketed. "For food—
The meals we've had no one can take from us.
I wish that everything on earth were just
As certain as the meals we've had. I wish
The meals we haven't had were, anyway.
What have you you know where to lay your hands on?"

"The bread we bought in passing at the store.
There's butter somewhere, too."

        "Let's rend the bread.
I'll light the fire for company for you;
You'll not have any other company
Till Ed begins to get out on a Sunday
To look us over and give us his idea
Of what wants pruning, shingling, breaking up.
He'll know what he would do if he were we,
And all at once. He'll plan for us and plan
To help us, but he'll take it out in planning.
Well, you can set the table with the loaf.
Let's see you find your loaf. I'll light the fire.
I like chairs occupying other chairs
Not offering a lady—"

"There again, Joe!
*You're tired.*"

         "I'm drunk-nonsensical tired out;
Don't mind a word I say. It's a day's work
To empty one house of all household goods
And fill another with 'em fifteen miles away,
Although you do no more than dump them down."

"Dumped down in paradise we are and happy."

"It's all so much what I have always wanted,
I can't believe it's what you wanted, too."

"Shouldn't you like to know?"

                    "I'd like to know
If it is what you wanted, then how much
You wanted it for me."

                    "A troubled conscience!
You don't want me to tell if *I* don't know."

"I don't want to find out what can't be known.
But who first said the word to come?"

                         "My dear,
It's who first thought the thought. You're searching, Joe,
For things that don't exist; I mean beginnings.
Ends and beginnings—there are no such things.
There are only middles."

              "What is this?"

                    "This life?
Our sitting here by lantern-light together
Amid the wreckage of a former home?
You won't deny the lantern isn't new.
The stove is not, and you are not to me,

Nor I to you."

          "Perhaps you never were?"

"It would take me forever to recite
All that's not new in where we find ourselves.
New is a word for fools in towns who think
Style upon style in dress and thought at last
Must get somewhere. I've heard you say as much.
No, this is no beginning."

                    "Then an end?"

"End is a gloomy word."

                    "Is it too late
To drag you out for just a good-night call
On the old peach trees on the knoll to grope
By starlight in the grass for a last peach
The neighbors may not have taken as their right
When the house wasn't lived in? I've been looking:
I doubt if they have left us many grapes.
Before we set ourselves to right the house,
The first thing in the morning, out we go
To go the round of apple, cherry, peach,
Pine, alder, pasture, mowing, well, and brook.
All of a farm it is."

          "I know this much:
I'm going to put you in your bed, if first
I have to make you build it. Come, the light."

When there was no more lantern in the kitchen,
The fire got out through crannies in the stove
And danced in yellow wrigglers on the ceiling,
As much at home as if they'd always danced there.

# THE TELEPHONE

"When I was just as far as I could walk
From here today,
There was an hour
All still
When leaning with my head against a flower
I heard you talk.
Don't say I didn't, for I heard you say—
You spoke from that flower on the window sill—
Do you remember what it was you said?"

"First tell me what it was you thought you heard."

"Having found the flower and driven a bee away,
I leaned my head,
And holding by the stalk,
I listened and I thought I caught the word—
What was it? Did you call me by my name?
Or did you say—
*Someone* said 'Come'—I heard it as I bowed."

"I may have thought as much, but not aloud."

"Well, so I came."

# MEETING AND PASSING

As I went down the hill along the wall
There was a gate I had leaned at for the view
And had just turned from when I first saw you
As you came up the hill. We met. But all
We did that day was mingle great and small
Footprints in summer dust as if we drew
The figure of our being less than two
But more than one as yet. Your parasol
Pointed the decimal off with one deep thrust.
And all the time we talked you seemed to see
Something down there to smile at in the dust.
(Oh, it was without prejudice to me!)
Afterward I went past what you had passed
Before we met and you what I had passed.

# HYLA BROOK

By June our brook's run out of song and speed
Sought for much after that, it will be found
Either to have gone groping underground
(And taken with it all the Hyla breed
That shouted in the mist a month ago,
Like ghost of sleigh-bells in a ghost of snow)—
Or flourished and come up in jewel-weed,
Weak foliage that is blown upon and bent
Even against the way its waters went.
Its bed is left a faded paper sheet
Of dead leaves stuck together by the heat—
A brook to none but who remember long.
This as it will be seen is other far
Than with brooks taken otherwhere in song.
We love the things we love for what they are.

# THE OVEN BIRD

There is a singer everyone has heard,
Loud, a mid-summer and a mid-wood bird,
Who makes the solid tree trunks sound again.
He says that leaves are old and that for flowers
Mid-summer is to spring as one to ten.
He says the early petal-fall is past
When pear and cherry bloom went down in showers
On sunny days a moment overcast;
And comes that other fall we name the fall.
He says the highway dust is over all.
The bird would cease and be as other birds
But that he knows in singing not to sing.
The question that he frames in all but words
Is what to make of a diminished thing.

# BOND AND FREE

Love has earth to which she clings
With hills and circling arms about—
Wall within wall to shut fear out.
But Thought has need of no such things,
For Thought has a pair of dauntless wings.

On snow and sand and turf, I see
Where Love has left a printed trace
With straining in the world's embrace.
And such is Love and glad to be.
But Thought has shaken his ankles free.

Thought cleaves the interstellar gloom
And sits in Sirius' disc all night,
Till day makes him retrace his flight,
With smell of burning on every plume,
Back past the sun to an earthly room.

His gains in heaven are what they are.
Yet some say Love by being thrall
And simply staying possesses all
In several beauty that Thought fares far
To find fused in another star.

# BIRCHES

When I see birches bend to left and right
Across the lines of straighter darker trees,
I like to think some boy's been swinging them.
But swinging doesn't bend them down to stay
As ice-storms do. Often you must have seen them
Loaded with ice a sunny winter morning
After a rain. They click upon themselves
As the breeze rises, and turn many-colored
As the stir cracks and crazes their enamel.
Soon the sun's warmth makes them shed crystal shells
Shattering and avalanching on the snow-crust—
Such heaps of broken glass to sweep away
You'd think the inner dome of heaven had fallen.
They are dragged to the withered bracken by the load,
And they seem not to break; though once they are bowed
So low for long, they never right themselves:
You may see their trunks arching in the woods
Years afterwards, trailing their leaves on the ground
Like girls on hands and knees that throw their hair
Before them over their heads to dry in the sun.
But I was going to say when Truth broke in
With all her matter-of-fact about the ice-storm
I should prefer to have some boy bend them
As he went out and in to fetch the cows—
Some boy too far from town to learn baseball,
Whose only play was what he found himself,
Summer or winter, and could play alone.
One by one he subdued his father's trees
By riding them down over and over again
Until he took the stiffness out of them,
And not one but hung limp, not one was left
For him to conquer. He learned all there was
To learn about not launching out too soon
And so not carrying the tree away
Clear to the ground. He always kept his poise
To the top branches, climbing carefully
With the same pains you use to fill a cup

Up to the brim, and even above the brim.
Then he flung outward, feet first, with a swish,
Kicking his way down through the air to the ground.
So was I once myself a swinger of birches.
And so I dream of going back to be.
It's when I'm weary of considerations,
And life is too much like a pathless wood
Where your face burns and tickles with the cobwebs
Broken across it, and one eye is weeping
From a twig's having lashed across it open.
I'd like to get away from earth awhile
And then come back to it and begin over.
May no fate willfully misunderstand me
And half grant what I wish and snatch me away
Not to return. Earth's the right place for love:
I don't know where it's likely to go better.
I'd like to go by climbing a birch tree,
And climb black branches up a snow-white trunk
*Toward* heaven, till the tree could bear no more,
But dipped its top and set me down again.
That would be good both going and coming back.
One could do worse than be a swinger of birches.

# PEA BRUSH

I walked down alone Sunday after church
  To the place where John has been cutting trees
To see for myself about the birch
  He said I could have to bush my peas.

The sun in the new-cut narrow gap
  Was hot enough for the first of May,
And stifling hot with the odor of sap
  From stumps still bleeding their life away.

The frogs that were peeping a thousand shrill
  Wherever the ground was low and wet,
The minute they heard my step went still
  To watch me and see what I came to get.

Birch boughs enough piled everywhere!—
  All fresh and sound from the recent ax.
Time someone came with cart and pair
  And got them off the wild flowers' backs.

They might be good for garden things
  To curl a little finger round,
The same as you seize cat's-cradle strings,
  And lift themselves up off the ground.

Small good to anything growing wild,
  They were crooking many a trillium
That had budded before the boughs were piled
  And since it was coming up had to come.

# PUTTING IN THE SEED

You come to fetch me from my work tonight
When supper's on the table, and we'll see
If I can leave off burying the white
Soft petals fallen from the apple tree
(Soft petals, yes, but not so barren quite,
Mingled with these, smooth bean and wrinkled pea;)
And go along with you ere you lose sight
Of what you came for and become like me,
Slave to a springtime passion for the earth.
How Love burns through the Putting in the Seed
On through the watching for that early birth
When, just as the soil tarnishes with weed,
The sturdy seedling with arched body comes
Shouldering its way and shedding the earth crumbs.

# A TIME TO TALK

When a friend calls to me from the road
And slows his horse to a meaning walk,
I don't stand still and look around
On all the hills I haven't hoed,
And shout from where I am, "What is it?"
No, not as there is a time to talk.
I thrust my hoe in the mellow ground,
Blade-end up and five feet tall,
And plod: I go up to the stone wall
For a friendly visit.

# THE COW IN APPLE TIME

Something inspires the only cow of late
To make no more of a wall than an open gate,
And think no more of wall-builders than fools.
Her face is flecked with pomace and she drools
A cider syrup. Having tasted fruit,
She scorns a pasture withering to the root.
She runs from tree to tree where lie and sweeten
The windfalls spiked with stubble and worm-eaten.
She leaves them bitten when she has to fly.
She bellows on a knoll against the sky.
Her udder shrivels and the milk goes dry.

# AN ENCOUNTER

Once on the kind of day called "weather breeder,"
When the heat slowly hazes and the sun
By its own power seems to be undone,
I was half boring through, half climbing through
A swamp of cedar. Choked with oil of cedar
And scurf of plants, and weary and over-heated,
And sorry I ever left the road I knew,
I paused and rested on a sort of hook
That had me by the coat as good as seated,
And since there was no other way to look,
Looked up toward heaven, and there against the blue,
Stood over me a resurrected tree,
A tree that had been down and raised again—
A barkless specter. He had halted too,
As if for fear of treading upon me.
I saw the strange position of his hands—
Up at his shoulders, dragging yellow strands
Of wire with something in it from men to men.
"You here?" I said. "Where aren't you nowadays
And what's the news you carry—if you know?
And tell me where you're off for—Montreal?
Me? I'm not off for anywhere at all.
Sometimes I wander out of beaten ways
Half looking for the orchid Calypso."

# RANGE-FINDING

The battle rent a cobweb diamond-strung
And cut a flower beside a ground bird's nest
Before it stained a single human breast.
The stricken flower bent double and so hung.
And still the bird revisited her young.
A butterfly its fall had dispossessed
A moment sought in air his flower of rest,
Then lightly stooped to it and fluttering clung.
On the bare upland pasture there had spread
O'ernight 'twixt mullein stalks a wheel of thread
And straining cables wet with silver dew.
A sudden passing bullet shook it dry.
The indwelling spider ran to greet the fly,
But finding nothing, sullenly withdrew.

# THE HILL WIFE

## LONELINESS
### *Her Word*

One ought not to have to care
   So much as you and I
Care when the birds come round the house
   To seem to say good-by;

Or care so much when they come back
   With whatever it is they sing;
The truth being we are as much
   Too glad for the one thing

As we are too sad for the other here—
   With birds that fill their breasts
But with each other and themselves
   And their built or driven nests.

## HOUSE FEAR

Always—I tell you this they learned—
Always at night when they returned
To the lonely house from far away
To lamps unlighted and fire gone gray,
They learned to rattle the lock and key
To give whatever might chance to be
Warning and time to be off in flight:
And preferring the out- to the in-door night,
They learned to leave the house-door wide
Until they had lit the lamp inside.

## THE SMILE
### *Her Word*

I didn't like the way he went away.
That smile! It never came of being gay.
Still he smiled—did you see him?—I was sure!

Perhaps because we gave him only bread
And the wretch knew from that that we were poor.
Perhaps because he let us give instead
Of seizing from us as he might have seized.
Perhaps he mocked at us for being wed,
Or being very young (and he was pleased
To have a vision of us old and dead).
I wonder how far down the road he's got.
He's watching from the woods as like as not.

## THE OFT-REPEATED DREAM

She had no saying dark enough
   For the dark pine that kept
Forever trying the window-latch
   Of the room where they slept.

The tireless but ineffectual hands
   That with every futile pass
Made the great tree seem as a little bird
   Before the mystery of glass!

It never had been inside the room,
   And only one of the two
Was afraid in an oft-repeated dream
   Of what the tree might do.

## THE IMPULSE

It was too lonely for her there,
   And too wild,
And since there were but two of them,
   And no child,

And work was little in the house,
   She was free,
And followed where he furrowed field,
   Or felled tree.

She rested on a log and tossed
   The fresh chips,
With a song only to herself
   On her lips.

And once she went to break a bough
   Of black alder.
She strayed so far she scarcely heard
   When he called her—

And didn't answer—didn't speak—
   Or return.
She stood, and then she ran and hid
   In the fern.

He never found her, though he looked
   Everywhere,
And he asked at her mother's house
   Was she there.

Sudden and swift and light as that
   The ties gave,
And he learned of finalities
   Besides the grave.

# THE BONFIRE

"Oh, let's go up the hill and scare ourselves,
As reckless as the best of them tonight,
By setting fire to all the brush we piled
With pitchy hands to wait for rain or snow.
Oh, let's not wait for rain to make it safe.
The pile is ours: we dragged it bough on bough
Down dark converging paths between the pines.
Let's not care what we do with it tonight.
Divide it? No! But burn it as one pile
The way we piled it. And let's be the talk
Of people brought to windows by a light
Thrown from somewhere against their wallpaper.
Rouse them all, both the free and not so free
With saying what they'd like to do to us
For what they'd better wait till we have done.
Let's all but bring to life this old volcano,
If that is what the mountain ever was—
And scare ourselves. Let wild fire loose we will…"

"And scare you too?" the children said together.

"Why wouldn't it scare me to have a fire
Begin in smudge with ropy smoke and know
That still, if I repent, I may recall it,
But in a moment not: a little spurt
Of burning fatness, and then nothing but
The fire itself can put it out, and that
By burning out, and before it burns out
It will have roared first and mixed sparks with stars,
And sweeping round it with a flaming sword,
Made the dim trees stand back in wider circle—
Done so much and I know not how much more
I mean it shall not do if I can bind it.
Well if it doesn't with its draft bring on
A wind to blow in earnest from some quarter,
As once it did with me upon an April.
The breezes were so spent with winter blowing

They seemed to fail the bluebirds under them
Short of the perch their languid flight was toward
And my flame made a pinnacle to heaven
As I walked once around it in possession.
But the wind out of doors—you know the saying.
There came a gust. You used to think the trees
Made wind by fanning since you never knew
It blow but that you saw the trees in motion.
Something or someone watching made that gust.
It put the flame tip-down and dabbed the grass
Of over-winter with the least tip-touch
Your tongue gives salt or sugar in your hand.
The place it reached to blackened instantly.
The black was almost all there was by daylight,
That and the merest curl of cigarette smoke—
And a flame slender as the hepaticas,
Blood-root, and violets so soon to be now.
But the black spread like black death on the ground,
And I think the sky darkened with a cloud
Like winter and evening coming on together.
There were enough things to be thought of then.
Where the field stretches toward the north
And setting sun to Hyla brook, I gave it
To flames without twice thinking, where it verges
Upon the road, to flames too, though in fear
They might find fuel there, in withered brake,
Grass its full length, old silver goldenrod,
And alder and grape vine entanglement,
To leap the dusty deadline. For my own
I took what front there was beside. I knelt
And thrust hands in and held my face away.
Fight such a fire by rubbing not by beating.
A board is the best weapon if you have it.
I had my coat. And oh, I knew, I knew,
And said out loud, I couldn't bide the smother
And heat so close in; but the thought of all
The woods and town on fire by me, and all
The town turned out to fight for me—that held me.
I trusted the brook barrier, but feared

The road would fail; and on that side the fire
Died not without a noise of crackling wood—
Of something more than tinder-grass and weed—
That brought me to my feet to hold it back
By leaning back myself, as if the reins
Were round my neck and I was at the plow.
I won! But I'm sure no one ever spread
Another color over a tenth the space
That I spread coal-black over in the time
It took me. Neighbors coming home from town
Couldn't believe that so much black had come there
While they had backs turned, that it hadn't been there
When they had passed an hour or so before
Going the other way and they not seen it.
They looked about for someone to have done it.
But there was no one. I was somewhere wondering
Where all my weariness had gone and why
I walked so light on air in heavy shoes
In spite of a scorched Fourth-of-July feeling.
Why wouldn't I be scared remembering that?"

"If it scares you, what will it do to us?"

"Scare you. But if you shrink from being scared,
What would you say to war if it should come?
That's what for reasons I should like to know—
If you can comfort me by any answer."

"Oh, but war's not for children—it's for men."

"Now we are digging almost down to China.
My dears, my dears, you thought that—we all thought it.
So your mistake was ours. Haven't you heard, though,
About the ships where war has found them out
At sea, about the towns where war has come
Through opening clouds at night with droning speed
Further o'erhead than all but stars and angels,—
And children in the ships and in the towns?
Haven't you heard what we have lived to learn?

Nothing so new—something we had forgotten:
*War is for everyone, for children too.*
I wasn't going to tell you and I mustn't.
The best way is to come up hill with me
And have our fire and laugh and be afraid."

# A GIRL'S GARDEN

A neighbor of mine in the village
  Likes to tell how one spring
When she was a girl on the farm, she did
  A childlike thing.

One day she asked her father
  To give her a garden plot
To plant and tend and reap herself,
  And he said, "Why not?"

In casting about for a corner
  He thought of an idle bit
Of walled-off ground where a shop had stood,
  And he said, "Just it."

And he said, "That ought to make you
  An ideal one-girl farm,
And give you a chance to put some strength
  On your slim-jim arm."

It was not enough of a garden,
  Her father said, to plow;
So she had to work it all by hand,
  But she don't mind now.

She wheeled the dung in the wheelbarrow
  Along a stretch of road;
But she always ran away and left
  Her not-nice load,

And hid from anyone passing.
  And then she begged the seed.
She says she thinks she planted one
  Of all things but weed.

A hill each of potatoes,
  Radishes, lettuce, peas,

Tomatoes, beets, beans, pumpkins, corn
  And even fruit trees.

And yes, she has long mistrusted
  That a cider apple tree
In bearing there today is hers,
  Or at least may be.

Her crop was a miscellany
  When all was said and done,
A little bit of everything,
  A great deal of none.

*Now* when she sees in the village
  How village things go,
Just when it seems to come in right,
  She says, "*I* know!

"It's as when I was a farmer—"
  Oh, never by way of advice!
And she never sins by telling the tale
  To the same person twice.

## LOCKED OUT
### As Told to a Child

When we locked up the house at night,
We always locked the flowers outside
And cut them off from window light.
The time I dreamed the door was tried
And brushed with buttons upon sleeves,
The flowers were out there with the thieves.
Yet nobody molested them!
We did find one nasturtium
Upon the steps with bitten stem.
I may have been to blame for that:
I always thought it must have been
Some flower I played with as I sat
At dusk to watch the moon down early.

# THE LAST WORD OF A BLUEBIRD
## As Told to a Child

As I went out a Crow
In a low voice said, "Oh,
I was looking for you.
How do you do?
I just came to tell you
To tell Lesley (will you?)
That her little Bluebird
Wanted me to bring word
That the north wind last night
That made the stars bright
And made ice on the trough
Almost made him cough
His tail feathers off.
He just had to fiy!
But he sent her Good-by,
And said to be good,
And wear her red hood,
And look for skunk tracks
In the snow with an ax—
And do everything!
And perhaps in the spring
He would come back and sing."

# "OUT, OUT—"

The buzz saw snarled and rattled in the yard
And made dust and dropped stove-length sticks of wood,
Sweet-scented stuff when the breeze drew across it.
And from there those that lifted eyes could count
Five mountain ranges one behind the other
Under the sunset far into Vermont.
And the saw snarled and rattled, snarled and rattled,
As it ran light, or had to bear a load.
And nothing happened: day was all but done.
Call it a day, I wish they might have said
To please the boy by giving him the half hour
That a boy counts so much when saved from work.
His sister stood beside them in her apron
To tell them "Supper." At the word, the saw,
As if to prove saws knew what supper meant,
Leaped out at the boy's hand, or seemed to leap—
He must have given the hand. However it was,
Neither refused the meeting. But the hand!
The boy's first outcry was a rueful laugh,
As he swung toward them holding up the hand
Half in appeal, but half as if to keep
The life from spilling. Then the boy saw all—
Since he was old enough to know, big boy
Doing a man's work, though a child at heart—
He saw all spoiled. "Don't let him cut my hand off—
The doctor, when he comes. Don't let him, sister!"
So. But the hand was gone already.
The doctor put him in the dark of ether.
He lay and puffed his lips out with his breath.
And then—the watcher at his pulse took fright.
No one believed. They listened at his heart.
Little—less—nothing!—and that ended it.
No more to build on there. And they, since they
Were not the one dead, turned to their affairs.

# BROWN'S DESCENT

### or

### The Willy-Nilly Slide

Brown lived at such a lofty farm
    That everyone for miles could see
His lantern when he did his chores
    In winter after half-past three.

And many must have seen him make
    His wild descent from there one night,
'Cross lots, 'cross walls, 'cross everything,
    Describing rings of lantern light.

Between the house and barn the gale
    Got him by something he had on
And blew him out on the icy crust
    That cased the world, and he was gone!

Walls were all buried, trees were few:
    He saw no stay unless he stove
A hole in somewhere with his heel.
    But though repeatedly he strove

And stamped and said things to himself,
    And sometimes something seemed to yield,
He gained no foothold, but pursued
    His journey down from field to field.

Sometimes he came with arms outspread
    Like wings, revolving in the scene
Upon his longer axis, and
    With no small dignity of mien.

Faster or slower as he chanced,
    Sitting or standing as he chose,
According as he feared to risk
    His neck, or thought to spare his clothes.

He never let the lantern drop.
    And some exclaimed who saw afar
The figures he described with it,
    "I wonder what those signals are

"Brown makes at such an hour of night!
    He's celebrating something strange.
I wonder if he's sold his farm,
    Or been made Master of the Grange."

He reeled, he lurched, he bobbed, he checked;
    He fell and made the lantern rattle
(But saved the light from going out.)
    So halfway down he fought the battle,

Incredulous of his own bad luck.
    And then becoming reconciled
To everything, he gave it up
    And came down like a coasting child.

"Well—I—be—" that was all he said,
    As standing in the river road,
He looked back up the slippery slope
    (Two miles it was) to his abode.

Sometimes as an authority
    On motor-cars, I'm asked if I
Should say our stock was petered out,
    And this is my sincere reply:

Yankees are what they always were.
    Don't think Brown ever gave up hope
Of getting home again because
    He couldn't climb that slippery slope;

Or even thought of standing there
    Until the January thaw
Should take the polish off the crust.
    He bowed with grace to natural law,

And then went round it on his feet,
    After the manner of our stock;
Not much concerned for those to whom,
    At that particular time o'clock,

It must have looked as if the course
    He steered was really straight away
From that which he was headed for—
    Not much concerned for them, I say;

No more so than became a man—
    *And* politician at odd seasons.
I've kept Brown standing in the cold
    While I invested him with reasons;

But now he snapped his eyes three times;
    Then shook his lantern, saying, "Ile's
'Bout out!" and took the long way home
    By road, a matter of several miles.

# THE GUM-GATHERER

There overtook me and drew me in
To his down-hill, early-morning stride,
And set me five miles on my road
Better than if he had had me ride,
A man with a swinging bag for load
And half the bag wound round his hand.
We talked like barking above the din
Of water we walked along beside.
And for my telling him where I'd been
And where I lived in mountain land
To be coming home the way I was,
He told me a little about himself.
He came from higher up in the pass
Where the grist of the new-beginning brooks
Is blocks split off the mountain mass—
And hopeless grist enough it looks
Ever to grind to soil for grass.
(The way it is will do for moss.)
There he had built his stolen shack.
It had to be a stolen shack
Because of the fears of fire and loss
That trouble the sleep of lumber folk:
Visions of half the world burned black
And the sun shrunken yellow in smoke.
We know who when they come to town
Bring berries under the wagon seat,
Or a basket of eggs between their feet;
What this man brought in a cotton sack
Was gum, the gum of the mountain spruce.
He showed me lumps of the scented stuff
Like uncut jewels, dull and rough.
It comes to market golden brown;
But turns to pink between the teeth.

I told him this is a pleasant life
To set your breast to the bark of trees
That all your days are dim beneath,

And reaching up with a little knife,
To loose the resin and take it down
And bring it to market when you please.

# THE LINE-GANG

Here come the line-gang pioneering by.
They throw a forest down less cut than broken.
They plant dead trees for living, and the dead
They string together with a living thread.
They string an instrument against the sky
Wherein words whether beaten out or spoken
Will run as hushed as when they were a thought
But in no hush they string it: they go past
With shouts afar to pull the cable taut,
To hold it hard until they make it fast,
To ease away—they have it. With a laugh,
An oath of towns that set the wild at naught
They bring the telephone and telegraph.

# THE VANISHING RED

He is said to have been the last Red Man
In Acton. And the Miller is said to have laughed—
If you like to call such a sound a laugh.
But he gave no one else a laugher's license.
For he turned suddenly grave as if to say,
"Whose business,—if I take it on myself,
Whose business—but why talk round the barn?—
When it's just that I hold with getting a thing done with."
You can't get back and see it as he saw it.
It's too long a story to go into now.
You'd have to have been there and lived it.
Then you wouldn't have looked on it as just a matter
Of who began it between the two races.

Some guttural exclamation of surprise
The Red Man gave in poking about the mill
Over the great big thumping shuffling millstone
Disgusted the Miller physically as coming
From one who had no right to be heard from.
"Come, John," he said, "you want to see the wheel-pit?"

He took him down below a cramping rafter,
And showed him, through a manhole in the floor,
The water in desperate straits like frantic fish,
Salmon and sturgeon, lashing with their tails.
Then he shut down the trap door with a ring in it
That jangled even above the general noise,
And came upstairs alone—and gave that laugh,
And said something to a man with a meal-sack
That the man with the meal-sack didn't catch—then.
Oh, yes, he showed John the wheel-pit all right.

# SNOW

The three stood listening to a fresh access
Of wind that caught against the house a moment,
Gulped snow, and then blew free again—the Coles
Dressed, but disheveled from some hours of sleep,
Meserve belittled in the great skin coat he wore.

Meserve was first to speak. He pointed backward
Over his shoulder with his pipe-stem, saying,
"You can just see it glancing off the roof
Making a great scroll upward toward the sky,
Long enough for recording all our names on.—
I think I'll just call up my wife and tell her
I'm here—so far—and starting on again.
I'll call her softly so that if she's wise
And gone to sleep, she needn't wake to answer."
Three times he barely stirred the bell, then listened.
"Why, Lett, still up? Lett, I'm at Cole's. I'm late.
I called you up to say Good-night from here
Before I went to say Good-morning there.—
I thought I would.—I know, but, Lett—I know—
I could, but what's the sense? The rest won't be
So bad.—Give me an hour for it.—Ho, ho,
Three hours to here! But that was all up hill;
The rest is down.—Why no, no, not a wallow:
They kept their heads and took their time to it
Like darlings, both of them. They're in the barn.—
My dear, I'm coming just the same. I didn't
Call you to ask you to invite me home.—"
He lingered for some word she wouldn't say,
Said it at last himself, "Good-night," and then,
Getting no answer, closed the telephone.
The three stood in the lamplight round the table
With lowered eyes a moment till he said,
"I'll just see how the horses are."

                              "Yes, do,"
Both the Coles said together. Mrs. Cole

Added: "You can judge better after seeing.—
I want you here with me, Fred. Leave him here,
Brother Meserve. You know to find your way
Out through the shed."

                        "I guess I know my way,
I guess I know where I can find my name
Carved in the shed to tell me who I am
If it don't tell me where I am. I used
To play—"

                "You tend your horses and come back.
Fred Cole, you're going to let him!"

                              "Well, aren't you?
How can you help yourself?"

                          "I called him Brother.
Why did I call him that?"

                        "It's right enough.
That's all you ever heard him called round here.
He seems to have lost off his Christian name."

"Christian enough I should call that myself.
He took no notice, did he? Well, at least
I didn't use it out of love of him,
The dear knows. I detest the thought of him
With his ten children under ten years old.
I hate his wretched little Racker Sect,
All's ever I heard of it, which isn't much.
But that's not saying—Look, Fred Cole, it's twelve.
Isn't it, now? He's been here half an hour.
He says he left the village store at nine.
Three hours to do four miles—a mile an hour
Or not much better. Why, it doesn't seem
As if a man could move that slow and move.
Try to think what he did with all that time.
And three miles more to go!"

"Don't let him go.
Stick to him, Helen. Make him answer you.
That sort of man talks straight on all his life
From the last thing he said himself, stone deaf
To anything anyone else may say.
I should have thought, though, you could make him hear
    you."

"What is he doing out a night like this?
Why can't he stay at home?"

                    "He had to preach."

"It's no night to be out."

                "He may be small,
He may be good, but one thing's sure, he's tough."

"And strong of stale tobacco."

                    "He'll pull through."

"You only say so. Not another house
Or shelter to put into from this place
To theirs. I'm going to call his wife again."

"Wait and he may. Let's see what he will do.
Let's see if he will think of her again.
But then I doubt he's thinking of himself.
He doesn't look on it as anything."

"He shan't go—there!"

                "It *is* a night, my dear."

"One thing: he didn't drag God into it."

"He don't consider it a case for God."

"You think so, do you? You don't know the kind.
He's getting up a miracle this minute.
Privately—to himself, right now, he's thinking
He'll make a case of it if he succeeds,
But keep still if he fails."

                    "Keep still all over.
He'll be dead—dead and buried."

                        "Such a trouble!
Not but I've every reason not to care
What happens to him if it only takes
Some of the sanctimonious conceit
Out of one of those pious scalawags."

"Nonsense to that! You want to see him safe."

"You like the runt."

            "Don't you a little?"

                              "Well,
I don't like what he's doing, which is what
You like, and like him for."

                    "Oh, yes you do.
You like your fun as well as anyone;
Only you women have to put these airs on
To impress men. You've got us so ashamed
Of being men we can't look at a good fight
Between two boys and not feel bound to stop it.
Let the man freeze an ear or two, I say.—
He's here. I leave him all to you. Go in
And save his life.—All right, come in, Meserve.
Sit down, sit down. How did you find the horses?"

"Fine, fine."

"And ready for some more? My wife here
Says it won't do. You've got to give it up."

"Won't you to please me? Please! If I say please?
Mr. Meserve, I'll leave it to *your* wife.
What *did* your wife say on the telephone?"

Meserve seemed to heed nothing but the lamp
Or something not far from it on the table.
By straightening out and lifting a forefinger,
He pointed with his hand from where it lay
Like a white crumpled spider on his knee:
"That leaf there in your open book! It moved
Just then, I thought. It's stood erect like that,
There on the table, ever since I came,
Trying to turn itself backward or forward,
I've had my eye on it to make out which;
If forward, then it's with a friend's impatience—
You see I know—to get you on to things
It wants to see how you will take, if backward
It's from regret for something you have passed
And failed to see the good of. Never mind,
Things must expect to come in front of us
A many times—I don't say just how many—
That varies with the things—before we see them.
One of the lies would make it out that nothing
Ever presents itself before us twice.
Where would we be at last if that were so?
Our very life depends on everything's
Recurring till we answer from within.
The thousandth time may prove the charm.—That leaf!
It can't turn either way. It needs the wind's help.
But the wind didn't move it if it moved.
It moved itself. The wind's at naught in here.
It couldn't stir so sensitively poised
A thing as that. It couldn't reach the lamp
To get a puff of black smoke from the flame,
Or blow a rumple in the collie's coat.
You make a little foursquare block of air,

Quiet and light and warm, in spite of all
The illimitable dark and cold and storm,
And by so doing give these three, lamp, dog,
And book-leaf, that keep near you, their repose;
Though for all anyone can tell, repose
May be the thing you haven't, yet you give it.
So false it is that what we haven't we can't give;
So false, that what we always say is true.
I'll have to turn the leaf if no one else will.
It won't lie down. Then let it stand. Who cares?"

"I shouldn't want to hurry you, Meserve,
But if you're going—say you'll stay, you know.
But let me raise this curtain on a scene,
And show you how it's piling up against you.
You see the snow-white through the white of frost?
Ask Helen how far up the sash it's climbed
Since last we read the gauge."

                              "It looks as if
Some pallid thing had squashed its features flat
And its eyes shut with overeagerness
To see what people found so interesting
In one another, and had gone to sleep
Of its own stupid lack of understanding,
Or broken its white neck of mushroom stuff
Short off, and died against the window-pane."

"Brother Meserve, take care, you'll scare yourself
More than you will us with such nightmare talk.
It's you it matters to, because it's you
Who have to go out into it alone."

"Let him talk, Helen, and perhaps he'll stay."

"Before you drop the curtain—I'm reminded:
You recollect the boy who came out here
To breathe the air one winter—had a room

Down at the Averys'? Well, one sunny morning
After a downy storm, he passed our place
And found me banking up the house with snow.
And I was burrowing in deep for warmth,
Piling it well above the window-sills.
The snow against the window caught his eye.
'Hey, that's a pretty thought'—those were his words.
'So you can think it's six feet deep outside,
While you sit warm and read up balanced rations.
You can't get too much winter in the winter.'
Those were his words. And he went home and all
But banked the daylight out of Avery's windows.
Now you and I would go to no such length.
At the same time you can't deny it makes
It not a mite worse, sitting here, we three,
Playing our fancy, to have the snowline run
So high across the pane outside. There where
There is a sort of tunnel in the frost
More like a tunnel than a hole—way down
At the far end of it you see a stir
And quiver like the frayed edge of the drift
Blown in the wind. I *like* that—I like *that*.
Well, now I leave you, people."

                              "Come, Meserve,
We thought you were deciding not to go—
The ways you found to say the praise of comfort
And being where you are. You want to stay."

"I'll own it's cold for such a fall of snow.
This house is frozen brittle, all except
This room you sit in. If you think the wind
Sounds further off, it's not because it's dying;
You're further under in the snow—that's all—
And feel it less. Hear the soft bombs of dust
It bursts against us at the chimney mouth,
And at the eaves. I like it from inside
More than I shall out in it. But the horses
Are rested and it's time to say good-night,

And let you get to bed again. Good-night,
Sorry I had to break in on your sleep."

"Lucky for you you did. Lucky for you
You had us for a halfway station
To stop at. If you were the kind of man
Paid heed to women, you'd take my advice
And for your family's sake stay where you are.
But what good is my saying it over and over?
You've done more than you had a right to think
You could do—*now.* You know the risk you take
In going on."

        "Our snow-storms as a rule
Aren't looked on as man-killers, and although
I'd rather be the beast that sleeps the sleep
Under it all, his door sealed up and lost,
Than the man fighting it to keep above it,
Yet think of the small birds at roost and not
In nests. Shall I be counted less than they are?
Their bulk in water would be frozen rock
In no time out tonight. And yet tomorrow
They will come budding boughs from tree to tree
Flirting their wings and saying Chickadee,
As if not knowing what you meant by the word storm."

"But why when no one wants you to go on?
Your wife—she doesn't want you to. We don't,
And you yourself don't want to. Who else is there?"

"Save us from being cornered by a woman.
Well, there's—" She told Fred afterward that in
The pause right there, she thought the dreaded word
Was coming, "God." But no, he only said,
"Well, there's—the storm. That says I must go on.
That wants me as a war might if it came.
Ask any man."

He threw her that as something
To last her till he got outside the door.
He had Cole with him to the barn to see him off.
When Cole returned he found his wife still standing
Beside the table near the open book,
Not reading it.

        "Well, what kind of a man
Do you call that?" she said.

          "He had the gift
Of words, or is it tongues, I ought to say?"

"Was ever such a man for seeing likeness?"

"Or disregarding people's civil questions—
What? We've found out in one hour more about him
Than we had seeing him pass by in the road
A thousand times. If that's the way he preaches!
You didn't think you'd keep him after all.
Oh, I'm not blaming you. He didn't leave you
Much say in the matter, and I'm just as glad
We're not in for a night of him. No sleep
If he had stayed. The least thing set him going.
It's quiet as an empty church without him."

"But how much better off are we as it is?
We'll have to sit here till we know he's safe."

"Yes, I suppose you'll want to, but I shouldn't.
He knows what he can do, or he wouldn't try.
Get into bed I say, and get some rest.
He won't come back, and if he telephones,
It won't be for an hour or two."

        "Well then.
We can't be any help by sitting here
And living his fight through with him, I suppose."

· · ·

Cole had been telephoning in the dark.
Mrs. Cole's voice came from an inner room:
"Did she call you or you call her?"

                              "She me.
You'd better dress: you won't go back to bed.
We must have been asleep: it's three and after."

"Had she been ringing long? I'll get my wrapper.
I want to speak to her."

                    "All she said was,
He hadn't come and had he really started."

"She knew he had, poor thing, two hours ago."

"He had the shovel. He'll have made a fight."

"Why did I ever let him leave this house!"

"Don't begin that. You did the best you could
To keep him—though perhaps you didn't quite
Conceal a wish to see him show the spunk
To disobey you. Much his wife'll thank you."

"Fred, after all I said! You shan't make out
That it was any way but what it was.
Did she let on by any word she said
She didn't thank me?"

                    "When I told her 'Gone,'
'Well then,' she said, and 'Well then'—like a threat.
And then her voice came scraping slow: 'Oh, you,
Why did you let him go?'"

                         "Asked why we let him?
You let me there. I'll ask her why she let him.

She didn't dare to speak when he was here.
Their number's—twenty-one? The thing won't work.
Someone's receiver's down. The handle stumbles.
The stubborn thing, the way it jars your arm!
It's theirs. She's dropped it from her hand and gone."

"Try speaking. Say 'Hello!'"

                              "Hello. Hello."

"What do you hear?"

                         "I hear an empty room—
You know—it sounds that way. And yes, I hear—
I think I hear a clock—and windows rattling.
No step though. If she's there she's sitting down."

"Shout, she may hear you."

                              "Shouting is no good."

"Keep speaking then."

                         "Hello. Hello. Hello.
You don't suppose—? She wouldn't go outdoors?"

"I'm half afraid that's just what she might do."

"And leave the children?"

                              "Wait and call again.
You can't hear whether she has left the door
Wide open and the wind's blown out the lamp
And the fire's died and the room's dark and cold?"

"One of two things, either she's gone to bed
Or gone outdoors."

                         "In which case both are lost.

Do you know what she's like? Have you ever met her?
It's strange she doesn't want to speak to us."

        "Fred, see if you can hear what I hear. Come."

"A clock maybe."

        "Don't you hear something else?"

"Not talking."

        "No."

        "Why, yes, I hear—what is it?"

"What do you say it is?"

        "A baby's crying!
Frantic it sounds, though muffled and far off.
Its mother wouldn't let it cry like that,
Not if she's there."

        "What do you make of it?"

"There's only one thing possible to make,
That is, assuming—that she has gone out.
Of course she hasn't though." They both sat down
Helpless. "There's nothing we can do till morning."

"Fred, I shan't let you think of going out."

"Hold on." The double bell began to chirp.
They started up. Fred took the telephone.
"Hello, Meserve. You're there, then!—And your wife?
Good! Why I asked—she didn't seem to answer.
He says she went to let him in the barn.—
We're glad. Oh, say no more about it, man.
Drop in and see us when you're passing."

                                        "Well,
She has him then, though what she wants him for
I *don't* see."

                    "Possibly not for herself.
Maybe she only wants him for the children."

"The whole to-do seems to have been for nothing.
What spoiled our night was to him just his fun.
What did he come in for?—To talk and visit?
Thought he'd just call to tell us it was snowing.
If he thinks he is going to make our house
A halfway coffee house 'twixt town and nowhere—"

"I thought you'd feel you'd been too much concerned."

"You think you haven't been concerned yourself."

"If you mean he was inconsiderate
To rout us out to think for him at midnight
And then take our advice no more than nothing,
Why, I agree with you. But let's forgive him.
We've had a share in one night of his life.
What'll you bet he ever calls again?"

# THE SOUND OF TREES

I wonder about the trees.
Why do we wish to bear
Forever the noise of these
More than another noise
So close to our dwelling place?
We suffer them by the day
Till we lose all measure of pace,
And fixity in our joys,
And acquire a listening air.
They are that that talks of going
But never gets away;
And that talks no less for knowing,
As it grows wiser and older,
That now it means to stay.
My feet tug at the floor
And my head sways to my shoulder
Sometimes when I watch trees sway,
From the window or the door.
I shall set forth for somewhere,
I shall make the reckless choice
Some day when they are in voice
And tossing so as to scare
The white clouds over them on.
I shall have less to say,
But I shall be gone.

# NEW HAMPSHIRE

# NEW HAMPSHIRE

I met a lady from the South who said
(You won't believe she said it, but she said it):
"None of my family ever worked, or had
A thing to sell." I don't suppose the work
Much matters. You may work for all of me.
I've seen the time I've had to work myself.
The having anything to sell is what
Is the disgrace in man or state or nation.

I met a traveler from Arkansas
Who boasted of his state as beautiful
For diamonds and apples. "Diamonds
And apples in commercial quantities?"
I asked him, on my guard. "Oh, yes," he answered,
Off his. The time was evening in the Pullman.
"I see the porter's made your bed," I told him.

I met a Californian who would
Talk California—a state so blessed,
He said, in climate, none had ever died there
A natural death, and Vigilance Committees
Had had to organize to stock the graveyards
And vindicate the state's humanity.
"Just the way Stefansson runs on," I murmured,
"About the British Arctic. That's what comes
Of being in the market with a climate."

I met a poet from another state,
A zealot full of fluid inspiration,
Who in the name of fluid inspiration,
But in the best style of bad salesmanship,
Angrily tried to make me write a protest
(In verse I think) against the Volstead Act.
He didn't even offer me a drink
Until I asked for one to steady *him*.
This is called having an idea to sell.

It never could have happened in New Hampshire.

The only person really soiled with trade
I ever stumbled on in old New Hampshire
Was someone who had just come back ashamed
From selling things in California.
He'd built a noble mansard roof with balls
On turrets like Constantinople, deep
In woods some ten miles from a railroad station,
As if to put forever out of mind
The hope of being, as we say, received.
I found him standing at the close of day
Inside the threshold of his open barn,
Like a lone actor on a gloomy stage—
And recognized him through the iron gray
In which his face was muffled to the eyes
As an old boyhood friend, and once indeed
A drover with me on the road to Brighton.
His farm was "grounds," and not a farm at all;
His house among the local sheds and shanties
Rose like a factor's at a trading station.
And he was rich, and I was still a rascal.
I couldn't keep from asking impolitely,
Where had he been and what had he been doing?
How did he get so? (Rich was understood.)
In dealing in "old rags" in San Francisco.
Oh it was terrible as well could be.
We both of us turned over in our graves.

Just specimens is all New Hampshire has,
One each of everything as in a show-case
Which naturally she doesn't care to sell.

She had one President (pronounce him Purse,
And make the most of it for better or worse.
He's your one chance to score against the state).
She had one Daniel Webster. He was all
The Daniel Webster ever was or shall be.
She had the Dartmouth needed to produce him.

I call her old. She has one family
Whose claim is good to being settled here
Before the era of colonization,
And before that of exploration even.
John Smith remarked them as he coasted by
Dangling their legs and fishing off a wharf
At the Isles of Shoals, and satisfied himself
They weren't Red Indians, but veritable
Pre-primitives of the white race, dawn people,
Like those who furnished Adam's sons with wives;
However uninnocent they may have been
In being there so early in our history.
They'd been there then a hundred years or more.
Pity he didn't ask what they were up to
At that date with a wharf already built,
And take their name. They've since told me their name—
Today an honored one in Nottingham.
As for what they were up to more than fishing—
Suppose they weren't behaving Puritanly,
The hour had not yet struck for being good,
Mankind had not yet gone on the Sabbatical.
It became an explorer of the deep
Not to explore too deep in others' business.

Did you but know of him, New Hampshire has
One real reformer who would change the world
So it would be accepted by two classes,
Artists the minute they set up as artists,
Before, that is, they are themselves accepted,
And boys the minute they get out of college.
I can't help thinking those are tests to go by.

And she has one I don't know what to call him,
Who comes from Philadelphia every year
With a great flock of chickens of rare breeds
He wants to give the educational
Advantages of growing almost wild
Under the watchful eye of hawk and eagle—
Dorkings because they're spoken of by Chaucer,

Sussex because they're spoken of by Herrick.

She has a touch of gold. New Hampshire gold—
You may have heard of it. I had a farm
Offered me not long since up Berlin way
With a mine on it that was worked for gold;
But not gold in commercial quantities,
Just enough gold to make the engagement rings
And marriage rings of those who owned the farm.
What gold more innocent could one have asked for?
One of my children ranging after rocks
Lately brought home from Andover or Canaan
A specimen of beryl with a trace
Of radium. I know with radium
The trace would have to be the merest trace
To be below the threshold of commercial;
But trust New Hampshire not to have enough
Of radium or anything to sell.

A specimen of everything, I said.
She has one witch—old style. She lives in Colebrook.
(The only other witch I ever met
Was lately at a cut-glass dinner in Boston.
There were four candles and four people present.
The witch was young, and beautiful (new style),
And open-minded. She was free to question
Her gift for reading letters locked in boxes.
Why was it so much greater when the boxes
Were metal than it was when they were wooden?
It made the world seem so mysterious.
The S'ciety for Psychical Research
Was cognizant. Her husband was worth millions.
I think he owned some shares in Harvard College.)

New Hampshire *used* to have at Salem
A company we called the White Corpuscles,
Whose duty was at any hour of night
To rush in sheets and fools' caps where they smelled
A thing the least bit doubtfully perscented

And give someone the Skipper Ireson's Ride.

One each of everything as in a show-case.
More than enough land for a specimen
You'll say she has, but there there enters in
Something else to protect her from herself.
There quality makes up for quantity.
Not even New Hampshire farms are much for sale.
The farm I made my home on in the mountains
I had to take by force rather than buy.
I caught the owner outdoors by himself
Raking up after winter, and I said,
"I'm going to put you off this farm: I want it."
"Where are you going to put me? In the road?"
"I'm going to put you on the farm next to it."
"Why won't the farm next to it do for you?"
"I like this better." It was really better.

Apples? New Hampshire has them, but unsprayed,
With no suspicion in stem-end or blossom-end
Of vitriol or arsenate of lead,
And so not good for anything but cider.
Her unpruned grapes are flung like lariats
Far up the birches out of reach of man.

A state producing precious metals, stones,
And—writing; none of these except perhaps
The precious literature in quantity
Or quality to worry the producer
About disposing of it. Do you know,
Considering the market, there are more
Poems produced than any other thing?
No wonder poets sometimes have to *seem*
So much more business-like than business men.
Their wares are so much harder to get rid of.

She's one of the two best states in the Union.
Vermont's the other. And the two have been
Yoke-fellows in the sap-yoke from of old

In many Marches. And they lie like wedges,
Thick end to thin end and thin end to thick end,
And are a figure of the way the strong
Of mind and strong of arm should fit together,
One thick where one is thin and vice versa.
New Hampshire raises the Connecticut
In a trout hatchery near Canada,
But soon divides the river with Vermont.
Both are delightful states for their absurdly
Small towns—Lost Nation, Bungey, Muddy Boo,
Poplin, Still Corners (so called not because
The place is silent all day long, nor yet
Because it boasts a whisky still—because
It set out once to be a city and still
Is only corners, cross-roads in a wood).
And I remember one whose name appeared
Between the pictures on a movie screen
Election night once in Franconia,
When everything had gone Republican
And Democrats were sore in need of comfort:
Easton goes Democratic, Wilson 4
Hughes 2. And everybody to the saddest
Laughed the loud laugh, the big laugh at the little.
New York (five million) laughs at Manchester,
Manchester (sixty or seventy thousand) laughs
At Littleton (four thousand), Littleton
Laughs at Franconia (seven hundred), and
Franconia laughs, I fear,—did laugh that night—
At Easton. What has Easton left to laugh at,
And like the actress exclaim, "Oh, my God" at?
There's Bungey; and for Bungey there are towns,
Whole townships named but without population.

Anything I can say about New Hampshire
Will serve almost as well about Vermont,
Excepting that they differ in their mountains.
The Vermont mountains stretch extended straight;
New Hampshire mountains curl up in a coil.

I had been coming to New Hampshire mountains.
And here I am and what am I to say?
Here first my theme becomes embarrassing.
Emerson said, "The God who made New Hampshire
Taunted the lofty land with little men."
Another Massachusetts poet said,
"I go no more to summer in New Hampshire.
I've given up my summer place in Dublin."
But when I asked to know what ailed New Hampshire,
She said she couldn't stand the people in it,
The little men (it's Massachusetts speaking).
And when I asked to know what ailed the people,
She said, "Go read your own books and find out."
I may as well confess myself the author
Of several books against the world in general.
To take them as against a special state
Or even nation's to restrict my meaning.
I'm what is called a sensibilitist,
Or otherwise an environmentalist.
I refuse to adapt myself a mite
To any change from hot to cold, from wet
To dry, from poor to rich, or back again.
I make a virtue of my suffering
From nearly everything that goes on round me.
In other words, I know wherever I am,
Being the creature of literature I am,
I shall not lack for pain to keep me awake.
Kit Marlowe taught me how to say my prayers:
"Why, this is Hell, nor am I out of it."
Samoa, Russia, Ireland, I complain of,
No less than England, France, and Italy.
Because I wrote my novels in New Hampshire
Is no proof that I aimed them at New Hampshire.

When I left Massachusetts years ago
Between two days, the reason why I sought
New Hampshire, not Connecticut,
Rhode Island, New York, or Vermont was this:
Where I was living then, New Hampshire offered

The nearest boundary to escape across.
I hadn't an illusion in my hand-bag
About the people being better there
Than those I left behind. I thought they weren't.
I thought they couldn't be. And yet they were.
I'd sure had no such friends in Massachusetts
As Hall of Windham, Gay of Atkinson,
Bartlett of Raymond (now of Colorado),
Harris of Derry, and Lynch of Bethlehem.

The glorious bards of Massachusetts seem
To want to make New Hampshire people over.
They taunt the lofty land with little men.
I don't know what to say about the people.
For art's sake one could almost wish them worse
Rather than better. How are we to write
The Russian novel in America
As long as life goes so unterribly?
There is the pinch from which our only outcry
In literature to date is heard to come.
We get what little misery we can
Out of not having cause for misery.
It makes the guild of novel writers sick
To be expected to be Dostoievskis
On nothing worse than too much luck and comfort.
This is not sorrow, though; it's just the vapors,
And recognized as such in Russia itself
Under the new régime, and so forbidden.
If well it is with Russia, then feel free
To say so or be stood against the wall
And shot. It's Pollyanna now or death.
This, then, is the new freedom we hear tell of;
And very sensible. No state can build
A literature that shall at once be sound
And sad on a foundation of well-being.

To show the level of intelligence
Among us: it was just a Warren farmer
Whose horse had pulled him short up in the road

By me, a stranger. This is what he said,
From nothing but embarrassment and want
Of anything more sociable to say:
"You hear those hound-dogs sing on Moosilauke?
Well they remind me of the hue and cry
We've heard against the Mid-Victorians
And never rightly understood till Bryan
Retired from politics and joined the chorus.
The matter with the Mid-Victorians
Seems to have been a man named John L. Darwin."
"Go 'long," I said to him, he to his horse.

I knew a man who failing as a farmer
Burned down his farmhouse for the fire insurance,
And spent the proceeds on a telescope
To satisfy a life-long curiosity
About our place among the infinities.
And how was that for other-worldliness?

If I must choose which I would elevate—
The people or the already lofty mountains,
I'd elevate the already lofty mountains.
The only fault I find with old New Hampshire
Is that her mountains aren't quite high enough.
I was not always so; I've come to be so.
How, to my sorrow, how have I attained
A height from which to look down critical
On mountains? What has given me assurance
To say what height becomes New Hampshire mountains,
Or any mountains? Can it be some strength
I feel as of an earthquake in my back
To heave them higher to the morning star?
Can it be foreign travel in the Alps?
Or having seen and credited a moment
The solid molding of vast peaks of cloud
Behind the pitiful reality
Of Lincoln, Lafayette, and Liberty?
Or some such sense as says how high shall jet
The fountain in proportion to the basin?

No, none of these has raised me to my throne
Of intellectual dissatisfaction,
But the sad accident of having seen
Our actual mountains given in a map
Of early times as twice the height they are—
Ten thousand feet instead of only five—
Which shows how sad an accident may be.
Five thousand is no longer high enough.
Whereas I never had a good idea
About improving people in the world,
Here I am over-fertile in suggestion,
And cannot rest from planning day or night
How high I'd thrust the peaks in summer snow
To tap the upper sky and draw a flow
Of frosty night air on the vale below
Down from the stars to freeze the dew as starry.

The more the sensibilitist I am
The more I seem to want my mountains wild;
The way the wiry gang-boss liked the log-jam.
After he'd picked the lock and got it started,
He dodged a log that lifted like an arm
Against the sky to break his back for him,
Then came in dancing, skipping, with his life
Across the roar and chaos, and the words
We saw him say along the zigzag journey
Were doubtless as the words we heard him say
On coming nearer: "Wasn't she an *i*-deal
Son-of-a-bitch? You bet she was an *i*-deal."

For all her mountains fall a little short,
Her people not quite short enough for Art,
She's still New Hampshire, a most restful state.

Lately in converse with a New York alec
About the new school of the pseudo-phallic,
I found myself in a close corner where
I had to make an almost funny choice.
"Choose you which you will be—a prude, or puke,

Mewling and puking in the public arms."
"Me for the hills where I don't have to choose."
"But if you had to choose, which would you be?"
I wouldn't be a prude afraid of nature.
I know a man who took a double ax
And went alone against a grove of trees;
But his heart failing him, he dropped the ax
And ran for shelter quoting Matthew Arnold:
"Nature is cruel, man is sick of blood;
There's been enough shed without shedding mine.
Remember Birnam Wood! The wood's in flux!"
He had a special terror of the flux
That showed itself in dendrophobia.
The only decent tree had been to mill
And educated into boards, he said.
He knew too well for any earthly use
The line where man leaves off and nature starts,
And never over-stepped it save in dreams.
He stood on the safe side of the line talking;
Which is sheer Matthew Arnoldism,
The cult of one who owned himself "a foiled,
Circuitous wanderer," and "took dejectedly
His seat upon the intellectual throne."
Agreed in frowning on these improvised
Altars the woods are full of nowadays,
Again as in the days when Ahaz sinned
By worship under green trees in the open.
Scarcely a mile but that I come on one,
A black-cheeked stone and stick of rain-washed charcoal.
Even to say the groves were God's first temples
Comes too near to Ahaz' sin for safety.
Nothing not built with hands of course is sacred;
But here is not a question of what's sacred;
Rather of what to face or run away from.
I'd hate to be a runaway from nature.
And neither would I choose to be a puke
Who cares not what he does in company,
And, when he can't do anything, falls back
On words, and tries his worst to make words speak

Louder than actions, and sometimes achieves it.
It seems a narrow choice the age insists on.
How about being a good Greek, for instance?
That course, they tell me, isn't offered this year.
"Come, but this isn't choosing—puke or prude?"
Well, if I have to choose one or the other,
I choose to be a plain New Hampshire farmer
With an income in cash of say a thousand
(From say a publisher in New York City).
It's restful to arrive at a decision,
And restful just to think about New Hampshire.
At present I am living in Vermont.

# A STAR IN A STONE-BOAT

### For Lincoln MacVeagh

Never tell me that not one star of all
That slip from heaven at night and softly fall
Has been picked up with stones to build a wall.

Some laborer found one faded and stone cold,
And saving that its weight suggested gold,
And tugged it from his first too certain hold,

He noticed nothing in it to remark.
He was not used to handling stars thrown dark
And lifeless from an interrupted arc.

He did not recognize in that smooth coal
The one thing palpable beside the soul
To penetrate the air in which we roll.

He did not see how like a flying thing
It brooded ant-eggs, and had one large wing,
One not so large for flying in a ring,

And a long Bird of Paradise's tail,
(Though these when not in use to fly and trail
It drew back in its body like a snail);

Nor know that he might move it from the spot,
The harm was done; from having been star-shot
The very nature of the soil was hot

And burning to yield flowers instead of grain,
Flowers fanned and not put out by all the rain
Poured on them by his prayers prayed in vain.

He moved it roughly with an iron bar,
He loaded an old stone-boat with the star
And not, as you might think, a flying car,

Such as even poets would admit perforce
More practical than Pegasus the horse
If it could put a star back in its course.

He dragged it through the plowed ground at a pace
But faintly reminiscent of the race
Of jostling rock in interstellar space.

It went for building stone, and I, as though
Commanded in a dream, forever go
To right the wrong that this should have been so.

Yet ask where else it could have gone as well,
I do not know—I cannot stop to tell:
He might have left it lying where it fell.

From following walls I never lift my eye
Except at night to places in the sky
Where showers of charted meteors let fly.

Some may know what they seek in school and church,
And why they seek it there; for what I search
I must go measuring stone walls, perch on perch;

Sure that though not a star of death and birth,
So not to be compared, perhaps, in worth
To such resorts of life as Mars and Earth,

Though not, I say, a star of death and sin,
It yet has poles, and only needs a spin
To show its worldly nature and begin

To chafe and shuffle in my calloused palm
And run off in strange tangents with my arm
As fish do with the line in first alarm.

Such as it is, it promises the prize
Of the one world complete in any size
That I am like to compass, fool or wise.

# THE CENSUS-TAKER

I came an errand one cloud-blowing evening
To a slab-built, black-paper-covered house
Of one room and one window and one door,
The only dwelling in a waste cut over
A hundred square miles round it in the mountains:
And that not dwelt in now by men or women.
(It never had been dwelt in, though, by women,
So what is this I make a sorrow of?)
I came as census-taker to the waste
To count the people in it and found none,
None in the hundred miles, none in the house,
Where I came last with some hope, but not much
After hours' overlooking from the cliffs
An emptiness flayed to the very stone.
I found no people that dared show themselves,
None not in hiding from the outward eye.
The time was autumn, but how anyone
Could tell the time of year when every tree
That could have dropped a leaf was down itself
And nothing but the stump of it was left
Now bringing out its rings in sugar of pitch;
And every tree up stood a rotting trunk
Without a single leaf to spend on autumn,
Or branch to whistle after what was spent.
Perhaps the wind the more without the help
Of breathing trees said something of the time
Of year or day the way it swung a door
Forever off the latch, as if rude men
Passed in and slammed it shut each one behind him
For the next one to open for himself.
I counted nine I had no right to count
(But this was dreamy unofficial counting)
Before I made the tenth across the threshold.
Where was my supper? Where was anyone's?
No lamp was lit. Nothing was on the table.
The stove was cold—the stove was off the chimney—
And down by one side where it lacked a leg.

The people that had loudly passed the door
Were people to the ear but not the eye.
They were not on the table with their elbows.
They were not sleeping in the shelves of bunks.
I saw no men there and no bones of men there.
I armed myself against such bones as might be
With the pitch-blackened stub of an ax-handle
I picked up off the straw-dust covered floor.
Not bones, but the ill-fitted window rattled.
The door was still because I held it shut
While I thought what to do that could be done—
About the house—about the people not there.
This house in one year fallen to decay
Filled me with no less sorrow than the houses
Fallen to ruin in ten thousand years
Where Asia wedges Africa from Europe.
Nothing was left to do that I could see
Unless to find that there was no one there
And declare to the cliffs too far for echo,
"The place is desert and let whoso lurks
In silence, if in this he is aggrieved,
Break silence now or be forever silent.
Let him say why it should not be declared so."
The melancholy of having to count souls
Where they grow fewer and fewer every year
Is extreme where they shrink to none at all.
It must be I want life to go on living.

# THE STAR-SPLITTER

"You know Orion always comes up sideways.
Throwing a leg up over our fence of mountains,
And rising on his hands, he looks in on me
Busy outdoors by lantern-light with something
I should have done by daylight, and indeed,
After the ground is frozen, I should have done
Before it froze, and a gust flings a handful
Of waste leaves at my smoky lantern chimney
To make fun of my way of doing things,
Or else fun of Orion's having caught me.
Has a man, I should like to ask, no rights
These forces are obliged to pay respect to?"
So Brad McLaughlin mingled reckless talk
Of heavenly stars with hugger-mugger farming,
Till having failed at hugger-mugger farming,
He burned his house down for the fire insurance
And spent the proceeds on a telescope
To satisfy a life-long curiosity
About our place among the infinities.

"What do you want with one of those blame things?"
I asked him well beforehand. "Don't you get one!"
"Don't call it blamed; there isn't anything
More blameless in the sense of being less
A weapon in our human fight," he said.
"I'll have one if I sell my farm to buy it."
There where he moved the rocks to plow the ground
And plowed between the rocks he couldn't move,
Few farms changed hands; so rather than spend years
Trying to sell his farm and then not selling,
He burned his house down for the fire insurance
And bought the telescope with what it came to.
He had been heard to say by several:
"The best thing that we're put here for's to see;
The strongest thing that's given us to see with's
A telescope. Someone in every town
Seems to me owes it to the town to keep one.

In Littleton it may as well be me."
After such loose talk it was no surprise
When he did what he did and burned his house down.

Mean laughter went about the town that day
To let him know we weren't the least imposed on,
And he could wait—we'd see to him tomorrow.
But the first thing next morning we reflected
If one by one we counted people out
For the least sin, it wouldn't take us long
To get so we had no one left to live with.
For to be social is to be forgiving.
Our thief, the one who does our stealing from us,
We don't cut off from coming to church suppers,
But what we miss we go to him and ask for.
He promptly gives it back, that is if still
Uneaten, unworn out, or undisposed of.
It wouldn't do to be too hard on Brad
About his telescope. Beyond the age
Of being given one for Christmas gift,
He had to take the best way he knew how
To find himself in one. Well, all we said was
He took a strange thing to be roguish over.
Some sympathy was wasted on the house,
A good old-timer dating back along;
But a house isn't sentient; the house
Didn't feel anything. And if it did,
Why not regard it as a sacrifice,
And an old-fashioned sacrifice by fire,
Instead of a new-fashioned one at auction?

Out of a house and so out of a farm
At one stroke (of a match), Brad had to turn
To earn a living on the Concord railroad,
As under-ticket-agent at a station
Where his job, when he wasn't selling tickets,
Was setting out up track and down, not plants
As on a farm, but planets, evening stars
That varied in their hue from red to green.

He got a good glass for six hundred dollars.
His new job gave him leisure for star-gazing.
Often he bid me come and have a look
Up the brass barrel, velvet black inside,
At a star quaking in the other end.
I recollect a night of broken clouds
And underfoot snow melted down to ice,
And melting further in the wind to mud.
Bradford and I had out the telescope.
We spread our two legs as we spread its three,
Pointed our thoughts the way we pointed it,
And standing at our leisure till the day broke,
Said some of the best things we ever said.
That telescope was christened the Star-splitter,
Because it didn't do a thing but split
A star in two or three the way you split
A globule of quicksilver in your hand
With one stroke of your finger in the middle.
It's a star-splitter if there ever was one
And ought to do some good if splitting stars
'Sa thing to be compared with splitting wood.

We've looked and looked, but after all where are we?
Do we know any better where we are,
And how it stands between the night tonight
And a man with a smoky lantern chimney?
How different from the way it ever stood?

# MAPLE

Her teacher's certainty it must be Mabel
Made Maple first take notice of her name.
She asked her father and he told her "Maple—
Maple is right."

          "But teacher told the school
There's no such name."

           "Teachers don't know as much
As fathers about children, you tell teacher.
You tell her that it's M-A-P-L-E.
You ask her if she knows a maple tree.
Well, you were named after a maple tree.
Your mother named you. You and she just saw
Each other in passing in the room upstairs,
One coming this way into life, and one
Going the other out of life—you know?
So you can't have much recollection of her.
She had been having a long look at you.
She put her finger in your cheek so hard
It must have made your dimple there, and said,
'Maple.' I said it too: 'Yes, for her name.'
She nodded. So we're sure there's no mistake.
I don't know what she wanted it to mean,
But it seems like some word she left to bid you
Be a good girl—be like a maple tree.
How like a maple tree's for us to guess.
Or for a little girl to guess sometime.
Not now—at least I shouldn't try too hard now.
By and by I will tell you all I know
About the different trees, and something, too,
About your mother that perhaps may help."
Dangerous self-arousing words to sow.
Luckily all she wanted of her name then
Was to rebuke her teacher with it next day,
And give the teacher a scare as from her father.
Anything further had been wasted on her,

Or so he tried to think to avoid blame.
She would forget it. She all but forgot it.
What he sowed with her slept so long a sleep,
And came so near death in the dark of years,
That when it woke and came to life again
The flower was different from the parent seed.
It came back vaguely at the glass one day,
As she stood saying her name over aloud,
Striking it gently across her lowered eyes
To make it go well with the way she looked.
What was it about her name? Its strangeness lay
In having too much meaning. Other names,
As Lesley, Carol, Irma, Marjorie,
Signified nothing. Rose could have a meaning,
But hadn't as it went. (She knew a Rose.)
This difference from other names it was
Made people notice it—and notice her.
(They either noticed it, or got it wrong.)
Her problem was to find out what it asked
In dress or manner of the girl who bore it.
If she could form some notion of her mother—
What she had thought was lovely, and what good.
This was her mother's childhood home;
The house one story high in front, three stories
On the end it presented to the road.
(The arrangement made a pleasant sunny cellar.)
Her mother's bedroom was her father's yet,
Where she could watch her mother's picture fading.
Once she found for a bookmark in the Bible
A maple leaf she thought must have been laid
In wait for her there. She read every word
Of the two pages it was pressed between
As if it was her mother speaking to her.
But forgot to put the leaf back in closing
And lost the place never to read again.
She was sure, though, there had been nothing in it.

So she looked for herself, as everyone
Looks for himself, more or less outwardly.

And her self-seeking, fitful though it was,
May still have been what led her on to read,
And think a little, and get some city schooling.
She learned shorthand, whatever shorthand may
Have had to do with it—she sometimes wondered
So, till she found herself in a strange place
For the name Maple to have brought her to,
Taking dictation on a paper pad,
And in the pauses when she raised her eyes
Watching out of a nineteenth story window
An airship laboring with unship-like motion
And a vague all-disturbing roar above the river
Beyond the highest city built with hands.
Someone was saying in such natural tones
She almost wrote the words down on her knee,
"Do you know you remind me of a tree—
A maple tree?"

              "Because my name is Maple?"

"Isn't it Mabel? I thought it was Mabel."

"No doubt you've heard the office call me Mabel.
I have to let them call me what they like."

They were both stirred that he should have divined
Without the name her personal mystery.
It made it seem as if there must be something
She must have missed herself. So they were married,
And took the fancy home with them to live by.

They went on pilgrimage once to her father's
(The house one story high in front, three stories
On the side it presented to the road)
To see if there was not some special tree
She might have overlooked. They could find none,
Not so much as a single tree for shade,
Let alone grove of trees for sugar orchard.
She told him of the bookmark maple leaf

In the big Bible, and all she remembered
Of the place marked with it—"Wave offering,
Something about wave offering, it said."

"You've never asked your father outright, have you?"

"I have, and been put off sometime, I think."
(This was her faded memory of the way
Once long ago her father had put himself off.)

"Because no telling but it may have been
Something between your father and your mother
Not meant for us at all."

     "Not meant for me?
Where would the fairness be in giving me
A name to carry for life, and never know
The secret of?"

     "And then it may have been
Something a father couldn't tell a daughter
As well as could a mother. And again
It may have been their one lapse into fancy
'Twould be too bad to make him sorry for
By bringing it up to him when he was too old.
Your father feels us round him with our questing,
And holds us off unnecessarily,
As if he didn't know what little thing
Might lead us on to a discovery.
It was as personal as he could be
About the way he saw it was with you
To say your mother, had she lived, would be
As far again as from being born to bearing."

"Just one look more with what you say in mind,
And I give up"; which last look came to nothing.
But, though they now gave up the search forever,
They clung to what one had seen in the other
By inspiration. It proved there was something.

They kept their thoughts away from when the maples
Stood uniform in buckets, and the steam
Of sap and snow rolled off the sugar house.
When they made her related to the maples,
It was the tree the autumn fire ran through
And swept of leathern leaves, but left the bark
Unscorched, unblackened, even, by any smoke.
They always took their holidays in autumn.
Once they came on a maple in a glade,
Standing alone with smooth arms lifted up,
And every leaf of foliage she'd worn
Laid scarlet and pale pink about her feet.
But its age kept them from considering this one.
Twenty-five years ago at Maple's naming
It hardly could have been a two-leaved seedling
The next cow might have licked up out at pasture.
Could it have been another maple like it?
They hovered for a moment near discovery,
Figurative enough to see the symbol,
But lacking faith in anything to mean
The same at different times to different people.
Perhaps a filial diffidence partly kept them
From thinking it could be a thing so bridal.
And anyway it came too late for Maple.
She used her hands to cover up her eyes.
"We would not see the secret if we could now:
We are not looking for it any more."

Thus had a name with meaning, given in death,
Made a girl's marriage, and ruled in her life.
No matter that the meaning was not clear.
A name with meaning could bring up a child,
Taking the child out of the parents' hands.
Better a meaningless name, I should say,
As leaving more to nature and happy chance.
Name children some names and see what you do.

# THE AX-HELVE

I've known ere now an interfering branch
Of alder catch my lifted ax behind me.
But that was in the woods, to hold my hand
From striking at another alder's roots,
And that was, as I say, an alder branch.
This was a man, Baptiste, who stole one day
Behind me on the snow in my own yard
Where I was working at the chopping-block,
And cutting nothing not cut down already.
He caught my ax expertly on the rise,
When all my strength put forth was in his favor,
Held it a moment where it was, to calm me,
Then took it from me—and I let him take it.
I didn't know him well enough to know
What it was all about. There might be something
He had in mind to say to a bad neighbor
He might prefer to say to him disarmed.
But all he had to tell me in French-English
Was what he thought of—not me, but my ax,
Me only as I took my ax to heart.
It was the bad ax-helve someone had sold me—
"Made on machine," he said, plowing the grain
With a thick thumbnail to show how it ran
Across the handle's long drawn serpentine,
Like the two strokes across a dollar sign.
"You give her one good crack, she's snap raght off.
Den where's your hax-ead flying t'rough de hair?"
Admitted; and yet, what was that to him?

"Come on my house and I put you one in
What's las' awhile—good hick'ry what's grow crooked.
De second growt' I cut myself—tough, tough!"

Something to sell? That wasn't how it sounded.

"Den when you say you come? It's cost you nothing.
Tonaght?"

As well tonight as any night.

Beyond an over-warmth of kitchen stove
My welcome differed from no other welcome.
Baptiste knew best why I was where I was.
So long as he would leave enough unsaid,
I shouldn't mind his being overjoyed
(If overjoyed he was) at having got me
Where I must judge if what he knew about an ax
That not everybody else knew was to count
For nothing in the measure of a neighbor.
Hard if, though cast away for life with Yankees,
A Frenchman couldn't get his human rating!

Mrs. Baptiste came in and rocked a chair
That had as many motions as the world:
One back and forward, in and out of shadow,
That got her nowhere; one more gradual,
Sideways, that would have run her on the stove
In time, had she not realized her danger
And caught herself up bodily, chair and all,
And set herself back where she started from.
"She ain't spick too much Henglish—dat's too bad."

I was afraid, in brightening first on me,
Then on Baptiste, as if she understood
What passed between us, she was only feigning.
Baptiste was anxious for her; but no more
Than for himself, so placed he couldn't hope
To keep his bargain of the morning with me
In time to keep me from suspecting him
Of really never having meant to keep it.

Needlessly soon he had his ax-helves out,
A quiverful to choose from, since he wished me
To have the best he had, or had to spare—
Not for me to ask which, when what he took
Had beauties he had to point me out at length
To insure their not being wasted on me.

He liked to have it slender as a whipstock,
Free from the least knot, equal to the strain
Of bending like a sword across the knee.
He showed me that the lines of a good helve
Were native to the grain before the knife
Expressed them, and its curves were no false curves
Put on it from without. And there its strength lay
For the hard work. He chafed its long white body
From end to end with his rough hand shut round it.
He tried it at the eye-hole in the ax-head.
"Hahn, hahn," he mused, "don't need much taking down."
Baptiste knew how to make a short job long
For love of it, and yet not waste time either.

Do you know, what we talked about was knowledge?
Baptiste on his defense about the children
He kept from school, or did his best to keep—
Whatever school and children and our doubts
Of laid-on education had to do
With the curves of his ax-helves and his having
Used these unscrupulously to bring me
To see for once the inside of his house.
Was I desired in friendship, partly as someone
To leave it to, whether the right to hold
Such doubts of education should depend
Upon the education of those who held them?

But now he brushed the shavings from his knee
And stood the ax there on its horse's hoof,
Erect, but not without its waves, as when
The snake stood up for evil in the Garden,—
Top-heavy with a heaviness his short,
Thick hand made light of, steel-blue chin drawn down
And in a little—a French touch in that.
Baptiste drew back and squinted at it, pleased;
"See how she's cock her head!"

# THE GRINDSTONE

Having a wheel and four legs of its own
Has never availed the cumbersome grindstone
To get it anywhere that I can see.
These hands have helped it go, and even race;
Not all the motion, though, they ever lent,
Not all the miles it may have thought it went,
Have got it one step from the starting place.
It stands beside the same old apple tree.
The shadow of the apple tree is thin
Upon it now, its feet are fast in snow.
All other farm machinery's gone in,
And some of it on no more legs and wheel
Than the grindstone can boast to stand or go.
(I'm thinking chiefly of the wheelbarrow.)
For months it hasn't known the taste of steel,
Washed down with rusty water in a tin.
But standing outdoors hungry, in the cold,
Except in towns at night, is not a sin.
And, anyway, its standing in the yard
Under a ruinous live apple tree
Has nothing any more to do with me,
Except that I remember how of old
One summer day, all day I drove it hard,
And someone mounted on it rode it hard,
And he and I between us ground a blade.

I gave it the preliminary spin,
And poured on water (tears it might have been),
And when it almost gaily jumped and flowed,
A Father-Time-like man got on and rode,
Armed with a scythe and spectacles that glowed.
He turned on will-power to increase the load
And slow me down—and I abruptly slowed,
Like coming to a sudden railroad station.
I changed from hand to hand in desperation.
I wondered what machine of ages gone
This represented an improvement on.

For all I knew it may have sharpened spears
And arrowheads itself. Much use for years
Had gradually worn it an oblate
Spheroid that kicked and struggled in its gait,
Appearing to return me hate for hate;
(But I forgive it now as easily
As any other boyhood enemy
Whose pride has failed to get him anywhere).
I wondered who it was the man thought ground—
The one who held the wheel back or the one
Who gave his life to keep it going round?
I wondered if he really thought it fair
For him to have the say when we were done.
Such were the bitter thoughts to which I turned.

Not for myself was I so much concerned.
Oh no!—although, of course, I could have found
A better way to pass the afternoon
Than grinding discord out of a grindstone,
And beating insects at their gritty tune.
Nor was I for the man so much concerned.
Once when the grindstone almost jumped its bearing
It looked as if he might be badly thrown
And wounded on his blade. So far from caring,
I laughed inside, and only cranked the faster,
(It ran as if it wasn't greased but glued);
I'd welcome any moderate disaster
That might be calculated to postpone
What evidently nothing could conclude.
The thing that made me more and more afraid
Was that we'd ground it sharp and hadn't known.
And now were only wasting precious blade.
And when he raised it dripping once and tried
The creepy edge of it with wary touch,
And viewed it over his glasses funny-eyed,
Only disinterestedly to decide
It needed a turn more, I could have cried
Wasn't there danger of a turn too much?
Mightn't we make it worse instead of better?

I was for leaving something to the whetter.
What if it wasn't all it should be? I'd
Be satisfied if he'd be satisfied.

# PAUL'S WIFE

To drive Paul out of any lumber camp
All that was needed was to say to him,
"How is the wife, Paul?"—and he'd disappear.
Some said it was because he had no wife,
And hated to be twitted on the subject;
Others because he'd come within a day
Or so of having one, and then been jilted;
Others because he'd had one once, a good one,
Who'd run away with someone else and left him;
And others still because he had one now
He only had to be reminded of,—
He was all duty to her in a minute:
He had to run right off to look her up,
As if to say, "That's so, how is my wife?
I hope she isn't getting into mischief."
No one was anxious to get rid of Paul.
He'd been the hero of the mountain camps
Ever since, just to show them, he had slipped
The bark of a whole tamarack off whole,
As clean as boys do off a willow twig
To make a willow whistle on a Sunday
In April by subsiding meadow brooks.
They seemed to ask him just to see him go,
"How is the wife, Paul?" and he always went.
He never stopped to murder anyone
Who asked the question. He just disappeared—
Nobody knew in what direction,
Although it wasn't usually long
Before they heard of him in some new camp,
The same Paul at the same old feats of logging.
The question everywhere was why should Paul
Object to being asked a civil question—
A man you could say almost anything to
Short of a fighting word. You have the answers.
And there was one more not so fair to Paul:
That Paul had married a wife not his equal.
Paul was ashamed of her. To match a hero,

She would have had to be a heroine;
Instead of which she was some half-breed squaw.
But if the story Murphy told was true,
She wasn't anything to be ashamed of.

You know Paul could do wonders. Everyone's
Heard how he thrashed the horses on a load
That wouldn't budge until they simply stretched
Their rawhide harness from the load to camp.
Paul told the boss the load would be all right,
"The sun will bring your load in"—and it did—
By shrinking the rawhide to natural length.
That's what is called a stretcher. But I guess
The one about his jumping so's to land
With both his feet at once against the ceiling,
And then land safely right side up again,
Back on the floor, is fact or pretty near fact.
Well, this is such a yarn. Paul sawed his wife
Out of a white-pine log. Murphy was there,
And, as you might say, saw the lady born.
Paul worked at anything in lumbering.
He'd been hard at it taking boards away
For—I forget—the last ambitious sawyer
To want to find out if he couldn't pile
The lumber on Paul till Paul begged for mercy.
They'd sliced the first slab off a big butt log,
And the sawyer had slammed the carriage back
To slam end on again against the saw teeth.
To judge them by the way they caught themselves
When they saw what had happened to the log,
They must have had a guilty expectation
Something was going to go with their slambanging.
Something had left a broad black streak of grease
On the new wood the whole length of the log
Except, perhaps, a foot at either end.
But when Paul put his finger in the grease,
It wasn't grease at all, but a long slot.
The log was hollow. They were sawing pine.
"First time I ever saw a hollow pine.

That comes of having Paul around the place.
Take it to hell for me," the sawyer said.
Everyone had to have a look at it,
And tell Paul what he ought to do about it.
(They treated it as his.) "You take a jack-knife,
And spread the opening, and you've got a dug-out
All dug to go a-fishing in." To Paul
The hollow looked too sound and clean and empty
Ever to have housed birds or beasts or bees.
There was no entrance for them to get in by.
It looked to him like some new kind of hollow
He thought he'd *better* take his jack-knife to.
So after work that evening he came back
And let enough light into it by cutting
To see if it was empty. He made out in there
A slender length of pith, or was it pith?
It might have been the skin a snake had cast
And left stood up on end inside the tree
The hundred years the tree must have been growing.
More cutting and he had this in both hands,
And, looking from it to the pond nearby,
Paul wondered how it would respond to water.
Not a breeze stirred, but just the breath of air
He made in walking slowly to the beach
Blew it once off his hands and almost broke it.
He laid it at the edge where it could drink.
At the first drink it rustled and grew limp.
At the next drink it grew invisible.
Paul dragged the shallows for it with his fingers,
And thought it must have melted. It was gone.
And then beyond the open water, dim with midges,
Where the log drive lay pressed against the boom,
It slowly rose a person, rose a girl,
Her wet hair heavy on her like a helmet,
Who, leaning on a log looked back at Paul.
And that made Paul in turn look back
To see if it was anyone behind him
That she was looking at instead of him.
Murphy had been there watching all the time,

But from a shed where neither of them could see him.
There was a moment of suspense in birth
When the girl seemed too water-logged to live,
Before she caught her first breath with a gasp
And laughed. Then she climbed slowly to her feet,
And walked off talking to herself or Paul
Across the logs like backs of alligators,
Paul taking after her around the pond.

Next evening Murphy and some other fellows
Got drunk, and tracked the pair up Catamount,
From the bare top of which there is a view
To other hills across a kettle valley.
And there, well after dark, let Murphy tell it,
They saw Paul and his creature keeping house.
It was the only glimpse that anyone
Has had of Paul and her since Murphy saw them
Falling in love across the twilight mill-pond.
More than a mile across the wilderness
They sat together halfway up a cliff
In a small niche let into it, the girl
Brightly, as if a star played on the place,
Paul darkly, like her shadow. All the light
Was from the girl herself, though, not from a star,
As was apparent from what happened next.
All those great ruffians put their throats together,
And let out a loud yell, and threw a bottle,
As a brute tribute of respect to beauty.
Of course the bottle fell short by a mile,
But the shout reached the girl and put her light out.
She went out like a firefly, and that was all.

So there were witnesses that Paul was married,
And not to anyone to be ashamed of.
Everyone had been wrong in judging Paul.
Murphy told me Paul put on all those airs
About his wife to keep her to himself.
Paul was what's called a terrible possessor.
Owning a wife with him meant owning her.

She wasn't anybody else's business,
Either to praise her, or so much as name her,
And he'd thank people not to think of her.
Murphy's idea was that a man like Paul
Wouldn't be spoken to about a wife
In any way the world knew how to speak.

# WILD GRAPES

What tree may not the fig be gathered from?
The grape may not be gathered from the birch?
It's all you know the grape, or know the birch.
As a girl gathered from the birch myself
Equally with my weight in grapes, one autumn,
I ought to know what tree the grape is fruit of.
I was born, I suppose, like anyone,
And grew to be a little boyish girl
My brother could not always leave at home.
But that beginning was wiped out in fear
The day I swung suspended with the grapes,
And was come after like Eurydice
And brought down safely from the upper regions;
And the life I live now's an extra life
I can waste as I please on whom I please.
So if you see me celebrate two birthdays,
And give myself out as two different ages,
One of them five years younger than I look—

One day my brother led me to a glade
Where a white birch he knew of stood alone,
Wearing a thin head-dress of pointed leaves,
And heavy on her heavy hair behind,
Against her neck, an ornament of grapes.
Grapes, I knew grapes from having seen them last year.
One bunch of them, and there began to be
Bunches all round me growing in white birches,
The way they grew round Leif the Lucky's German;
Mostly as much beyond my lifted hands, though,
As the moon used to seem when I was younger,
And only freely to be had for climbing.
My brother did the climbing; and at first
Threw me down grapes to miss and scatter
And have to hunt for in sweet fern and hardhack;
Which gave him some time to himself to eat,
But not so much, perhaps, as a boy needed.
So then, to make me wholly self-supporting,

He climbed still higher and bent the tree to earth
And put it in my hands to pick my own grapes.
"Here, take a tree-top, I'll get down another.
Hold on with all your might when I let go."
I said I had the tree. It wasn't true.
The opposite was true. The tree had me.
The minute it was left with me alone
It caught me up as if I were the fish
And it the fishpole. So I was translated
To loud cries from my brother of "Let go!
Don't you know anything, you girl? Let go!"
But I, with something of the baby grip
Acquired ancestrally in just such trees
When wilder mothers than our wildest now
Hung babies out on branches by the hands
To dry or wash or tan, I don't know which,
(You'll have to ask an evolutionist)—
I held on uncomplainingly for life.
My brother tried to make me laugh to help me.
"What are you doing up there in those grapes?
Don't be afraid. A few of them won't hurt you.
I mean, they won't pick you if you don't them."
Much danger of my picking anything!
By that time I was pretty well reduced
To a philosophy of hang-and-let-hang.
"Now you know how it feels," my brother said,
"To be a bunch of fox-grapes, as they call them,
That when it thinks it has escaped the fox
By growing where it shouldn't—on a birch,
Where a fox wouldn't think to look for it—
And if he looked and found it, couldn't reach it—
Just then come you and I to gather it.
Only you have the advantage of the grapes
In one way: you have one more stem to cling by,
And promise more resistance to the picker."

One by one I lost off my hat and shoes,
And still I clung. I let my head fall back,
And shut my eyes against the sun, my ears

Against my brother's nonsense; "Drop," he said,
"I'll catch you in my arms. It isn't far."
(Stated in lengths of him it might not be.)
"Drop or I'll shake the tree and shake you down."
Grim silence on my part as I sank lower,
My small wrists stretching till they showed the banjo
	strings.
"Why, if she isn't serious about it!
Hold tight awhile till I think what to do.
I'll bend the tree down and let you down by it."
I don't know much about the letting down;
But once I felt ground with my stocking feet
And the world came revolving back to me,
I know I looked long at my curled-up fingers,
Before I straightened them and brushed the bark off.
My brother said: "Don't you weigh anything?
Try to weigh something next time, so you won't
Be run off with by birch trees into space."

It wasn't my not weighing anything
So much as my not knowing anything—
My brother had been nearer right before.
I had not taken the first step in knowledge;
I had not learned to let go with the hands,
As still I have not learned to with the heart,
And have no wish to with the heart—nor need,
That I can see. The mind—is not the heart.
I may yet live, as I know others live,
To wish in vain to let go with the mind—
Of cares, at night, to sleep; but nothing tells me
That I need learn to let go with the heart.

# PLACE FOR A THIRD

Nothing to say to all those marriages!
She had made three herself to three of his.
The score was even for them, three to three.
But come to die she found she cared so much:
She thought of children in a burial row;
Three children in a burial row were sad.
One man's three women in a burial row
Somehow made her impatient with the man.
And so she said to Laban, "You have done
A good deal right; don't do the last thing wrong.
Don't make me lie with those two other women."

Laban said, No, he would not make her lie
With anyone but that she had a mind to,
If that was how she felt, of course, he said.
She went her way. But Laban having caught
This glimpse of lingering person in Eliza,
And anxious to make all he could of it
With something he remembered in himself,
Tried to think how he could exceed his promise,
And give good measure to the dead, though thankless.
If that was how she felt, he kept repeating.
His first thought under pressure was a grave
In a new boughten grave plot by herself,
Under he didn't care how great a stone:
He'd sell a yoke of steers to pay for it.
And weren't there special cemetery flowers,
That, once grief sets to growing, grief may rest;
The flowers will go on with grief awhile,
And no one seem neglecting or neglected?
A prudent grief will not despise such aids.
He thought of evergreen and everlasting.
And then he had a thought worth many of these.
Somewhere must be the grave of the young boy
Who married her for playmate more than helpmate,
And sometimes laughed at what it was between them.
How would she like to sleep her last with him?

Where was his grave? Did Laban know his name?

He found the grave a town or two away,
The headstone cut with *John, Beloved Husband*,
Beside it room reserved, the say a sister's,
A never-married sister's of that husband,
Whether Eliza would be welcome there.
The dead was bound to silence: ask the sister.
So Laban saw the sister, and, saying nothing
Of where Eliza wanted *not* to lie,
And who had thought to lay her with her first love,
Begged simply for the grave. The sister's face
Fell all in wrinkles of responsibility.
She wanted to do right. She'd have to think.
Laban was old and poor, yet seemed to care;
And she was old and poor—but she cared, too.
They sat. She cast one dull, old look at him,
Then turned him out to go on other errands
She said he might attend to in the village,
While she made up her mind how much she cared—
And how much Laban cared—and why he cared,
(She made shrewd eyes to see where he came in.)
She'd looked Eliza up her second time,
A widow at her second husband's grave,
And offered her a home to rest awhile
Before she went the poor man's widow's way,
Housekeeping for the next man out of wedlock.
She and Eliza had been friends through all.
Who was she to judge marriage in a world
Whose Bible's so confused in marriage counsel?
The sister had not come across this Laban;
A decent product of life's ironing-out;
She must not keep him waiting. Time would press
Between the death day and the funeral day.
So when she saw him coming in the street
She hurried her decision to be ready
To meet him with his answer at the door.
Laban had known about what it would be

From the way she had set her poor old mouth,
To do, as she had put it, what was right.

She gave it through the screen door closed between them:
"No, not with John. There wouldn't be no sense.
Eliza's had too many other men."

Laban was forced to fall back on his plan
To buy Eliza a plot to lie alone in:
Which gives him for himself a choice of lots
When his time comes to die and settle down.

# TWO WITCHES

## I.
### The Witch of Coös

I stayed the night for shelter at a farm
Behind the mountain, with a mother and son,
Two old-believers. They did all the talking.

MOTHER. Folks think a witch who has familiar spirits
She could call up to pass a winter evening,
But won't, should be burned at the stake or something.
Summoning spirits isn't "Button, button,
Who's got the button," I would have them know.

SON. Mother can make a common table rear
And kick with two legs like an army mule.

MOTHER. And when I've done it, what good have I done?
Rather than tip a table for you, let me
Tell you what Ralle the Sioux Control once told me.
He said the dead had souls, but when I asked him
How could that be—I thought the dead were souls,
He broke my trance. Don't that make you suspicious
That there's something the dead are keeping back?
Yes, there's something the dead are keeping back.

SON. You wouldn't want to tell him what we have
Up attic, mother?

MOTHER. Bones—a skeleton.

SON. But the headboard of mother's bed is pushed
Against the attic door: the door is nailed.
It's harmless. Mother hears it in the night
Halting perplexed behind the barrier
Of door and headboard. Where it wants to get
Is back into the cellar where it came from.

MOTHER. We'll never let them, will we, son? We'll never!

SON. It left the cellar forty years ago
And carried itself like a pile of dishes
Up one flight from the cellar to the kitchen,
Another from the kitchen to the bedroom,
Another from the bedroom to the attic,
Right past both father and mother, and neither stopped it.
Father had gone upstairs; mother was downstairs.
I was a baby: I don't know where I was.

MOTHER. The only fault my husband found with me—
I went to sleep before I went to bed,
Especially in winter when the bed
Might just as well be ice and the clothes snow.
The night the bones came up the cellar-stairs
Toffile had gone to bed alone and left me,
But left an open door to cool the room off
So as to sort of turn me out of it.
I was just coming to myself enough
To wonder where the cold was coming from,
When I heard Toffile upstairs in the bedroom
And thought I heard him downstairs in the cellar.
The board we had laid down to walk dry-shod on
When there was water in the cellar in spring
Struck the hard cellar bottom. And then someone
Began the stairs, two footsteps for each step,
The way a man with one leg and a crutch,
Or a little child, comes up. It wasn't Toffile:
It wasn't anyone who could be there.
The bulkhead double-doors were double-locked
And swollen tight and buried under snow.
The cellar windows were banked up with sawdust
And swollen tight and buried under snow.
It was the bones. I knew them—and good reason.
My first impulse was to get to the knob
And hold the door. But the bones didn't try
The door; they halted helpless on the landing,
Waiting for things to happen in their favor.

The faintest restless rustling ran all through them.
I never could have done the thing I did
If the wish hadn't been too strong in me
To see how they were mounted for this walk.
I had a vision of them put together
Not like a man, but like a chandelier.
So suddenly I flung the door wide on him.
A moment he stood balancing with emotion,
And all but lost himself. (A tongue of fire
Flashed out and licked along his upper teeth.
Smoke rolled inside the sockets of his eyes.)
Then he came at me with one hand outstretched,
The way he did in life once; but this time
I struck the hand off brittle on the floor,
And fell back from him on the floor myself.
The finger-pieces slid in all directions.
(Where did I see one of those pieces lately?
Hand me my button-box—it must be there.)
I sat up on the floor and shouted, "Toffile,
It's coming up to you." It had its choice
Of the door to the cellar or the hall.
It took the hall door for the novelty,
And set off briskly for so slow a thing,
Still going every which way in the joints, though,
So that it looked like lightning or a scribble,
From the slap I had just now given its hand.
I listened till it almost climbed the stairs
From the hall to the only finished bedroom,
Before I got up to do anything;
Then ran and shouted, "Shut the bedroom door,
Toffile, for my sake!" "Company?" he said,
"Don't make me get up; I'm too warm in bed."
So lying forward weakly on the handrail
I pushed myself upstairs, and in the light
(The kitchen had been dark) I had to own
I could see nothing. "Toffile, I don't see it.
It's with us in the room though. It's the bones."
"What bones?" "The cellar bones—out of the grave."
That made him throw his bare legs out of bed

And sit up by me and take hold of me.
I wanted to put out the light and see
If I could see it, or else mow the room,
With our arms at the level of our knees,
And bring the chalk-pile down. "I'll tell you what—
It's looking for another door to try.
The uncommonly deep snow has made him think
Of his old song, *The Wild Colonial Boy,*
He always used to sing along the tote road.
He's after an open door to get outdoors.
Let's trap him with an open door up attic."
Toffile agreed to that, and sure enough,
Almost the moment he was given an opening,
The steps began to climb the attic stairs.
I heard them. Toffile didn't seem to hear them.
"Quick!" I slammed to the door and held the knob.
"Toffile, get nails." I made him nail the door shut,
And push the headboard of the bed against it.
Then we asked was there anything
Up attic that we'd ever want again.
The attic was less to us than the cellar.
If the bones liked the attic, let them have it.
Let them stay in the attic. When they sometimes
Come down the stairs at night and stand perplexed
Behind the door and headboard of the bed,
Brushing their chalky skull with chalky fingers,
With sounds like the dry rattling of a shutter,
That's what I sit up in the dark to say—
To no one any more since Toffile died.
Let them stay in the attic since they went there.
I promised Toffile to be cruel to them
For helping them be cruel once to him.

SON. We think they had a grave down in the cellar.

MOTHER. We know they had a grave down in the cellar.

SON. We never could find out whose bones they were.

MOTHER. Yes, we could too, son. Tell the truth for once.
They were a man's his father killed for me.
I mean a man he killed instead of me.
The least I could do was to help dig their grave.
We were about it one night in the cellar.
Son knows the story: but 'twas not for him
To tell the truth, suppose the time had come.
Son looks surprised to see me end a lie
We'd kept all these years between ourselves
So as to have it ready for outsiders.
But tonight I don't care enough to lie—
I don't remember why I ever cared.
Toffile, if he were here, I don't believe
Could tell you why he ever cared himself....

She hadn't found the finger-bone she wanted
Among the buttons poured out in her lap.
I verified the name next morning: Toffile.
The rural letter box said Toffile Lajway.

II.

THE PAUPER WITCH OF GRAFTON

Now that they've got it settled whose I be,
I'm going to tell them something they won't like:
They've got it settled wrong, and I can prove it.
Flattered I must be to have two towns fighting
To make a present of me to each other.
They don't dispose me, either one of them,
To spare them any trouble. Double trouble's
Always the witch's motto anyway.
I'll double theirs for both of them—you watch me.
They'll find they've got the whole thing to do over,
That is, if facts is what they want to go by.
They set a lot (now don't they?) by a record
Of Arthur Amy's having once been up
For Hog Reeve in March Meeting here in Warren.
I could have told them any time this twelvemonth
The Arthur Amy I was married to

Couldn't have been the one they say was up
In Warren at March Meeting for the reason
He wa'n't but fifteen at the time they say.
The Arthur Amy I was married to
Voted the only times he ever voted,
Which wasn't many, in the town of Wentworth.
One of the times was when 'twas in the warrant
To see if the town wanted to take over
The tote road to our clearing where we lived.
I'll tell you who'd remember—Heman Lapish.
Their Arthur Amy was the father of mine.
So now they've dragged it through the law courts once
I guess they'd better drag it through again.
Wentworth and Warren's both good towns to live in,
Only I happen to prefer to live
In Wentworth from now on; and when all's said,
Right's right, and the temptation to do right
When I can hurt someone by doing it
Has always been too much for me, it has.
I know of some folks that'd be set up
At having in their town a noted witch:
But most would have to think of the expense
That even I would be. They ought to know
That as a witch I'd often milk a bat
And that'd be enough to last for days.
It'd make my position stronger, think,
If I was to consent to give some sign
To make it surer that I was a witch?
It wa'n't no sign, I s'pose, when Mallice Huse
Said that I took him out in his old age
And rode all over everything on him
Until I'd had him worn to skin and bones,
And if I'd left him hitched unblanketed
In front of one Town Hall, I'd left him hitched
In front of every one in Grafton County.
Some cried shame on me not to blanket him,
The poor old man. It would have been all right
If someone hadn't said to gnaw the posts
He stood beside and leave his trade mark on them,

So they could recognize them. Not a post
That they could hear tell of was scarified.
They made him keep on gnawing till he whined.
Then that same smarty someone said to look—
He'd bet Huse was a cribber and had gnawed
The crib he slept in—and as sure's you're born
They found he'd gnawed the four posts of his bed,
All four of them to splinters. What did that prove?
Not that he hadn't gnawed the hitching posts
He said he had besides. Because a horse
Gnaws in the stable ain't no proof to me
He don't gnaw trees and posts and fences too.
But everybody took it for a proof.
I was a strapping girl of twenty then.
The smarty someone who spoiled everything
Was Arthur Amy. You know who he was.
That was the way he started courting me.
He never said much after we were married,
But I mistrusted he was none too proud
Of having interfered in the Huse business.
I guess he found he got more out of me
By having me a witch. Or something happened
To turn him round. He got to saying things
To undo what he'd done and make it right,
Like, "No, she ain't come back from kiting yet.
Last night was one of her nights out. She's kiting.
She thinks when the wind makes a night of it
She might as well herself." But he liked best
To let on he was plagued to death with me:
If anyone had seen me coming home
Over the ridgepole, 'stride of a broomstick,
As often as he had in the tail of the night,
He guessed they'd know what he had to put up with.
Well, I showed Arthur Amy signs enough
Off from the house as far as we could keep
And from barn smells you can't wash out of plowed ground
With all the rain and snow of seven years;
And I don't mean just skulls of Rogers' Rangers
On Moosilauke, but woman signs to man,

Only bewitched so I would last him longer.
Up where the trees grow short, the mosses tall,
I made him gather me wet snow berries
On slippery rocks beside a waterfall.
I made him do it for me in the dark.
And he liked everything I made him do.
I hope if he is where he sees me now
He's so far off he can't see what I've come to.
You *can* come down from everything to nothing.
All is, if I'd a-known when I was young
And full of it, that this would be the end,
It doesn't seem as if I'd had the courage
To make so free and kick up in folks' faces.
I might have, but it doesn't seem as if.

# AN EMPTY THREAT

I stay;
But it isn't as if
There wasn't always Hudson's Bay
And the fur trade,
A small skiff
And a paddle blade.

I can just see my tent pegged,
And me on the floor,
Crosslegged,
And a trapper looking in at the door
With furs to sell.

His name's Joe,
Alias John,
And between what he doesn't know
And won't tell
About where Henry Hudson's gone,
I can't say he's much help;
But we get on.

The seal yelp
On an ice cake.
It's not men by some mistake?

No,
There's not a soul
For a wind-break
Between me and the North Pole—

Except always John-Joe,
My French Indian Esquimaux,
And he's off setting traps,
In one himself perhaps.

Give a head shake
Over so much bay

Thrown away
In snow and mist
That doesn't exist,
I was going to say,
For God, man or beast's sake,
Yet does perhaps for all three.

Don't ask Joe
What it is to him.
It's sometimes dim
What it is to me,
Unless it be
It's the old captain's dark fate
Who failed to find or force a strait
In its two-thousand-mile coast;
And his crew left him where he failed,
And nothing came of all he sailed.

It's to say, "You and I"
To such a ghost,
"You and I
Off here
With the dead race of the Great Auk!"
And, "Better defeat almost,
If seen clear,
Than life's victories of doubt
That need endless talk talk
To make them out."

# A FOUNTAIN, A BOTTLE, A DONKEY'S EARS, AND SOME BOOKS

Old Davis owned a solid mica mountain
In Dalton that would some day make his fortune.
There'd been some Boston people out to see it:
And experts said that deep down in the mountain
The mica sheets were big as plate glass windows.
He'd like to take me there and show it to me.

"I'll tell you what you show me. You remember
You said you knew the place where once, on Kinsman,
The early Mormons made a settlement
And built a stone baptismal font outdoors—
But Smith, or someone, called them off the mountain
To go West to a worse fight with the desert.
You said you'd seen the stone baptismal font.
Well, take me there."

                        "Some day I will."

                                "Today."

"Huh, that old bathtub, what is that to see?
Let's talk about it."

                        "Let's go see the place."

"To shut you up I'll tell you what I'll do:
I'll find that fountain if it takes all summer,
And both of our united strengths, to do it."

"You've lost it, then?"

                        "Not so but I can find it.
No doubt it's grown up some to woods around it.
The mountain may have shifted since I saw it
In eighty-five."

"As long ago as that?"

"If I remember rightly, it had sprung
A leak and emptied then. And forty years
Can do a good deal to bad masonry.
You won't see any Mormon swimming in it.
But you have said it, and we're off to find it.
Old as I am, I'm going to let myself
Be dragged by you all over everywhere—"

"I thought you were a guide."

                                        "I am a guide,
And that's why I can't decently refuse you."

We made a day of it out of the world,
Ascending to descend to reascend.
The old man seriously took his bearings,
And spoke his doubts in every open place.

We came out on a look-off where we faced
A cliff, and on the cliff a bottle painted,
Or stained by vegetation from above,
A likeness to surprise the thrilly tourist.

"Well, if I haven't brought you to the fountain,
At least I've brought you to the famous Bottle."

"I won't accept the substitute. It's empty."

"So's everything."

                        "I want my fountain."

"I guess you'd find the fountain just as empty.
And anyway this tells me where I am."

"Hadn't you long suspected where you were?"

"You mean miles from that Mormon settlement?
Look here, you treat your guide with due respect
If you don't want to spend the night outdoors.
I vow we must be near the place from where
The two converging slides, the avalanches,
On Marshall, look like donkey's ears.
We may as well see that and save the day."

"Don't donkey's ears suggest we shake our own?"

"For God's sake, aren't you fond of viewing nature?
You don't like nature. All you like is books.
What signify a donkey's ears and bottle,
However natural? Give you your books!
Well then, right here is where I show you books.
Come straight down off this mountain just as fast
As we can fall and keep a-bouncing on our feet.
It's hell for knees unless done hell-for-leather."

"Be ready," I thought, "for almost anything."

We struck a road I didn't recognize,
But welcomed for the chance to lave my shoes
In dust once more. We followed this a mile,
Perhaps, to where it ended at a house
I didn't know was there. It was the kind
To bring me to for broad-board paneling.
I never saw so good a house deserted.

"Excuse me if I ask you in a window
That happens to be broken," Davis said.
"The outside doors as yet have held against us.
I want to introduce you to the people
Who used to live here. They were Robinsons.
You must have heard of Clara Robinson,
The poetess who wrote the book of verses
And had it published. It was all about
The posies on her inner window sill,
And the birds on her outer window sill,

And how she tended both, or had them tended:
She never tended anything herself.
She was 'shut in' for life. She lived her whole
Life long in bed, and wrote her things in bed.
I'll show you how she had her sills extended
To entertain the birds and hold the flowers.
Our business first's up attic with her books."

We trod uncomfortably on crunching glass
Through a house stripped of everything
Except, it seemed, the poetess's poems.
Books, I should say!—if books are what is needed.
A whole edition in a packing-case,
That, overflowing like a horn of plenty,
Or like the poetess's heart of love,
Had spilled them near the window toward the light
Where driven rain had wet and swollen them.
Enough to stock a village library—
Unfortunately all of one kind, though.
They had been brought home from some publisher
And taken thus into the family.
Boys and bad hunters had known what to do
With stone and lead to unprotected glass:
Shatter it inward on the unswept floors.
How had the tender verse escaped their outrage?
By being invisible for what it was,
Or else by some remoteness that defied them
To find out what to do to hurt a poem.
Yet oh! the tempting flatness of a book,
To send it sailing out the attic window
Till it caught wind, and, opening out its covers,
Tried to improve on sailing like a tile
By flying like a bird (silent in flight,
But all the burden of its body song),
Only to tumble like a stricken bird,
And lie in stones and bushes unretrieved.
Books were not thrown irreverently about.
They simply lay where someone now and then,
Having tried one, had dropped it at his feet

And left it lying where it fell rejected.
Here were all those the poetess's life
Had been too short to sell or give away.

"Take one," Old Davis bade me graciously.

"Why not take two or three?"

                              "Take all you want.
Good-looking books like that." He picked one fresh
In virgin wrapper from deep in the box,
And stroked it with a horny-handed kindness.
He read in one and I read in another,
Both either looking for or finding something.

The attic wasps went missing by like bullets.

I was soon satisfied for the time being.

All the way home I kept remembering
The small book in my pocket. It was there.
The poetess had sighed, I knew, in heaven
At having eased her heart of one more copy—
Legitimately. My demand upon her,
Though slight, was a demand. She felt the tug.
In time she would be rid of all her books.

## I WILL SING YOU ONE-O

It was long I lay
Awake that night
Wishing the tower
Would name the hour
And tell me whether
To call it day
(Though not yet light)
And give up sleep.
The snow fell deep
With the hiss of spray;
Two winds would meet,
One down one street,
One down another,
And fight in a smother
Of dust and feather.
I could not say,
But feared the cold
Had checked the pace
Of the tower clock
By tying together
Its hands of gold
Before its face.

Then came one knock!
A note unruffled
Of earthly weather,
Though strange and muffled.
The tower said, "One!"
And then a steeple.
They spoke to themselves
And such few people
As winds might rouse
From sleeping warm
(But not unhouse).
They left the storm
That struck *en masse*
My window glass

Like a beaded fur.
In that grave One
They spoke of the sun
And moon and stars,
Saturn and Mars
And Jupiter.
Still more unfettered,
They left the named
And spoke of the lettered,
The sigmas and taus
Of constellations.
They filled their throats
With the furthest bodies
To which man sends his
Speculation,
Beyond which God is;
The cosmic motes
Of yawning lenses.
Their solemn peals
Were not their own:
They spoke for the clock
With whose vast wheels
Theirs interlock.
In that grave word
Uttered alone
The utmost star
Trembled and stirred,
Though set so far
Its whirling frenzies
Appear like standing
In one self station.
It has not ranged,
And save for the wonder
Of once expanding
To be a nova,
It has not changed
To the eye of man
On planets over
Around and under

It in creation
Since man began
To drag down man
And nation nation.

# FRAGMENTARY BLUE

Why make so much of fragmentary blue
In here and there a bird, or butterfly,
Or flower, or wearing-stone, or open eye,
When heaven presents in sheets the solid hue?

Since earth is earth, perhaps, not heaven (as yet)—
Though some savants make earth include the sky;
And blue so far above us comes so high,
It only gives our wish for blue a whet.

# FIRE AND ICE

Some say the world will end in fire,
Some say in ice.
From what I've tasted of desire
I hold with those who favor fire.
But if it had to perish twice,
I think I know enough of hate
To say that for destruction ice
Is also great
And would suffice.

# IN A DISUSED GRAVEYARD

The living come with grassy tread
To read the gravestones on the hill;
The graveyard draws the living still,
But never any more the dead.

The verses in it say and say:
"The ones who living come today
To read the stones and go away
Tomorrow dead will come to stay."

So sure of death the marbles rhyme,
Yet can't help marking all the time
How no one dead will seem to come.
What is it men are shrinking from?

It would be easy to be clever
And tell the stones: Men hate to die
And have stopped dying now forever.
I think they would believe the lie.

## DUST OF SNOW

The way a crow
Shook down on me
The dust of snow
From a hemlock tree

Has given my heart
A change of mood
And saved some part
Of a day I had rued.

# TO E. T.

I slumbered with your poems on my breast
Spread open as I dropped them half-read through
Like dove wings on a figure on a tomb
To see, if in a dream they brought of you,

I might not have the chance I missed in life
Through some delay, and call you to your face
First soldier, and then poet, and then both,
Who died a soldier-poet of your race.

I meant, you meant, that nothing should remain
Unsaid between us, brother, and this remained—
And one thing more that was not then to say:
The Victory for what it lost and gained.

You went to meet the shell's embrace of fire
On Vimy Ridge; and when you fell that day
The war seemed over more for you than me,
But now for me than you—the other way.

How over, though, for even me who knew
The foe thrust back unsafe beyond the Rhine,
If I was not to speak of it to you
And see you pleased once more with words of mine?

# NOTHING GOLD CAN STAY

Nature's first green is gold,
Her hardest hue to hold.
Her early leaf's a flower;
But only so an hour.
Then leaf subsides to leaf.
So Eden sank to grief,
So dawn goes down to day.
Nothing gold can stay.

# THE RUNAWAY

Once when the snow of the year was beginning to fall,
We stopped by a mountain pasture to say, "Whose colt?"
A little Morgan had one forefoot on the wall,
The other curled at his breast. He dipped his head
And snorted at us. And then he had to bolt.
We heard the miniature thunder where he fled,
And we saw him, or thought we saw him, dim and gray,
Like a shadow against the curtain of falling flakes.
"I think the little fellow's afraid of the snow.
He isn't winter-broken. It isn't play
With the little fellow at all. He's running away.
I doubt if even his mother could tell him, 'Sakes,
It's only weather.' He'd think she didn't know!
Where is his mother? He can't be out alone."
And now he comes again with clatter of stone,
And mounts the wall again with whited eyes
And all his tail that isn't hair up straight.
He shudders his coat as if to throw off flies.
"Whoever it is that leaves him out so late,
When other creatures have gone to stall and bin,
Ought to be told to come and take him in."

# THE AIM WAS SONG

Before man came to blow it right
  The wind once blew itself untaught,
And did its loudest day and night
  In any rough place where it caught.

Man came to tell it what was wrong:
  It hadn't found the place to blow;
It blew too hard—the aim was song.
  And listen—how it ought to go!

He took a little in his mouth,
  And held it long enough for north
To be converted into south,
  And then by measure blew it forth.

By measure. It was word and note,
  The wind the wind had meant to be—
A little through the lips and throat.
  The aim was song—the wind could see.

## STOPPING BY WOODS ON A SNOWY EVENING

Whose woods these are I think I know.
His house is in the village though;
He will not see me stopping here
To watch his woods fill up with snow.

My little horse must think it queer
To stop without a farmhouse near
Between the woods and frozen lake
The darkest evening of the year.

He gives his harness bells a shake
To ask if there is some mistake.
The only other sound's the sweep
Of easy wind and downy flake.

The woods are lovely, dark and deep,
But I have promises to keep,
And miles to go before I sleep,
And miles to go before I sleep.

# FOR ONCE, THEN, SOMETHING

Others taunt me with having knelt at well-curbs
Always wrong to the light, so never seeing
Deeper down in the well than where the water
Gives me back in a shining surface picture
Me myself in the summer heaven godlike
Looking out of a wreath of fern and cloud puffs.
*Once*, when trying with chin against a well-curb,
I discerned, as I thought, beyond the picture,
Through the picture, a something white, uncertain,
Something more of the depths—and then I lost it.
Water came to rebuke the too clear water.
One drop fell from a fern, and lo, a ripple
Shook whatever it was lay there at bottom,
Blurred it, blotted it out. What was that whiteness?
Truth? A pebble of quartz? For once, then, something.

## BLUE-BUTTERFLY DAY

It is blue-butterfly day here in spring,
And with these sky-flakes down in flurry on flurry
There is more unmixed color on the wing
Than flowers will show for days unless they hurry.

But these are flowers that fly and all but sing:
And now from having ridden out desire
They lie closed over in the wind and cling
Where wheels have freshly sliced the April mire.

# THE ONSET

Always the same, when on a fated night
At last the gathered snow lets down as white
As may be in dark woods, and with a song
It shall not make again all winter long
Of hissing on the yet uncovered ground,
I almost stumble looking up and round,
As one who overtaken by the end
Gives up his errand, and lets death descend
Upon him where he is, with nothing done
To evil, no important triumph won,
More than if life had never been begun.

Yet all the precedent is on my side:
I know that winter death has never tried
The earth but it has failed: the snow may heap
In long storms an undrifted four feet deep
As measured against maple, birch, and oak,
It cannot check the peeper's silver croak;
And I shall see the snow all go down hill
In water of a slender April rill
That flashes tail through last year's withered brake
And dead weeds, like a disappearing snake.
Nothing will be left white but here a birch,
And there a clump of houses with a church.

# TO EARTHWARD

Love at the lips was touch
As sweet as I could bear;
And once that seemed too much;
I lived on air

That crossed me from sweet things,
The flow of—was it musk
From hidden grapevine springs
Down hill at dusk?

I had the swirl and ache
From sprays of honeysuckle
That when they're gathered shake
Dew on the knuckle.

I craved strong sweets, but those
Seemed strong when I was young;
The petal of the rose
It was that stung.

Now no joy but lacks salt
That is not dashed with pain
And weariness and fault;
I crave the stain

Of tears, the aftermark
Of almost too much love,
The sweet of bitter bark
And burning clove.

When stiff and sore and scarred
I take away my hand
From leaning on it hard
In grass and sand,

The hurt is not enough:
I long for weight and strength

To feel the earth as rough
To all my length.

# GOOD-BY AND KEEP COLD

This saying good-by on the edge of the dark
And the cold to an orchard so young in the bark
Reminds me of all that can happen to harm
An orchard away at the end of the farm
All winter, cut off by a hill from the house.
I don't want it girdled by rabbit and mouse,
I don't want it dreamily nibbled for browse
By deer, and I don't want it budded by grouse.
(If certain it wouldn't be idle to call
I'd summon grouse, rabbit, and deer to the wall
And warn them away with a stick for a gun.)
I don't want it stirred by the heat of the sun.
(We made it secure against being, I hope,
By setting it out on a northerly slope.)
No orchard's the worse for the wintriest storm;
But one thing about it, it mustn't get warm.
"How often already you've had to be told,
Keep cold, young orchard. Good-by and keep cold.
Dread fifty above more than fifty below."
I have to be gone for a season or so.
My business awhile is with different trees,
Less carefully nurtured, less fruitful than these,
And such as is done to their wood with an ax—
Maples and birches and tamaracks.
I wish I could promise to lie in the night
And think of an orchard's arboreal plight
When slowly (and nobody comes with a light)
Its heart sinks lower under the sod.
But something has to be left to God.

# TWO LOOK AT TWO

Love and forgetting might have carried them
A little further up the mountainside
With night so near, but not much further up.
They must have halted soon in any case
With thoughts of the path back, how rough it was
With rock and washout, and unsafe in darkness;
When they were halted by a tumbled wall
With barbed-wire binding. They stood facing this,
Spending what onward impulse they still had
In one last look the way they must not go,
On up the failing path, where, if a stone
Or earthslide moved at night, it moved itself;
No footstep moved it. "This is all," they sighed,
"Good-night to woods." But not so; there was more.
A doe from round a spruce stood looking at them
Across the wall, as near the wall as they.
She saw them in their field, they her in hers.
The difficulty of seeing what stood still,
Like some up-ended boulder split in two,
Was in her clouded eyes: they saw no fear there.
She seemed to think that two thus they were safe.
Then, as if they were something that, though strange,
She could not trouble her mind with too long,
She sighed and passed unscared along the wall.
"*This*, then, is all. What more is there to ask?"
But no, not yet. A snort to bid them wait.
A buck from round the spruce stood looking at them
Across the wall as near the wall as they.
This was an antlered buck of lusty nostril,
Not the same doe come back into her place.
He viewed them quizzically with jerks of head,
As if to ask, "Why don't you make some motion?
Or give some sign of life? Because you can't.
I doubt if you're as living as you look."
Thus till he had them almost feeling dared
To stretch a proffering hand—and a spell-breaking.
Then he too passed unscared along the wall.

Two had seen two, whichever side you spoke from.
"This *must* be all." It was all. Still they stood,
A great wave from it going over them,
As if the earth in one unlooked-for favor
Had made them certain earth returned their love.

## NOT TO KEEP

They sent him back to her. The letter came
Saying…And she could have him. And before
She could be sure there was no hidden ill
Under the formal writing, he was there,
Living. They gave him back to her alive—
How else? They are not known to send the dead—
And not disfigured visibly. His face?
His hands? She had to look, to look and ask,
"What is it, dear?" And she had given all
And still she had all—*they* had—they the lucky!
Wasn't she glad now? Everything seemed won,
And all the rest for them permissible ease.
She had to ask, "What was it, dear?"

                                "Enough,
Yet not enough. A bullet through and through,
High in the breast. Nothing but what good care
And medicine and rest, and you a week,
Can cure me of to go again." The same
Grim giving to do over for them both.
She dared no more than ask him with her eyes
How was it with him for a second trial.
And with his eyes he asked her not to ask.
They had given him back to her, but not to keep.

# A BROOK IN THE CITY

The farmhouse lingers, though averse to square
With the new city street it has to wear
A number in. But what about the brook
That held the house as in an elbow-crook?
I ask as one who knew the brook, its strength
And impulse, having dipped a finger length
And made it leap my knuckle, having tossed
A flower to try its currents where they crossed.
The meadow grass could be cemented down
From growing under pavements of a town;
The apple trees be sent to hearth-stone flame.
Is water wood to serve a brook the same?
How else dispose of an immortal force
No longer needed? Staunch it at its source
With cinder loads dumped down? The brook was thrown
Deep in a sewer dungeon under stone
In fetid darkness still to live and run—
And all for nothing it had ever done
Except forget to go in fear perhaps.
No one would know except for ancient maps
That such a brook ran water. But I wonder
If from its being kept forever under
The thoughts may not have risen that so keep
This new-built city from both work and sleep.

# THE KITCHEN CHIMNEY

Builder, in building the little house,
In every way you may please yourself;
But please please me in the kitchen chimney:
Don't build me a chimney upon a shelf.

However far you must go for bricks,
Whatever they cost a-piece or a pound,
Buy me enough for a full-length chimney,
And build the chimney clear from the ground.

It's not that I'm greatly afraid of fire,
But I never heard of a house that throve
(And I know of one that didn't thrive)
Where the chimney started above the stove.

And I dread the ominous stain of tar
That there always is on the papered walls,
And the smell of fire drowned in rain
That there always is when the chimney's false.

A shelf's for a clock or vase or picture,
But I don't see why it should have to bear
A chimney that only would serve to remind me
Of castles I used to build in air.

# LOOKING FOR A SUNSET BIRD IN WINTER

The west was getting out of gold,
The breath of air had died of cold,
When shoeing home across the white,
I thought I saw a bird alight.

In summer when I passed the place
I had to stop and lift my face;
A bird with an angelic gift
Was singing in it sweet and swift.

No bird was singing in it now.
A single leaf was on a bough,
And that was all there was to see
In going twice around the tree.

From my advantage on a hill
I judged that such a crystal chill
Was only adding frost to snow
As gilt to gold that wouldn't show.

A brush had left a crooked stroke
Of what was either cloud or smoke
From north to south across the blue;
A piercing little star was through.

# A BOUNDLESS MOMENT

He halted in the wind, and—what was that
Far in the maples, pale, but not a ghost?
He stood there bringing March against his thought,
And yet too ready to believe the most.

"Oh, that's the Paradise-in-bloom," I said;
And truly it was fair enough for flowers
Had we but in us to assume in March
Such white luxuriance of May for ours.

We stood a moment so in a strange world,
Myself as one his own pretense deceives;
And then I said the truth (and we moved on).
A young beech clinging to its last year's leaves.

# EVENING IN A SUGAR ORCHARD

From where I lingered in a lull in March
Outside the sugar-house one night for choice,
I called the fireman with a careful voice
And bade him leave the pan and stoke the arch:
"O fireman, give the fire another stoke,
And send more sparks up chimney with the smoke."
I thought a few might tangle, as they did,
Among bare maple boughs, and in the rare
Hill atmosphere not cease to glow,
And so be added to the moon up there.
The moon, though slight, was moon enough to show
On every tree a bucket with a lid,
And on black ground a bear-skin rug of snow.
The sparks made no attempt to be the moon.
They were content to figure in the trees
As Leo, Orion, and the Pleiades.
And that was what the boughs were full of soon.

# GATHERING LEAVES

Spades take up leaves
No better than spoons,
And bags full of leaves
Are light as balloons.

I make a great noise
Of rustling all day
Like rabbit and deer
Running away.

But the mountains I raise
Elude my embrace,
Flowing over my arms
And into my face.

I may load and unload
Again and again
Till I fill the whole shed,
And what have I then?

Next to nothing for weight,
And since they grew duller
From contact with earth,
Next to nothing for color.

Next to nothing for use.
But a crop is a crop,
And who's to say where
The harvest shall stop?

# THE VALLEY'S SINGING DAY

The sound of the closing outside door was all.
You made no sound in the grass with your footfall,
As far as you went from the door, which was not far;
But you had awakened under the morning star
The first song-bird that awakened all the rest.
He could have slept but a moment more at best.
Already determined dawn began to lay
In place across a cloud the slender ray
For prying beneath and forcing the lids of sight,
And loosing the pent-up music of over-night.
But dawn was not to begin their "pearly-pearly"
(By which they mean the rain is pearls so early,
Before it changes to diamonds in the sun),
Neither was song that day to be self-begun.
You had begun it, and if there needed proof—
I was asleep still under the dripping roof,
My window curtain hung over the sill to wet;
But I should awake to confirm your story yet;
I should be willing to say and help you say
That once you had opened the valley's singing day.

# MISGIVING

All crying, "We will go with you, O Wind!"
The foliage follow him, leaf and stem;
But a sleep oppresses them as they go,
And they end by bidding him stay with them.

Since ever they flung abroad in spring
The leaves had promised themselves this flight,
Who now would fain seek sheltering wall,
Or thicket, or hollow place for the night.

And now they answer his summoning blast
With an ever vaguer and vaguer stir,
Or at utmost a little reluctant whirl
That drops them no further than where they were.

I only hope that when I am free
As they are free to go in quest
Of the knowledge beyond the bounds of life
It may not seem better to me to rest.

# A HILLSIDE THAW

To think to know the country and not know
The hillside on the day the sun lets go
Ten million silver lizards out of snow!
As often as I've seen it done before
I can't pretend to tell the way it's done.
It looks as if some magic of the sun
Lifted the rug that bred them on the floor
And the light breaking on them made them run.
But if I thought to stop the wet stampede,
And caught one silver lizard by the tail,
And put my foot on one without avail,
And threw myself wet-elbowed and wet-kneed
In front of twenty others' wriggling speed,—
In the confusion of them all aglitter,
And birds that joined in the excited fun
By doubling and redoubling song and twitter,
I have no doubt I'd end by holding none.

It takes the moon for this. The sun's a wizard
By all I tell, but so's the moon a witch.
From the high west she makes a gentle cast
And suddenly, without a jerk or twitch,
She has her spell on every single lizard.
I fancied when I looked at six o'clock
The swarm still ran and scuttled just as fast.
The moon was waiting for her chill effect.
I looked at nine: the swarm was turned to rock
In every lifelike posture of the swarm,
Transfixed on mountain slopes almost erect.
Across each other and side by side they lay.
The spell that so could hold them as they were
Was wrought through trees without a breath of storm
To make a leaf, if there had been one, stir.
It was the moon's: she held them until day,
One lizard at the end of every ray.
The thought of my attempting such a stay!

## PLOWMEN

A plow, they say, to plow the snow.
They cannot mean to plant it, no—
Unless in bitterness to mock
At having cultivated rock.

## ON A TREE FALLEN ACROSS THE ROAD
(to hear us talk)

The tree the tempest with a crash of wood
Throws down in front of us is not to bar
Our passage to our journey's end for good,
But just to ask us who we think we are

Insisting always on our own way so.
She likes to halt us in our runner tracks,
And make us get down in a foot of snow
Debating what to do without an ax.

And yet she knows obstruction is in vain:
We will not be put off the final goal
We have it hidden in us to attain,
Not though we have to seize earth by the pole

And, tired of aimless circling in one place,
Steer straight off after something into space.

# OUR SINGING STRENGTH

It snowed in spring on earth so dry and warm
The flakes could find no landing place to form.
Hordes spent themselves to make it wet and cold,
And still they failed of any lasting hold.
They made no white impression on the black.
They disappeared as if earth sent them back.
Not till from separate flakes they changed at night
To almost strips and tapes of ragged white
Did grass and garden ground confess it snowed,
And all go back to winter but the road.
Next day the scene was piled and puffed and dead.
The grass lay flattened under one great tread.
Borne down until the end almost took root,
The rangey bough anticipated fruit
With snowballs cupped in every opening bud.
The road alone maintained itself in mud,
Whatever its secret was of greater heat
From inward fires or brush of passing feet.

In spring more mortal singers than belong
To any one place cover us with song.
Thrush, bluebird, blackbird, sparrow, and robin throng;
Some to go further north to Hudson's Bay,
Some that have come too far north back away,
Really a very few to build and stay.
Now was seen how these liked belated snow.
The fields had nowhere left for them to go;
They'd soon exhausted all there was in flying;
The trees they'd had enough of with once trying
And setting off their heavy powder load.
They could find nothing open but the road.
So there they let their lives be narrowed in
By thousands the bad weather made akin.
The road became a channel running flocks
Of glossy birds like ripples over rocks.
I drove them under foot in bits of flight
That kept the ground, almost disputing right

Of way with me from apathy of wing,
A talking twitter all they had to sing.
A few I must have driven to despair
Made quick asides, but having done in air
A whir among white branches great and small
As in some too much carven marble hall
Where one false wing beat would have brought down all,
Came tamely back in front of me, the Drover,
To suffer the same driven nightmare over.
One such storm in a lifetime couldn't teach them
That back behind pursuit it couldn't reach them;
None flew behind me to be left alone.

Well, something for a snowstorm to have shown
The country's singing strength thus brought together,
That though repressed and moody with the weather
Was none the less there ready to be freed
And sing the wildflowers up from root and seed.

# THE LOCKLESS DOOR

It went many years,
But at last came a knock,
And I thought of the door
With no lock to lock.

I blew out the light,
I tip-toed the floor,
And raised both hands
In prayer to the door.

But the knock came again.
My window was wide;
I climbed on the sill
And descended outside.

Back over the sill
I bade a "Come in"
To whatever the knock
At the door may have been.

So at a knock
I emptied my cage
To hide in the world
And alter with age.

# THE NEED OF BEING VERSED IN
## COUNTRY THINGS

The house had gone to bring again
To the midnight sky a sunset glow.
Now the chimney was all of the house that stood,
Like a pistil after the petals go.

The barn opposed across the way,
That would have joined the house in flame
Had it been the will of the wind, was left
To bear forsaken the place's name.

No more it opened with all one end
For teams that came by the stony road
To drum on the floor with scurrying hoofs
And brush the mow with the summer load.

The birds that came to it through the air
At broken windows flew out and in,
Their murmur more like the sigh we sigh
From too much dwelling on what has been.

Yet for them the lilac renewed its leaf,
And the aged elm, though touched with fire;
And the dry pump flung up an awkward arm;
And the fence post carried a strand of wire.

For them there was really nothing sad.
But though they rejoiced in the nest they kept,
One had to be versed in country things
Not to believe the phoebes wept.

# ANNOTATIONS

## A BOY'S WILL

Frost said about this book: "These were poems of youth, written separately, between 1892–1912, not in a design to be together.... The poetry itself represented evasiveness, furtiveness."

When *A Boy's Will* was published in 1913, it contained three poems that he excluded from the reprint of this book in his *Collected Poems* in 1930: "Asking for Roses," "In Equal Sacrifice," and "Spoils of the Dead."

The 1949 edition of the *Complete Poems* and subsequent reprintings also omitted these poems.

From 1930 forward, Frost included "In Hardwood Groves" in the *A Boy's Will* section of *Collected Poems*. It's not in the first edition.

The Table of Contents of the first English and American editions of *A Boy's Will* includes brief prose glosses for thirty of the thirty-two poems, e.g., see below, "Into My Own." Frost did not use them in the *Collected Poems* or in the *Complete Poems*.

Into My Own

    The prose gloss for this poem in the first edition is: "The youth is persuaded that he will be rather more than less himself for having forsworn the world." Frost told a biographer that this poem represented "his first desire to escape from something, his fear of something."

Ghost House

    Copse: a small group of trees.

My November Guest

    Sodden: saturated with water, soaked through.

    Worsted: a fine smooth yarn spun from combed long-staple wool.

Love and a Question

    Woodbine: a climbing plant.

Stars

    Minerva: goddess of poetry, medicine, commerce, weaving, the crafts, and wisdom.

To the Thawing Wind

    Southwester: the southwest wind. The speaker calls upon this wind to bring rain, awaken nature, and inspire creativity.

Hermit's crucifix: a hermit lives in seclusion, often for religious reasons, away from society; a crucifix is a type of cross that features a representation of Jesus Christ crucified upon it. The term comes from the Latin *crucifixus*, "fixed to a cross."

A Prayer in Spring

Bill: the beak of a bird, a point. Frost said about this line that it was an example of his effort to "notice little fresh things."

Flower-Gathering

In the gloaming: the time of twilight or dusk. "Gloaming" is derived from Scots dialect, originally meaning "twilight," and traces back to Old English, where it is related to words meaning "to glow" or "to become dark" as evening approaches. A moment of transition, the fleeting beauty of the day giving way to night.

Waiting

Haycock: a conical heap of hay in a field.

Antiphony: sung, recited, or played alternately by two groups.

Purblind: having impaired or defective vision; slow or unable to understand.

In a Vale

Vale: a valley, used in place names or as a poetic term.

Fen: a low and marshy or frequently flooded area of land.

In Neglect

Seraphic: seraph, seraphim, an angelic being belonging to the highest order of the ninefold celestial hierarchy, associated with light and purity.

The Vantage Point

Hie: go quickly.

Bluet: a low-growing plant, with small four-petaled flowers.

Mowing

In a July 1913 letter, Frost said about this poem: "I come so near what I long to get that I almost despair of coming nearer." He added, about *A Boy's Will*: "I think I have made poetry. The language is appropriate to the virtues I celebrate."

Fay: a fairy.

Swale: a low or hollow place, especially a marshy depression between ridges.

The fact is…: Frost remarked about this line: "Doting on things, gloating on things, just dwelling on things. Not getting up things, not exaggerating things, not whooping things up, but just gloating."

Going for Water

Gnomes: a legendary dwarfish creature that guards the earth's underground treasures.

The Trial by Existence

This poem was first published in *The Independent* in 1906, under the name "Robert Frost." Prior to this, his name had included his middle initial "L."

Concourse: a large open area inside or in front of a public building.

Limns: depict or describe in painting or words; suffuse or highlight with a bright color or light.

On the rack: on an instrument of torture; suffering intense pain, distress, or strain.

The Tuft of Flowers

Frost made this comment: "*A Boy's Will* told how I was scared away from life and crept back to it through this poem. I was speaking literally."

Tuft: small bunch or cluster.

Whetstone: a fine-grained stone used for sharpening cutting tools.

Tremulous: shaking, quivering.

But from sheer morning…: Frost took pleasure in this line. He commented, "I don't get enough credit for these things."

Pan with Us

Pan: a god of flocks and herds, typically represented with the horns, ears, and legs of a goat on a man's body.

Zephyr: soft, gentle breeze; from late Old English *zefferus*, denoting a personification of the west wind, via Latin from Greek *zephuros*, "god of the west wind."

Homespun: cloth or yarn made or spun at home; simple and unsophisticated.

Pipes: a wind instrument consisting of a single tube with holes along its length that are covered by the fingers to produce different notes.

Sylvan: consisting of or associated with woods; pleasantly rural or pastoral.

Raveled: untangle; the noun "ravel" means a tangle, cluster, or knot.

The Demiurge's Laugh

Demiurge: a being responsible for the creation of the universe; in Platonic philosophy, the maker or creator of the world; in Gnosticism and other theological systems, a heavenly being, subordinate to the Supreme Being, the controller of the material world and antagonistic to all that is purely spiritual.

Demon: evil spirit or devil.

A Line-Storm Song

Line-Storm: a type of storm that occurs around the time of the equinoxes, characterized by violent weather conditions, including rain and wind.

Bruit: to make a loud noise or to spread by rumor or report; from Old French *bruit*, "noise," from *bruire*, "to roar."

Wilding brooch: refers to a wildflower, specifically goldenrod. Wilding implies something untamed or natural; a brooch is an ornament fastened to clothing with a hinged pin and catch.

Dry-shod: having dry feet or shoes.

Amain: with full force or speed, renewed intensity.

October

Frost said about the first line: "I was very much aware that I was giving it a prayer sound…. I wouldn't have put that 'mild' to that if I hadn't been prayerful."

Amethyst: a precious stone consisting of a violet or purple variety of quartz.

My Butterfly

Emulous: seeking to emulate or imitate someone or something; motivated by a spirit of rivalry.

Daft: silly, foolish, eccentric.

Like a limp rose-wreath in a fairy dance: Frost said about this line: "That's like a blush. Never thought of that before. Poetry is like a cry, I've said. But it's like a blush—you can get something you didn't know you had."

Dreaming fond: nostalgia for a more innocent, untroubled time.

Reckless zephyr: reckless means a lack of caution or care, a sense of impulsiveness and disregard for the potential consequences of one's actions; zephyr is a gentle breeze, particularly one that comes from the west, from Zephyrus, the Greek god of the west wind, often associated with mild and pleasant weather.

Eaves: the part of a roof that meets or overhangs the walls of a building.

Reluctance

On this poem and *A Boy's Will*, Frost said: "It's only seven or eight lines long but it so unmistakably sounds with the sound of that book, you know. You can tell if you've got an ear, you know. And the attitude toward life so concentrated in that little thing."

## NORTH OF BOSTON

In a talk on poetry, 1955, Frost spoke about "the luck of the name" (the title) and the form of the book: "I got it out of the advertisements in the *Boston Globe* years and years ago. It came back to me far from the *Boston Globe*. I was away off in England, and all of a sudden I just remembered that constantly in the advertisements that I used to read with interest—and still do—this phrase 'north of Boston' popped into my head—just the name. And I got a dozen poems together—a dozen or fifteen, I think it was—that hadn't been written toward that name and hadn't been written toward any particular ideas. They had been scattered among lyrics. They were blank-verse things scattered through twenty years. Then, all of a sudden, I put them together with some little dim notion of their belonging together—swept them together. They're not organic. Then I got that name on them."

"Literature," Frost said, "begins with geography."

Mending Wall

In a letter, Frost wrote: "In My 'Mending Wall' was my intention fulfilled with the characters portrayed and the atmosphere of the place? You might be amused by my answer."

Good fences make good neighbors: in 1962 Frost said about this line: "People are frequently misunderstanding it or misinterpreting it. The secret of what it means I keep."

The Death of the Hired Man

Frost told an interviewer in February 1918 that he wrote this poem "ten years ago in two hours, without changing a word, at a time when his nature was in equipoise." It was first published in *The New Republic*, February 6, 1915. The title of the poem was listed on the cover, but not Frost's name.

To a friend, Frost remarked it's "a little drama in which the gradual change in Warren is shown. It has four distinctly drawn characters; and it perfectly observes all the old unities."

Beholden: owing thanks or having a duty to someone in return for help or a service.

Piqued: stimulated from interest or curiosity; irritated or resentful.

Find water with a hazel prong: the practice of water dowsing or water witching; a traditional method of searching for underground water sources using a forked stick, often made from hazel wood.

The Mountain

Frost said this poem "was all done in one sitting and stands today pretty exactly as I wrote it."

Lunenburg: small town in Essex County, Vermont. Population in 1910: 880.

Sojourn: a temporary stay or visit.

Logged: part of the mountain was harvested for timber the previous winter, potentially creating an access route partway up the slope.

Hor: Mt. Hor, in southeastern Vermont, elevation 2650 feet.

A Hundred Collars

Lancaster: small town in New Hampshire, located along the Connecticut River.

Bow: small town in New Hampshire, ten miles south of Concord, the state capital.

Bill Taft: William Howard Taft (1857–1930), Republican nominee, elected president in 1908, defeated in 1912 for a second term.

Home Burial

"If—you—do!": In a letter, July 1914, Frost said he was proud of the sound of these words: "It is that particular kind of imagination that I cultivate rather than the kind that merely sees things, the hearing imagination rather than the seeing imagination though I should not want to be without the latter."

The Black Cottage

Daguerreotype: a photograph taken by an early photographic process employing an iodine-sensitized silvered plate and mercury vapor.

Gettysburg: a decisive battle of the Civil War, fought near the town of Gettysburg, Pennsylvania, in July 1863. A Union army under General George Meade repulsed the Confederate army of General Robert E. Lee and forced him to abandon his invasion of the north.

Fredericksburg: in northeastern Virginia, where in December 1862, Confederate forces won a major victory over the Union army.

Garrison: William Lloyd Garrison (1805–1879), social reformer and leader of New England abolitionism, editor and publisher of The Liberator, 1831–65, and a founder of the American Anti-Slavery Society in 1833.

Whittier: John Greenleaf Whittier (1807–1892), poet and abolitionist, best known for his poems on rural themes, especially "Snow-Bound" (1866).

Jefferson: Thomas Jefferson (1743–1826), author of the Declaration of Independence, July 4, 1776, "all men are created equal"; third president of the U.S., 1801–09.

Hades: the underworld; the abode of the spirits of the dead.

Creed: a formal statement of Christian beliefs; a set of beliefs or aims that guide someone's actions:

Tamarisk: shrub or small tree with tiny scale-like leaves borne on slender branches, giving it a feathery appearance.

A Servant to Servants

Wrapper: a loose-fitting garment or robe worn by women, typically as a house dress or informal covering over other clothes.

Willoughby: a lake in Vermont.

Stanchions: upright posts or bars used as supports in a barn or stable.

Oxbow: U-shaped frame that fits around an ox's neck and is used to attach the ox to a yoke or plow.

After Apple-Picking

Hoary: greyish-white.

The Code

Cock the hay: the process of gathering cut hay into small mounds or piles in the field.

Salem: town in New Hampshire; population in 1910: 2117.

Big jag: a large load of hay that needs to be unloaded.

The Generations of Men

Reconnoiter: to make an observation (usually a military one) of a region.

Like a Viola: that is, the genealogical discussion is intricate, perhaps difficult to follow, much like the complex harmonies of a viola in an orchestral piece.

We Yankees: a term of Dutch origin, refers to New Englanders, particularly those with long-established family roots in the region.

Myth of Chicamoztoc: the Stark family's ancestral home, represented by the cellar hole, is a place of origin and identity, as significant to them as Chicamoztoc was to the Mesoamerican peoples. Often referred to as the "Place of the Seven Caves," Chicomoztoc is a legendary site in Mesoamerican mythology, associated with the beginnings of the Mexica (Aztec) people.

Nausicaä: a character in Homer's *Odyssey*, a Phaeacian princess who encountered Odysseus when he washed ashore on her island.

The Housekeeper

Pumps: a woman's plain, lightweight shoe.

Lank: long, limp, straight.

Cock: male bird, a rooster.

Crystal Palace, London: a large building of prefabricated iron and glass resembling a giant greenhouse, designed by Joseph Paxton (1803–1865) for the Great Exhibition of 1851 in Hyde Park, London. This international exhibition showcased industrial and cultural achievements from around the world.

Wampum: small cylindrical beads traditionally made by some Indigenous peoples in North America from shells, strung together and worn as decoration or used ceremonially or in trading.

Rig: a horse-drawn carriage or wagon.

The Fear

Gig: a light, two-wheeled horse-drawn carriage designed for one or two passengers.

The Self-Seeker

Wheel-pit: the area in a mill or factory where a water wheel or turbine is located, a crucial part of the machinery that powers the mill.

Flora: the plants of a particular region, habitat, or geological period.

*Cyprepedium reginae*: the Showy Lady's Slipper orchid, a rare and beautiful wildflower native to North America.

*Sinus*: a small cavity or hollow space; in this context, a small pocket or depression in the plant structure.

The Wood-Pile

Clematis: a climbing plant of the buttercup family with white, pink, or purple flowers and feathery seeds.

I thought that only / Someone who lived in turning to fresh tasks: About these lines, Frost told a friend: "What I have most aspired to be."


Mountain Interval

Frost said about this book, "I talk about the whole world in terms of New England."

The Road Not Taken

The original title was "Two Roads."

In a letter, Frost wrote—he was in England at the time: "Two lonely cross-roads that themselves cross each I have walked several times this winter without meeting or overtaking so much as a single person on foot or on runners [long, narrow blades on sleds designed to slide over snow]. The practically unbroken condition of both for several days after a snow or a blow proves that neither is much traveled. Judge then how surprised I was the other evening as I came down one to see a man, who to my own unfamiliar eyes and in the dusk looked for all the world like myself, coming down the other, his approach to the point where our paths must intersect being so timed that unless one of us pulled up we must inevitably collide. I felt as if I was going to meet my own image in a slanting mirror. Or say I felt as we slowly converged on the same point with the same noiseless yet laborious stride as if we were two images about to float together with the uncrossing of someone's eyes. I verily expected to take up or absorb this other self and feel the stronger by the addition for the three-mile journey home. But I didn't go forward to the touch. I stood still in wonderment and let him pass by; and that too, with the fatal omission of not trying to find out by a comparison of lives and immediate and remote interests what could have brought us by crossing paths to the same point in a wilderness at the same moment of nightfall. Some purpose I doubt not, if we could but have made it out."

Frost said to his friend Edward Thomas: "No matter which road you take, you'll always sigh, and wish you'd taken another."

An Old Man's Winter Night

Clomping: walk heavily or noisily.

The Exposed Nest

Cutter bar: also known as a sickle bar, a component in agricultural machinery, such as mowers, binders, or combines. It consists of a bar with triangular guards along which a knife or blade operates to cut grass or crops.

Champing: the action of biting and chewing something in a loud or vigorous manner.

In the Home Stretch

Common law: a body of law that is developed through judicial decisions and precedents rather than through statutes or written legislation; a legal marriage without compliance with statutory requirements.

Stovepipe: a metal pipe, made of sheet steel, that is used to carry smoke away from a stove or to connect a stove to a chimney flue.

"Ten-step": a traditional outdoor children's game. The leader counts to ten, taking steps towards the other players. The players remain still during this counting. Upon reaching ten, the leader may call out a command or challenge that the other players must respond to.

Alder: birch tree with toothed leaves.

Hyla Brook

Hyla: a tree frog.

Bond and Free

Sirius: the brightest star in the sky.

Birches

Originally titled "Swinging Birches." Frost said: "I never go down the shoreline from Boston to New York without watching the birches to see if they live up to what I say about them in the poem."

Bracken: a tall fern.

Pea Brush

Pea brush: long, forked branches that are inserted into the soil near the base of pea plants. As the plants grow, they wind around these branches.

Cat's cradle: a children's game in which a loop of string is put around and between the fingers and complex patterns are formed; here, the way that pea plants curl their tendrils around supports.

Trillium: plant with a single-petalled flower and three leaves.

The Cow in Apple Time

Pomace: pulpy residue remaining after fruit has been crushed to extract its juice.

Udder: the mammary gland of female cattle, sheep, goats, horses.

An Encounter

"Weather breeder": a fine, serene day that is believed to precede and prepare for bad weather, particularly a storm.

Scurf: flaky deposit on a surface, e.g., of skin.

Montreal: a port city on the St. Lawrence River in Quebec, southeastern Canada.

Calypso: a nymph who kept Odysseus on her island for seven years; from Greek, literally "she who conceals."

Range-Finding

Frost told a biographer that he sent this poem to Edward Thomas, who was on the front lines of battle. Thomas wrote back "it was a surprisingly exact description of no man's land," the unoccupied area between opposing armies, often heavily contested and dangerous. This usage became prominent during World War I, where it described the territory between trench lines that was not controlled by either side. Thomas's widow said that when her husband left England to return to the war, he carried with him a copy of Shakespeare's sonnets and a copy of *Mountain Interval*. He was killed in action in northern France, April 9, 1917.

Mullein: plant with woolly leaves and tall spikes of yellow flowers.

The Hill Wife

Furrowed: make a rut, groove, or trail in the ground or on a surface.

Smudge: a smoky outdoor fire that is lit to keep off insects or protect plants against frost.

Brake: a thicket or an area of dense undergrowth, typically consisting of ferns or brushwood.

A Girl's Garden

Slim-jim: a long, thin, tool, a thin strip of metal.

Dung: the excrement of animals; manure.

Miscellany: a group or collection of different items; a mixture.

Locked Out

Bitten: broken, damaged, or partially severed.

"Out, Out—"

Frost based this poem on a tragic accident that took the life of a child. He and his family were living in Franconia, New Hampshire; the child was in Bethlehem, six miles away. The incident was reported in the March 31, 1910, edition of *The Courier* of Littleton, New Hampshire:

Raymond Tracy Fitzgerald, one of the twin sons of Michael G. and Margaret Fitzgerald of Bethlehem, died at his home Thursday afternoon, March 24, as a result of an accident by which one of his hands was badly hurt in a sawing machine. The young man was assisting in sawing up some wood in his own dooryard with a sawing machine and accidentally hit the loose pulley, causing the saw to descend upon his hand, cutting and lacerating it badly. Raymond was taken into the house and a physician was immediately summoned, but he died very suddenly from the effects of the shock, which produced heart failure.

Brown's Descent

Willy-Nilly Slide: refers to Brown's uncontrolled and involuntary descent down an icy slope. Willy-nilly originates from the archaic expression "will I, nill I," which means "whether I will or not."

Mien: a person's look or manner, indicating their character or mood.

Grange: a country house with attached farm buildings; an outlying farm; a barn.

Coasting child: a child coasting down a hill on a sled.

Petered out: gradually diminish or fade away; become exhausted or depleted; lose momentum or energy.

The Gum-Gatherer

About this poem, Frost said: "It is a favorite of mine if for no other reason than because it is the only poem I know of that has found a way to speak poetically of chewing gum."

Gum-Gatherer: someone who collects resin or sap from trees, likely spruce trees, to be used in making various products.

Grist: grain that is used to make flour; here, the rocky debris from the mountains that is slowly broken down by the water over time.

Resin: a sticky organic substance, exuded by some trees and other plants.

The Line-Gang

Line-Gang: a group of workers responsible for installing telephone and telegraph lines in rural areas.

The Vanishing Red

Red: an offensive term used about Native Americans and Indigenous People. The poem's title refers to their gradual disappearance, their extinction. Frost's poem reflects the early twentieth century belief in the "Vanishing Indian" myth—the idea that Native Americans were disappearing as a race as white civilization advanced. This concept was invoked to justify policies of forced assimilation and land seizure.

Frost said: "The place was Acton, Mass., a hundred or more years ago."

Acton: a town located in Middlesex County, Massachusetts, approximately 21 miles west-northwest of Boston.

Mill: a building equipped with machinery for grinding grain into flour.

Millstone: each of two circular stones used for grinding grain.

Wheel-pit: the area in a mill or factory where a water wheel or turbine is located.

Cramping rafter: the rafter is tight, confining; a space that is narrow or uncomfortable to move in.

Meal-sack: a large bag made of strong material, such as cloth or paper, used to store and transport bulk food items such as flour, sugar, or animal feed; here, "meal" refers to the edible part of grain ground to powder.

Snow

This poem was first published in *Poetry*, in November 1916. It was awarded the magazine's first prize of $100, which Frost said was his "first real prize in a long life."

Skin-coat: large fur coat, made from animal skins or pelts.

Racker Sect: name of the small religious group or denomination that Meserve belongs to.

Collie's coat: a sheepdog of a breed originating in Scotland, having a long, pointed nose and thick, long hair.

Downy storm: the soft, light quality of the falling snow.

Balanced rations: a well-proportioned diet, especially for livestock. In this context, it suggests reading about proper nutrition or dietary guidelines.

The Sound of Trees

Frost said about this poem that it was the "only one I wrote in England that had an English *subject*." It was first published in December 1914 in the journal *Poetry and Drama* with the title "The Sound of Trees." It was also published in August 1915 in *The Atlantic* magazine, with the same title. In 1916, however, in *Mountain Interval*, Frost changed the title to

"The Sound of the Trees." In printings of Frost's *Collected Poems* (1949), sometimes the poem is titled with a second "the," sometimes not.

## NEW HAMPSHIRE

New Hampshire

This very long poem is an unusual one in the Frost canon, self-reflective, humorous, satiric, a commentary on his own work, a rambling tribute to his home state, filled with names and references of a kind he rarely uses elsewhere. The first printing of the poem included many footnotes by Frost referring readers to other of his poems.

Frost said "he sat in the same chair and wrote all night. Had a good time writing scatteringly about New Hampshire—how the state has nothing to sell in commercial quantities."

Pullman: a type of railway passenger car designed for overnight travel, providing accommodations for passengers to sleep comfortably during their journey. The term originates from the Pullman Company, founded by George Pullman (1831–1897) in the late nineteenth century, which revolutionized rail travel by introducing luxurious sleeping cars.

Porter: a person employed to carry luggage and other loads, especially in a railroad station, airport, or hotel.

Vigilance Committees: groups of private citizens performing surveillance and law enforcement.

Stefansson: Vilhjalmur Stefansson (1879–1962), Canadian Arctic explorer and ethnologist.

Zealot: a person who is fanatical and uncompromising in pursuit of their religious, political, or other ideals.

British Arctic: the Arctic regions that were under British control or exploration at the time.

Volstead Act: a law that enforced the prohibition of the sale, transportation, and consumption of alcohol in the U.S. It took effect on January 17, 1920: it was repealed on December 5, 1933, with the ratification of the twenty-first amendment to the U.S. constitution.

Mansard roof: a roof that has four sloping sides, each of which becomes steeper halfway down, from the French architect François Mansart (1598–1666).

Turrets like Constantinople: a small tower on top of a larger tower or at the corner of a building or wall, typically of a castle; Constantinople is the former name of Istanbul, Turkey, from AD 330 (when it was given its name by Constantine the Great) until the early twentieth century.

Shanties: a small, crudely built shack.

Drover: a herder of livestock.

Brighton: Brighton, Massachusetts, a town near Boston known in the early nineteenth century for its cattle market.

"Grounds": the estate or property surrounding a house, particularly a large or impressive one.

Factor's at a trading station: a factor is an agent or representative of a company; trading station, a remote outpost where goods are bought, sold, or traded, often in frontier or colonial settings.

"Old rags": a colloquial term for second-hand clothing or textiles.

Purse: the reference here is to Franklin Pierce (1804–1869), the four-teenth President of the United States, 1853 to 1857, and the only president from New Hampshire. He pronounced his surname "purse."

Daniel Webster: Born in New Hampshire, Daniel Webster (1782–1852) was a prominent American statesman, lawyer, and orator; he served as a member of Congress, senator from Massachusetts, and secretary of state.

Dartmouth: Dartmouth College, established in 1769, located in Hanover, New Hampshire.

John Smith: Smith (1580–1631), born in England, was a leading pro-moter of English colonization, a founder of the colony of Jamestown, Virginia, in 1607. He explored and mapped parts of the east coast of North America in 1614, naming the region "New England." The refer-ence here is to his discovery of white settlers fishing off the coast of New Hampshire before its official founding.

Isles of Shoals: a group of small islands and tidal ledges situated approx-imately six miles from the coast, straddling the border of the states of Maine and New Hampshire.

Adam's sons: an allusion to the biblical story of Adam and Eve's descen-dants. In the Book of Genesis, it's said that Adam and Eve's sons needed wives, but where these wives came from isn't stated.

Nottingham: small town in New Hampshire.

Puritanly: derived from the term "Puritan," which refers to the strict religious sect that emerged in England during the late sixteenth and seventeenth centuries.

Sabbatical: an extended break from work, typically lasting from a few months to a year; the Sabbath is a day of religious observance and absti-nence, kept by Jews from Friday evening to Saturday evening, and by most Christians on Sunday.

Dorkings: an ancient breed of domestic chicken, originating in England.

Chaucer: Geoffrey Chaucer (c. 1342–1400), English poet, author of *The Canterbury Tales* (c. 1387–1400), a cycle of linked tales told by a group of pilgrims.

Sussex: breed of chickens.

Herrick: Robert Herrick (1591–1674), seventeenth century English lyric poet and cleric.

Berlin: city in northern New Hampshire.

Andover: a town located in Merrimack County, New Hampshire.

Canaan: a town in New Hampshire known for its mineral deposits, particularly beryl. Radium is not typically found in beryl, but Frost mentions it to emphasize the rarity and preciousness of the mineral specimen.

Colebrook: a town in northern New Hampshire, near the Canadian border.

Cut-glass dinner: a high-end, sophisticated setting; cut glass was often used for fine tableware.

S'ciety for Psychical Research: the Society for Psychical Research, a non-profit organization in the United Kingdom, formed in 1882, that studies paranormal phenomena.

Cognizant: having knowledge or being aware of.

White Corpuscles: a vigilante group in Salem, New Hampshire; the name is likely a metaphorical reference to white blood cells in the body that attack foreign invaders, suggesting that members of this group saw themselves as protectors of the community.

Sheets and fools' caps: the sheets probably refer to white sheets worn as disguises, like those used by the Ku Klux Klan, a white supremisist hate group; fools' caps were conical hats associated with dunces or fools, also used as disguises.

Skipper Ireson's Ride: refers to Captain Benjamin Ireson of Marblehead, Massachusetts, who was tarred and feathered in 1808 for abandoning a sinking ship and its crew. The poet John Greenleaf Whittier (1807–1892) wrote a popular ballad about this incident titled "Skipper Ireson's Ride" (1857).

Vitriol: cruel and bitter criticism.

Arsenate: lead arsenate, a pesticide that was commonly used on fruit crops, especially apples, in the early twentieth century.

Lariats: a rope used as a lasso or for tethering.

Wares: pottery, manufactured articles, goods or products offered for sale.

Yoke-fellows: refers to two animals, usually oxen, that are yoked together to pull a plow or wagon.

Sap-yoke: a wooden frame or pole used to carry buckets of maple sap from trees to the sugar house during maple syrup production.

Hatchery: a place where the hatching of fish or poultry eggs is artificially controlled for commercial purposes.

Lost Nation…: here and below, Frost refers to small towns and cities in New Hampshire.

Whisky still: alludes to the practice of making moonshine or illegal whisky, common in rural areas during Prohibition.

Wilson; Hughes: Woodrow Wilson (1856–1924), the twenty-eighth President of the United States (1913–1921), a Democrat; Charles Evans Hughes (1862–1948), the Republican nominee who ran against Wilson in the 1916 presidential election.

Emerson: Ralph Waldo Emerson (1803–1882), American writer, philosopher, and poet.

Sensibilitist: a person who is sensitive or attuned to emotional and aesthetic experiences.

Mite: a very small amount.

Kit Marlowe: Christopher Marlowe (1564–1593), playwright and poet. In Elizabethan England, "Kit" was a common nickname for Christopher.

Dostoyevskis: Fyodor Mikhailovich Dostoevsky (1821–1881), Russian novelist, author of *Crime and Punishment* (1866) and *The Brothers Karamazov* (1880).

Pollyanna: *Pollyanna* is a 1913 novel by Eleanor H. Porter (1868–1920) about an excessively optimistic orphan girl.

Warren farmer: Warren is a small town in Grafton County, New Hampshire.

Moosilauke: a mountain located in the White Mountains of New Hampshire, elevation 4,802 feet.

Mid-Victorians: refers to the middle period of Queen Victoria's reign, roughly 1850–1870; somewhat old-fashioned or conservative.

Bryan: William Jennings Bryan (1860–1925), a prominent Democrat and three-time presidential candidate. Silver Dollar refers to Bryan's advocacy for free silver and bimetallism, a major political issue in the 1890s.

John L. Darwin: the name "Darwin" likely alludes to Charles Darwin (1809–1882), the famous naturalist who proposed the theory of evolution. By creating a fictional "John L. Darwin," Frost might be playfully suggesting that this imaginary figure had some impact on Mid-Victorian society or thought.

Morning star: Venus, often visible as a bright object in the morning sky.

Alps: one of the highest and most extensive mountain ranges in Europe, stretching approximately 750 miles across eight countries.

Lincoln, Lafayette, and Liberty: Abraham Lincoln (1809–1865), sixteenth President of the United States, 1861–1865; Marquis de Lafayette (1757–1834), French aristocrat and military officer who fought in the American Revolutionary War; liberty, the concept of freedom, central to American ideals. These mountains are part of the Franconia Ridge in the White Mountains of New Hampshire, one of the most scenic and dramatic hikes in New England.

Gang-boss: a foreman or supervisor of a work crew, often in manual labor.

Log-jam: an accumulation of logs or trees that blocks a river; a situation where progress is blocked or impeded.

Pseudo-phallic: any structure found on an animal that, while superficially appearing to be a penis, is derived from a different developmental path.

Mewling and puking: an allusion to Shakespeare's famous "All the world's a stage" monologue in *As You Like It*, 2.7, which describes the seven ages of man. It begins: "At first, the infant, / Mewling and puking in the nurse's arms."

Matthew Arnold: English poet, essayist, and social critic (1822–1888).

Birnam Wood: in central Scotland, referred to in Shakespeare's tragedy *Macbeth* (c. 1606). The witches prophesy that Macbeth will not be defeated until Birnam Wood comes to Dunsinane (Macbeth's castle). Macduff's army later uses branches from Birnam Wood as camouflage when advancing on Dunsinane, making it appear as if the wood is moving.

Flux: flowing out, continuous change.

Dendrophobia: fear of trees.

"A foiled, circuitous wanderer": someone who has traveled extensively but perhaps unsuccessfully or without achieving their goals; the phrase comes from Matthew Arnold's poem "Sohrab and Rustum" (1853), dealing with an episode in a Persian epic.

Ahaz: King Ahaz of Judah, mentioned in the Bible (2 Kings 20:11 and Isaiah 38:8). The sundial of Ahaz refers to a miraculous event when the shadow on the sundial moved backwards as a sign from God.

A good Greek: alludes to classical Greek culture and philosophy, often associated with reason, balance, and moderation.

A Star in a Stone-Boat

Stone-boat: a simple farm implement used for hauling stones, often consisting of a flat wooden platform with a curved front edge that allows it to be dragged across fields.

Lincoln MacVeagh: an American diplomat, archaeologist, soldier, literary agent, and publisher (1890–1972). He worked for Henry Holt and Company, the publisher of Frost's books of poems.

Bird of Paradise: known for its colorful, elaborate plumage, with long, showy tail feathers.

Pegasus: in Greek mythology a legendary horse, a white stallion with large wings, a symbol of poetic inspiration and creativity.

The Census-Taker

Census-taker: Census takers gather demographic, economic, and housing data from households and businesses for government population censuses.

Waste cut: a vast area of land, where the forest has been cleared or logged; an uninhabited, desolate area.

Sugar of pitch: the sap or resin that oozes out of tree stumps, particularly pine trees, as they decay.

The Star-Splitter

Orion: Greek mythology, a giant and hunter who was changed at his death into a constellation of many bright stars.

Hugger-mugger: a disorderly, haphazard, or confused manner of doing something.

Littleton: a town in the White Mountains region of New Hampshire.

Sentient: able to perceive or feel things.

Concord railroad: Concord, New Hampshire, railway line.

Globule of quicksilver: Quicksilver (mercury) forms perfect spheres when in small amounts, and these can be divided with a finger, much as the telescope seems to divide stars.

Maple

Wave offering: refers to an Old Testament ritual described in the Bible, particularly in Leviticus. In this ritual, priests would lift or wave certain offerings before God as a symbolic gesture of dedication.

Sugar house: a cabin or small building where maple sap is boiled down to make maple syrup.

The Ax-Helve

Frost said about this poem: "This is as near as I like to come to talking about art, in a work of art—such as it is." He also said: "You know, Canadian woodchoppers make their own axe-handles, following the curve of the grain, and they're strong and beautiful. Art should follow lines in nature, like the grain of an axe-handle."

Ax-helve: the handle or shaft of an axe.

Horse's hoof: the shape of the bottom of the axe head, which often has a curved, hoof-like appearance.

Snake… Garden: in Genesis, the first book of the Bible, chapter 3, the serpent tempts Eve to eat fruit from the forbidden tree of knowledge of good and evil (1–5); Eve eats the fruit and gives some to Adam, who also eats it (6).

The Grindstone:

Grindstone: a tool used for sharpening metal tools and implements.

Father-Time: time is personified as an old man carrying a scythe, a tool used for cutting crops such as grass or wheat, with a long-curved blade at the end of a long pole, attached to which are one or two short handles.

Oblate Spheroid: a shape that is flattened at the poles, like a slightly squashed sphere.

Whetter: someone who sharpens blades or tools.

Paul's Wife

Twitted: tease, taunt, usually in a good-humored way.

Jilted: suddenly rejected or abandoned.

Tamarack: coniferous tree, known for its tough timber and resin.

Half-breed squaw: this is offensive and derogatory; it reflects racist attitudes towards Native American women that were common in the period when Frost's poem was written and published.

Yarn: a long, often exaggerated or incredible story.

Stretcher: a colloquial expression for a story that stretches the truth or seems unbelievable.

Sawyer: someone whose occupation involves sawing wood into planks or boards.

Dug-out: a hollowed-out log.

Midges: a small two-winged fly that is often seen in swarms near water or marshy areas where it breeds.

Catamount: refers to a mountain or hill, a name used for mountains in the northeastern United States, derived from "cat of the mountain," a term used for various wildcats like cougars or lynxes.

Kettle valley: a depression or hollow in the landscape formed by retreating glaciers.

Wild Grapes

Eurydice: in Greek mythology, Orpheus descended to the underworld to retrieve his wife Eurydice, who had died. He was allowed to lead her back to the world of the living on the condition that he did not look back at her until they reached the surface. He looked back too soon, and Eurydice was lost to him forever.

Glade: secluded clearing in a forest.

Leif the Lucky's German: Leif Erikson, the Norse explorer who is believed to have reached the coast of North America sometime around 970–1000 CE. Frost uses this historical allusion to describe how the grapes are growing abundantly around the speaker, as they might have grown around Leif Erikson's German foster-father in the newly discovered Vinland, which in Old Norse means "wine land," referring to wild grapes or berries found growing there.

Hardhack: a shrub that can form dense thickets.

Evolutionist: someone who accepts and supports the scientific theory of evolution, especially Charles Darwin's theory of the evolution of plant and animal species through natural selection. Darwin's *On the Origin of Species* was published in 1859.

Hang-and-let-hang: a passive acceptance of the situation, a surrender to circumstances.

Place for a Third

Boughten: an archaic form of the word "bought," purchased or obtained by buying, as opposed to something that is homemade or inherited.

Two Witches:

"Button, button…": a traditional children's game often referenced in literature and popular culture. Players form a circle, and one player hides a button in their hands while the others guess where it is.

Ralle the Sioux Control: a mysterious figure, here implying a connection to Native American spirituality or mysticism, specifically of the Sioux tribe. "Control" could imply that Ralle is a spirit guide or a medium's control spirit.

Bulkhead: a type of entrance, often with slanted doors, leading to a cellar or basement.

Brittle: easily broken or shattered; fragile or delicate; flexibility or resilience.

Joints: connections between bones.

Scribble: describes the erratic movement of the skeleton as it climbs the stairs.

*The Wild Colonial Boy*: an old Irish-Australian folk ballad.

Tote Road: a rough road or trail used for hauling supplies in logging operations or other rural industries; a path through the forest; a rural backroad or trail.

Hog Reeve in March meeting: a hog reeve was a minor town official in New England responsible for dealing with stray pigs and enforcing fencing laws; the annual town meeting was held in the month of March. The word "reeve" derives from the Old English term *gerefa*, which referred to a high-ranking official under Anglo-Saxon kings.

Wentworth: a town in Grafton County, New Hampshire. There is no Wentworth County.

Warrant: to guarantee or promise with certainty, assure or declare with confidence.

Grafton County: located in west central New Hampshire.

Scarified: cut and remove debris; mark or break up a surface; criticize severely and hurtfully.

Cribber: refers to a horse with a habit called cribbing, when it bites a fixed object (like a fence or stall door) with its incisors, arches its neck, and sucks in air.

Kiting: refers to a witch's supposed ability to fly on a broomstick.

Ridgepole: the highest horizontal beam or timber at the peak of a roof.

Rogers' Rangers: here, a metaphor to emphasize the witch's self-proclaimed power, independence, and versatility. Rogers' Rangers was a company of soldiers from New Hampshire raised by Major Robert Rogers (1731–1795) and attached to the British Army during the Seven Years' War (French and Indian War, 1754–1763). The unit was merged into the New England Colonies' army as an independent ranger company. Rangers were known for their adaptability, toughness, and ability to survive in harsh conditions.

All is, if I'd a-known when I was young: Frost marked this line in a friend's copy of his poems as an example of "the true New England vernacular."

An Empty Threat

Hudson's Bay: a large bay in northeastern Canada; historically significant for the fur trade; here, suggesting a remote, northern wilderness location. Henry Hudson (c. 1565–1611) was an English seaman and navigator, best known for his explorations of the Arctic and North America in the early seventeenth century.

Skiff: a shallow, flat-bottomed open boat with sharp bow and square stern.

Wind-break: a natural or artificial barrier that provides shelter from the wind.

French Indian Esquimaux: mixed French, Native American, and Inuit ("Esquimaux") ancestry.

Great Auk: a large, extinct, flightless auk (seabird) of the North Atlantic.

A Fountain, A Bottle, A Donkey's Ears, and Some Books

Mica mountain: a shiny silicate mineral with a layered structure, found as minute scales in granite and other rocks, or as crystals; here, a potential source of wealth.

Kinsman: Kinsman Notch, a mountain pass in the White Mountains of New Hampshire.

Mormons: members or followers of a millenarian Christian movement founded in the U.S. in 1830 by Joseph Smith Jr. (1805–1844); members of the Church of Jesus Christ of Latter-day Saints.

Settlement: a place, typically one that has been uninhabited, where people establish a community.

Baptismal font: a receptacle in a church for the water used in baptism, typically a freestanding stone structure.

Masonry: stonework.

Thrilly: easily excited or thrilled, suggesting naivety or eagerness for new experiences.

Marshall: a name associated with a conservation area located in the White Mountains region of New Hampshire.

Hell-for-leather: a phrase believed to originate from horseback riding, referring to the effect on a leather saddle when riding a horse as fast as possible; rapid movement, reckless behavior.

Lave: from Old English *lafian*, from Latin *lavare*, "to wash."

Sills: a shelf or slab of stone, wood, or metal at the foot of a window or doorway.

Horn of plenty: abundance and overflowing bounty, which are common associations with the horn of plenty or cornucopia, a goat's horn overflowing with flowers, fruit, and corn.

I Will Sing You One-O

*En masse*: French, "in a mass," in a group, all together.

Beaded fur: the texture and appearance of snow accumulating on the glass, comparing it to the intricate pattern of beads on fur.

Sigmas and taus: in this context, Frost is using Greek letters (sigma σ and tau τ) to represent stars or constellations.

Nova: a star showing a sudden large increase in brightness and then slowly returning to its original state.

Fragmentary Blue

In relation to this poem, Frost told a friend: "All we do in life is a clarification after we stir things up."

Savants: French, literally, "knowing person," present participle (used as a noun) of *savoir*; a very learned or talented person, especially one distinguished in a particular field of science or the arts.

Whet: sharpen the blade of a tool or weapon; excite, stimulate.

Fire and Ice

Frost was inspired by a conversation with the prominent astronomer Harlow Shapley (1885–1972) about how the world might end, either the sun exploding (fire) or the earth freezing (ice).

Dust of Snow

Rued: repent, bitterly regret.

To E. T.

E. T.: this poem is dedicated to Frost's close friend and fellow poet Edward Thomas (1878–1917), killed in World War I, in the Battle of Arras, northeastern France, April-May 1917. The toll of the dead and wounded was very high, with the British suffering 158,000 casualties and the Germans 130,000. It ended as a costly stalemate, with little change to the overall strategic situation on the Western Front.

Vimy Ridge: a site of fierce combat during the battle.

Rhine: a major river, 760 miles, in western Europe.

Nothing Gold Can Stay

Eden: the place where Adam and Eve lived in the Biblical account of Creation, from which they were expelled for disobediently eating the fruit of the tree of the knowledge of good and evil.

The Runaway

Frost said about this poem: "I added the moral at the end, just for the pleasure of the aggrieved tone of voice."

Little Morgan: the Morgan horse is one of the earliest horse breeds developed in the United States, tracing its lineage back to a stallion named Figure, owned by the teacher, composer, and horse breeder Justin Morgan (1747–1798).

Winter-broken: accustomed to winter conditions, especially snow.

Stall and bin: the stall is a stable or enclosed area where horses are kept;

bin is a storage area for feed or other supplies.

Stopping by Woods on a Snowy Evening

Frost told a friend that this poem was his "best bid for remembrance." Often asked about its meaning, he replied on one occasion: "That one I've been more bothered with than anybody has ever been with any poem in just the pressing it for more than it should be pressed for. It means enough without its being pressed. That's all right, you know. I don't say that somebody shouldn't press it, but I don't want it to be there."

For Once, Then, Something

Well-curbs: raised edge or a protective structure that surrounds the top of a well.

Blue-Butterfly Day

Mire: a stretch of swampy or boggy ground; soft and slushy mud or dirt.

The Onset

Peeper's silver croak: the peeper is a type of small frog.

Withered brake: refers to bracken or bracken fern, a type of fern that grows densely on woodland floors. During winter, these ferns turn brown and curl up, resembling dried paper.

To Earthward

This poem was important to Frost. He said about it: "one of the greatest changes my nature has undergone is of record in 'To Earthward.'"

Musk: a strong-smelling reddish-brown substance which is secreted by the male musk deer for scent-marking; also, musk plant or musk flower.

Honeysuckle: a climbing shrub with tubular flowers that are fragrant and of two colors or shades, opening in the evening for pollination by moths.

Clove: the dried flower bud of a tropical tree, used as a pungent aromatic spice.

Good-by and Keep Cold

Girdled: Girdling happens when the bark and cambium (plant tissue) layer of a tree are removed or severely damaged in a complete ring around the trunk or branch, the result of human, animal, or natural causes.

Browse: the tender shoots and leaves of trees and shrubs that animals feed on.

Grouse: a medium to large game bird with a plump body and feathered legs.

Arboreal: living in or related to trees.

Two Look at Two

Buck: male of deer or horned animal.

A Brook in the City

Elbow-crook: the bend of an elbow.

Hearth-stone: flat stone forming a fireplace.

Staunch: stop or restrict.

The Kitchen Chimney

Castles…: "castles built in air" is a well-known phrase referring to unrealistic or impractical plans and dreams.

A Boundless Moment

Paradise-in-bloom: not a specific type of flower, but here evokes the notion of a perfect, blooming paradise.

Evening in a Sugar Orchard

Stoke: add coal or other solid fuel to a fire

Leo, Orion, and the Pleiades: constellations, clusters of stars.

Misgiving

Fain: compelled by the circumstances; obliged; with pleasure, gladly.

A Hillside Thaw

Twitter: of a bird, to give a call consisting of repeated tremulous or quivering sounds.

Scuttled: run hurriedly or furtively with short quick steps.

The Need of Being Versed in Country Things

Phoebes: American bird, mainly with gray-brown or blackish plumage, known to nest on human structures and return to the same nesting sites year after year.

In an earlier version of the final two lines, Frost wrote:

But one had to be versed in New England Ways
Not to believe the Phoebes wept.

## ADDITIONAL POEMS

When *A Boy's Will* was published in 1913, it included three poems Frost decided to omit from the reprint of this book in his *Collected Poems* in 1930: "Asking for Roses," "In Equal Sacrifice," and "Spoils of the Dead." The 1949 edition of *Complete Poems* and subsequent reprintings also omitted them.

Below, are the three poems. You might enjoy reading and thinking about them and speculating about what might have prompted Frost to omit them.

In "Asking for Roses," the phrase "in the gloaming" refers to the period of twilight or dusk, specifically the time just after sunset when the light begins to fade but has not yet completely disappeared. "Old Herrick" is Robert Herrick (1591–1674), a prominent English poet and Anglican cleric, best known for lyrics on the themes of love, nature, and the passage of time.

"In Equal Sacrifice" centers on Sir James Douglas (1286–1330), a historical figure and loyal servant of Robert the Bruce (1274–1329), i.e., Robert I of Scotland, celebrated as a national hero in Scotland for his pivotal role in the Wars of Scottish Independence against England. Douglas here is depicted leaving his homeland to fight in the Holy Land, the area between the Mediterranean Sea and the eastern bank of the Jordan River, encompassing modern-day Israel, Palestine, parts of Jordan, and southern Syria. For Christians, this region was sacred because it was the birthplace of Jesus Christ and the site of his ministry, crucifixion, and resurrection. The "Moor": the Moors were a historical group of Muslim peoples, primarily of North African origin. They invaded and settled in the Iberian Peninsula (modern-day Spain and Portugal) during the early Middle Ages.

# ASKING FOR ROSES

A house that lacks, seemingly, mistress and master,
  With doors that none but the wind ever closes,
Its floor all littered with glass and with plaster;
  It stands in a garden of old-fashioned roses.

I pass by that way in the gloaming with Mary;
  "I wonder," I say, "who the owner of those is."
"Oh, no one you know," she answers me airy,
  "But one we must ask if we want any roses."

So we must join hands in the dew coming coldly
  There in the hush of the wood that reposes,
And turn and go up to the open door boldly,
  And knock to the echoes as beggars for roses.

"Pray, are you within there, Mistress Who-were-you?"
  'Tis Mary that speaks and our errand discloses.
"Pray, are you within there? Bestir you, bestir you!
  'Tis summer again; there's two come for roses.

"A word with you, that of the singer recalling—
  Old Herrick: a saying that every maid knows is
A flower unplucked is but left to the falling,
  And nothing is gained by not gathering roses."

We do not loosen our hands' intertwining
  (Not caring so very much what she supposes),
There when she comes on us mistily shining
  And grants us by silence the boon of her roses.

# IN EQUAL SACRIFICE

Thus of old the Douglas did:
He left his land as he was bid
With the royal heart of Robert the Bruce
In a golden case with a golden lid,

To carry the same to the Holy Land;
By which we see and understand
That that was the place to carry a heart
At loyalty and love's command,

And that was the case to carry it in.
The Douglas had not far to win
Before he came to the land of Spain,
Where long a holy war had been

Against the too-victorious Moor;
And there his courage could not endure
Not to strike a blow for God
Before he made his errand sure.

And ever it was intended so,
That a man for God should strike a blow,
No matter the heart he has in charge
For the Holy Land where hearts should go.

But when in battle the foe were met,
The Douglas found him sore beset,
With only strength of the fighting arm
For one more battle passage yet—

And that as vain to save the day
As bring his body safe away—
Only a signal deed to do
And a last sounding word to say.

The heart he wore in a golden chain
He swung and flung forth into the plain,

And followed it crying "Heart or death!"
And fighting over it perished fain.

So may another do of right,
Give a heart to the hopeless fight,
The more of right the more he loves;
So may another redouble might

For a few swift gleams of the angry brand,
Scorning greatly not to demand
In equal sacrifice with his
The heart he bore to the Holy Land.

# SPOILS OF THE DEAD

Two fairies it was
  On a still summer day
Came forth in the woods
  With the flowers to play.

The flowers they plucked
  They cast on the ground
For others, and those
  For still others they found.

Flower-guided it was
  That they came as they ran
On something that lay
  In the shape of a man.

The snow must have made
  The feathery bed
When this one fell
  On the sleep of the dead.

But the snow was gone
  A long time ago,
And the body he wore
  Nigh gone with the snow.

The fairies drew near
  And keenly espied
A ring on his hand
  And a chain at his side.

They knelt in the leaves
  And eerily played
With the glittering things,
  And were not afraid.

And when they went home
  To hide in their burrow,

They took them along
  To play with to-morrow.

When *you* came on death,
  Did you not come flower-guided
Like the elves in the wood?
  I remember that I did.

But I recognised death
  With sorrow and dread,
And I hated and hate
  The spoils of the dead.

# ROBERT FROST ON POETRY

S OMETIME IN THE 1930s, Frost made these cogent observations about his literary work and career. "Ward" might be Susan Hayes Ward, a New York literary figure who encouraged him early on. She was poetry editor of *The Independent*, a weekly magazine published in New York City. It was edited by her brother, William Hayes Ward, and it's possible that Frost is referring to him.

Frost's first published poem, "My Butterfly: An Elegy," appeared in the November 8, 1894, issue.

"Old Carl" is Carl Sandburg (1878–1967), an American poet, biographer, journalist, and editor. His books of poetry include *Chicago Poems* (1916), *Cornhuskers* (1918), and *Smoke and Steel* (1920).


Perhaps when that preacher friend of Ward's looked me up shortly after my first poem appeared in *The Independent* and talked to me about it, something providential was happening to me. I'm sure the old gentleman didn't have slightest idea he was having any effect on a very stubborn youngster who thought he knew what he knew. But something he said actually changed the whole course of my writing. It all became purposeful.

One day as we talked he said to me that when he read my poems it was just like hearing me talk. I didn't know until then what it was I was after. When he said that to me it all became clear. I was after poetry that talked. If my poems were talking poems—if to read one of them you heard a voice—that would be to my liking! So, I went to the great poets, Chaucer and Shakespeare to Coleridge and Wordsworth. And looked for this very thing in their lines. I will admit, when I have been quoted on the matter I been made to speak rather mistily. But one thing must always be kept in mind: Whenever I write a line it is because that line has already been spoken clearly by a voice within my mind, an audible voice.

There has been a great hue and cry raised over what I have had to say regarding voice posturing, or as I have sometimes called it, the sound of sense. When I first began to write poetry—before the illumination of what possibilities there are in the sound of sense came to me—I was writing largely, though not exclusively, after the pattern of the past. For every poet begins that way—following some pattern, or group of patterns. It is only when he has outgrown the pattern and sees clearly for himself his own way that he has really started to become. You may go back to all those early poems of mine in *A Boy's Will*, and some that are left out of it. You will find me there using the traditional clichés. Even "Into My Own" has an "as 'twere." In "Stars" there is a line "O'er the tumultuous snow"; while in my very first poem, "My Butterfly," I was even guilty of "theeing" and "thouing," a crime I have not committed since. For sentiment, perhaps, I have left all of these as first printed, though I have made one change, it will be observed, even in "My Butterfly," as it appears in *The Collected Poems*, transforming "'wildered" into "bewildered." The young poet is prone to echo all the pleasing sounds he has heard in his scattered reading. He is apt to look on the musical value of the lines, the metrical perfection, as all that matters. He has not listened for the voice within his mind, speaking the lines and giving them the value of sound.

There is another angle to this. It is suggested by a proneness to the unique. It is the value of current words in writing poetry. It has been a long time since I consciously fell into any of the clichés so common in verse. It has been a long time since I used any word not common in everyday speech. For example, I would never think of using the word "casement" for window in general. Whenever I have used that word, which I have occasionally, it was because I was writing about *that* kind of a window—never for window as such. In this, perhaps, I have unconsciously tried to do just what Chaucer did when the language was young and untried and virile. I have sought only those words I had met up with as a boy in New Hampshire, working on farms during the summer vacations. I listened to the men with whom I worked, and found that I could make out their conversation as they talked together out of ear-shot, even when I had not plainly heard the words they spoke. When I started to carry their conversation over into poetry, I could hear their voices, and the sound posture differentiated between one and the other. It was the sense of sound

I have been talking about. In some sort of way like this I have been able to write poetry, where characters talk, and, though not without infinite pains, to make it plain to the reader which character is saying the lines, without having to place his name before it, as is done in the drama.

Because I have been, what some might call, careless about the so-called proper beat and rhythm of my lines, there have been those who think I write free verse. Now, I am not dead set against *vers libre*; but you know there is no idea you cannot express beautifully and satisfactorily in the iambic pentameter. Much of my verse is written in this form—blank, unrhymed verse. I have always maintained that it takes form to properly perform, and free verse has no form, and so its performance is meager. These fellows, old Carl and the rest, think they are being free, but they aren't. The greatest freedom poetry can attain is having form, a frame, to work in. Free verse is batting a ball into space and wondering why it doesn't return to the batter. Poetry written in form is like batting a ball against the side of a wall and feeling it return to the bat. A picture frame with its four simple lines is necessary to the showing of a picture. Try it and see. The frame thus becomes a part, even, of the picture. Old Carl tries hard to write without form, but he has a form without knowing it. When he repeats himself, as he sometimes does, he is following a certain form, a slight form.

Source: Louis Mertins, *Robert Frost: Life and Talks-Walking*. Norman: University of Oklahoma Press, 1965. 197–198.

# BIOGRAPHICAL TIMELINE

Robert Frost lived for nearly nine decades. He traveled to and resided and worked in many places in the United States and abroad. He held a variety of academic appointments; he presented an extraordinary number of lectures and poetry readings; and he received many honors and more than forty honorary degrees. His relationships with his wife and children were complicated and often painful, and he suffered frequent periods of illness and hospitalizations. In this timeline, I've noted some, not all, of the important events and highlights. In Further Reading, I've listed biographies that tell the full story of Frost's personal life and literary career.

"I have made a lifetime study of what I can say."

"Poems are all that matter. The utmost of ambition is to lodge a few poems where they will be hard to get rid of."

"Writing, teaching a little, and farming.
The three strands of my life."

1874    Robert Lee Frost, named after Confederate general Robert E. Lee, born March 26, in San Francisco, California. "It's where I came from, the first place I really knew.... The first place in my memory, a place I still go back to in my dreams."

Parents: William Prescott Frost Jr. (1850–1885), born in Lawrence, Massachusetts, Harvard graduate (*cum laude*, Phi Beta Kappa, class of 1872), journalist, newspaper editor, minor political figure; and Isabelle Moodie (1844–1900), born in Edinburgh, Scotland, a schoolteacher.

"I suppose my father was a grafter, boodler [i.e., politician who receives *boodle*, slang for money, through corrupt means]. At least he wanted to be whether he ever was able to realize on his desires or not. He associated all the time with crooked politicians. It was taken as a matter of course."

1877–78    Attends Sunday school; mother gives him religious instruction and reads aloud Bible stories.

1880–82    In public school, begins first grade, withdraws because of illness; returns 1881, second grade, becomes ill; withdraws again and is taught at home.

"I hated school and wouldn't go if I could play off sick or get up some other excuse."

1883    Mother reads to him the works of many poets and authors, including Shakespeare, Wordsworth, Tennyson, Longfellow. He recalled his "favorite" was Emerson; he said, "Emerson was great. Great, great, great."

1885    May: father dies of tuberculosis.

Family relocates to live with father's family, in Lawrence, Massachusetts, and then with relatives in Amherst, Hillsborough County, New Hampshire.

Population of Lawrence: 44,654.

1886    Mother works as schoolteacher, fifth to eighth grades, Salem district school, New Hampshire; she continues to read literature to Frost and his sister Jeanie (1876–1929).

1888–89    Completes grammar school and enters Lawrence High School; becomes interested in Latin poetry and verse forms, and in astronomy, botany, and theory of evolution.

"I read Virgil, Homer, Horace, and the rest—all before I even went to college."

1890    "La Noche Triste" (The Sad Night), first published poem, Lawrence High School *Bulletin*, April.

1890–93    Mother teaches at four public schools in Methuen, Massachusetts.

1891    Editor of the high school *Bulletin*; meets and falls in love with fellow student Elinor Miriam White (b. 1872).

1892    Graduates from high school, co-valedictorian with Elinor White.

Begins first semester at Dartmouth College, Hanover, New Hampshire, withdraws in December. "I wasn't suited for the place."

Purchases copy of F. T. Palgrave's anthology, *The Golden Treasury of the Best Songs and Lyrical Poems in the English Language* (1861; rev. ed., 1891). "I liked discovering it on my own… A poem is best read in the light of all the other poems ever written."

"As for poems my favorites are and have been these: Keats's 'Hyperion', Shelley's 'Prometheus', Tennyson's 'Morte D'Arthur', and Browning's 'Saul'.… Besides these I am fond of the whole collection of Palgrave's."

In later years, Frost said his favorite poem was Milton's "Lycidas." On other occasions, he named Emerson's "Uriel" as "the greatest Western poem yet."

1893    Works in a mill in Lawrence; reads a "pocket Shakespeare" during breaks; teaches school in Methuen.

1894    Teaches, spring term, grammar school in Salem.

Fails to convince Elinor to marry him; in despair, travels in November to the Dismal Swamp (wetlands and dense forests) on the North Carolina/Virginia border; stays there for three weeks. "I was trying to throw my life away."

November 8: first published poem, "My Butterfly: An Elegy," front page, *The Independent* (New York City), paid $15.

"You're always believing ahead of your evidence. What was the evidence I could write a poem? I just believed it. The most creative thing in us is to believe in a thing."

1895    Living in Lawrence; works as reporter, tutor, teacher.

December: marries Elinor.

1896    In Lawrence; works as a teacher.

September: Elliott, son, born.

| | |
|---|---|
| 1897 | Lives in Cambridge, Massachusetts. |
| | September: begins studies at Harvard College. |
| 1898 | Reads book by Harvard professor and philosopher William James, *Psychology: Briefer Course* (1892); "my greatest inspiration, when I was a student, was a man whose classes I never attended." Later influenced by French philosopher Henri Bergson's *Creative Evolution* (1911). |
| 1899 | His teachers at Harvard include renowned philosophers Josiah Royce and George Santayana and literary scholar G. L. Kittredge. |
| | March: withdraws from Harvard. |
| | April: Lesley, daughter, born (d. 1983). |
| 1900 | July: Elliott dies of cholera; family moves to thirty-acre farm, Derry, New Hampshire, purchased for him by his grandfather, William Prescott Frost Sr.; he spends the next nine years there. |
| | Population of Derry: 3,587. |
| | November: mother dies of cancer. |
| | During this period, 1900–1909, Frost wrote nearly all the poems included in *A Boy's Will*, a number in *North of Boston*, and many in *Mountain Interval*. |
| 1901–02 | Works on farm; reads Henry David Thoreau's *Walden* (1854) for the first time. "In one book he surpasses everything we have had in America." |
| | After grandfather's death in July 1901, lives on Derry farm rent-free and receives an annuity, $500 per year for ten years, then $800 for subsequent years; the farm to become his property in 1911; not obliged to repay loans previously made to him by his grandfather. |
| 1902 | May: Carol, son, born. |
| 1903 | June: Irma, daughter, born (d. 1967). |
| 1905 | March: Marjorie, daughter, born. |
| 1906 | Teaches English literature at Pinkerton Academy in Derry. Says in a statement about its English curriculum: |

"Expression in oral reading rather than intelligent comment is made the test of appreciation."

1907    June: Elinor Bettina, daughter, born, lives only three days.

William James, *Pragmatism: A New Name for Some Old Ways of Thinking*

1909    Ezra Pound, *Personae*

1911    Leaves Pinkerton Academy; teaches at State Normal School, Plymouth, New Hampshire.

Population of Plymouth: 1,948.

November: sells farm in Derry.

1912    Resigns teaching position. "It'll never do to go on like this. I'll just turn into a machine, and what will happen to my poetry? We must get away, somewhere, anywhere—only away."

August: sails with family to England; focuses on poetry.

Prepares manuscript of first book of poems, *A Boy's Will*, which is accepted for publication. "To be a poet is a condition, not a profession."

Lives in rented cottage, Beaconsfield, Buckinghamshire, twenty-three miles north/northwest of London.

1912–13  Meets Ezra Pound, W. B. Yeats, Robert Bridges, and other poets and writers; becomes close friends with critic and essayist Edward Thomas and encourages him to pursue poetry.

"We had never lived among poets before, working poets."

1913    *A Boy's Will*; from 1894 to the appearance of this book, a period of nineteen years, Frost had published only fourteen poems.

1914    *North of Boston*

Does not want "a success with the critical few" but "to get outside to the general reader who buys books by the thousands."

Moves with family to Dymock, Gloucestershire, 120 miles west/northwest of London.

1914–18  July 1914–November 1918: World War I.

1915  February: leaves England, arrives in New York City; *North of Boston* (February) and *A Boy's Will* (April) published in the U.S. Family moves to farm in Franconia, New Hampshire.

May: first professional poetry reading, Tufts University, Medford, Massachusetts.

Meets poet E. A. Robinson and poet and editor Louis Untermeyer.

*North of Boston* is very successful; first year of sales, 20,000 copies.

1916  First speaking tour, in New England and along East coast.

*Mountain Interval*

1917  Moves family to Amherst, Massachusetts; begins teaching at Amherst College. "What we do in college is to get over our little mindedness. Education—to get it you have to hang around till you catch on."

Amherst College enrollment, 1916–17: 505 students; tuition, $140; room and board, $6–8 per week.

April: Edward Thomas killed in action, northern France. "The only brother I ever had.... He more than anyone else was accessory to what I had done and was doing. We were together to the exclusion of every other person and interest all through 1914—1914 was our year. I never had, I never shall have another such year of friendship."

T. S. Eliot, *Prufrock and Other Observations*; Ezra Pound, *Lustra and Other Poems*

1919  Elected president of New England Poetry Club.

1920  Resigns from teaching position at Amherst College. Buys farm in  South Shaftsbury, Vermont.

Ezra Pound, *Hugh Selwyn Mauberley*

1921  Begins association (which will continue for four decades) with Bread Loaf School of English, an intensive summer master's and continuing education program, Middlebury College, Vermont.

"To know a moment when you see it—that is to be a teacher. 'There you are—you've said it' is the most influencing thing you can say to a person."

1921–23   Poet in residence at the University of Michigan.

1922   T. S. Eliot, *The Waste Land*

1923   *Selected Poems*, dedicated to Edward Thomas. Returns to teaching at Amherst College.

*New Hampshire*

Wallace Stevens, *Harmonium*

1924–26   Pulitzer Prize for *New Hampshire*. "It is absurd to think that the only way to tell if a poem is lasting is to wait and see if it lasts. The right reader of a good poem can tell the moment it strikes him that he has taken an immortal wound—that he will never get over it."

1925   F. Scott Fitzgerald, *The Great Gatsby*; Ernest Hemingway, *In Our Time*

1926   New appointment at Amherst College.

"Long ago I gave up the idea of asking my students to tell me what I knew that I might discover if they knew as much as I did. Now in classes I ask questions in the correct sense of the word, for I want them to tell me something new, something I do not know."

Langston Hughes, *The Weary Blues*

1928   Travels with Elinor to England and Ireland. Meets T. S. Eliot.

*West-Running Brook*

W. B. Yeats, *The Tower*

1929   September: sister Jeanie dies in a state mental hospital, in Augusta, Maine. Frost moves to 150-acre "Gully Farm" in South Shaftsbury, Vermont.

William Faulkner, *The Sound and the Fury*

1930   Elected to membership in American Academy of Arts and Letters.

*Collected Poems*

"Every poem is the epitome of the great predicament; a figure of the will braving alien entanglements."

Hart Crane, *The Bridge*

1931    Pulitzer Prize for *Collected Poems.*

1934    May: Marjorie dies from complications following child-birth. "The noblest of all of us is dead and has taken our hearts out of the world with her."

Frost and Elinor travel to Key West, Florida. "We are on the point of the island exactly between the Gulf of Mexico and the Atlantic Ocean. The wave breaks twenty feet from our door."

1935    February: meets Wallace Stevens in Key West.

May: in an address at Milton Academy, in Milton, Massachusetts: "Writing free verse is like playing tennis with the net down."

1936    *A Further Range*

1937    Pulitzer Prize for *A Further Range.*

1938    March: Elinor dies of heart failure, age sixty-five, in Gainesville, Florida; she and Frost were married forty-two years; she "has been the unspoken half of everything I wrote."

Friends with Theodore Morrison, writer, critic, and director of Bread Loaf Writers Conference; forms close relationship (which will continue for many years) with Morrison's wife Kathleen (Kay). "Then came this girl stepping innocently into my days to give me something to think of besides dark regrets…. We wanted to marry. It was all decided. But you know how matters seem at times—others to think of."

1939    Awarded Gold Medal by National Institute of Arts and Letters in New York City; begins appointment to teach at Harvard.

*Collected Poems*, expanded edition.

John Steinbeck, *The Grapes of Wrath*

| | |
|---|---|
| 1940 | October: Carol, age thirty-eight, commits suicide. |
| 1941 | March: gives lecture, "The Role of a Poet in a Democracy," at the Library of Congress, Washington, DC. |
| | Moves to 35 Brewster Street, Cambridge, Massachusetts. |
| 1942 | *A Witness Tree* |
| 1943 | Pulitzer Prize for *A Witness Tree*; begins appointment (continues to 1949) at Dartmouth College. |
| 1945 | *A Masque of Reason* (comic/satiric play). |
| 1946 | Robert Lowell, *Lord Weary's Castle* |
| 1947 | *Steeple Bush*, dedicated to his six grandchildren; *A Masque of Mercy* (poetic drama). T. S. Eliot visits Frost in Cambridge. |
| 1948 | Accepts appointment to return to Amherst College to lecture, teach, and meet with students. |
| 1949 | *Complete Poems of Robert Frost* |
| | Arthur Miller, *Death of a Salesman* |
| 1952 | Ralph Ellison, *Invisible Man* |
| | Ernest Hemingway, *The Old Man and the Sea* |
| 1953 | Awarded Fellowship of the Academy of American Poets. |
| 1954 | Delegate to World Congress of Writers, São Paulo, Brazil. |
| 1954–57 | Travels in the United States and Europe, gives many readings ("barding around"), receives many honors. |
| 1955 | Philip Larkin, *The Less Deceived* |
| 1956 | Allen Ginsberg, *Howl and Other Poems* |
| 1957 | Ted Hughes, *The Hawk in the Rain* |
| 1958 | Receives Emerson-Thoreau Medal of the American Academy of Arts and Sciences. |
| 1959 | Honorary Consultant in the Humanities at the Library of Congress. |
| | Honored at dinner celebration, eighty-fifth birthday, New York City. |
| | Lorraine Hansberry, *A Raisin in the Sun* |

1960     Congressional Gold Medal.

1961     January: reads poem "The Gift Outright" at the inauguration of President John F. Kennedy. Travels to Greece, Israel, and England.

1962     *In the Clearing*

        March: birthday dinner in Washington, DC, guests include eminent writers and politicians.

        August: travels to Soviet Union and meets Nikita Khrushchev, the premier and the first secretary of the Communist Party. "We were charmed with each other. I'm very fond of him. He's a lovable man. I could talk out to him and he could talk out to me.... We were both so affable that we may both have been self-deceived."

1963     January: receives the Bollingen Prize for Poetry.

        January 29: dies in Boston hospital, from heart complications following prostate surgery; June 16, ashes interred in Frost family plot in Old Bennington Cemetery, Vermont. Gravestone inscription: "I had a lover's quarrel with the world."

### FROST'S CAREER AS A TEACHER

"I always go to farming when I can. I always make a failure,
and then I have to go to teaching."

1890s   Teaches in grammar schools.

1906–11  Pinkerton Academy, Derry, New Hampshire.

1911–12  New Hampshire State Normal School, Plymouth, New Hampshire.

1917–21  Amherst College, Amherst, Massachusetts.

1921–23  University of Michigan, Ann Arbor, Poet-in-Residence, then Fellow in Creative Arts.

1923–25  Amherst College, Professor of English.

1925–26  University of Michigan, Fellow in Letters.

1926–38  Amherst College.

1936     Charles Eliot Norton Lecturer, Harvard University, Cambridge, Massachusetts.

1939–40  Harvard, Ralph Waldo Emerson Fellow in Poetry.

1943–49  Dartmouth College, Hanover, New Hampshire, Ticknor Fellow in Humanities.

1949–63  Amherst College, Simpson Lecturer in Literature.

# FURTHER READING

## BOOKS OF POETRY

One of Robert Frost's biographers, Jeffrey Meyers, has noted: "Frost wrote about eight poems a year, averaged a book every seven years, and produced about four hundred poems during the fifty years (1913–1962) between his first and last volumes."

These are the books published in Frost's lifetime:

*A Boy's Will* (1913)
*North of Boston* (1914)
*Mountain Interval* (1916)
*New Hampshire* (1923)
*West-Running Brook* (1928)
*Collected Poems* (1930; expanded and updated, 1939)
*A Further Range* (1936)
*A Witness Tree* (1942)
*Steeple Bush* (1947)
*Complete Poems* (1949)
*In the Clearing* (1962)

## PRIMARY SOURCES

*Collected Poems, Prose, and Plays*, edited by Richard Poirier and Mark Richardson. New York: Library of America, 1995.

*The Collected Prose of Robert Frost*, edited by Mark Richardson. Cambridge, MA: Harvard University Press, 2007.

*Elected Friends: Robert Frost & Edward Thomas To One Another*, edited by Matthew Spencer. New York: Handsel Books, 2003.

*The Letters of Robert Frost*. 3 vols. to date, edited by Mark Richardson, Donald Sheehy, et al. Cambridge, MA: Harvard University Press, 2014–.

*The Notebooks of Robert Frost*, edited by Robert Faggen. Cambridge, MA: Harvard University Press, 2006.

*The Poetry of Robert Frost: The Collected Poems, Complete and Unabridged*, edited by Edward Connery Lathem. New York: Henry Holt and Company, 1979.

## REFERENCE

Cramer, Jeffrey S. *Robert Frost Among His Poems: A Literary Companion to the Poet's Own Biographical Contexts and Associations*. Jefferson, NC: McFarland, 1996.

Fagan, Deidre. *Critical Companion to Robert Frost: A Literary Reference to His Life and Work*. New York: Facts on File, 2007.

Faggen, Robert, ed. *The Cambridge Companion to Robert Frost*. New York: Cambridge University Press, 2001.

Marcus, Mordecai. *The Poems of Robert Frost: An Explication*. Boston: G.K. Hall, 1991; new ed., 2006.

Richardson, Mark, ed. *Robert Frost in Context*. New York: Cambridge University Press, 2014.

Smith, Virginia F. *A Scientific Companion to Robert Frost*. Clemson, SC: Clemson University Press, 2018.

Tuten, Nancy Lewis, and John Zubizarreta, eds. *The Robert Frost Encyclopedia*. Westport, CT: Greenwood Press, 2001.

## BIOGRAPHIES

Burnshaw, Stanley. *Robert Frost Himself*. New York: G. Braziller, 1986.

Hart, Henry. *The Life of Robert Frost: A Critical Biography*. Chichester, West Sussex, UK: Wiley Blackwell, 2017.

Meyers, Jeffrey. *Robert Frost: A Biography*. Boston: Houghton Mifflin, 1996.

Parini, Jay. *Robert Frost: A Life*. New York: Henry Holt, 1999.

Pritchard, William. *Frost: A Literary Life Reconsidered*. New York: Oxford University Press, 1984.

Sergeant, Elizabeth Shepley. *Robert Frost: Trial by Existence*. New York: Holt, Rinehart, and Winston, 1960.

Thompson, Lawrance, and R. H. Winnick. *Robert Frost: A Biography*. New York: Holt, Rinehart, and Winston, 1981. This is a one-volume condensed edition of a three-volume biography, 1966–1976.

## CRITICAL STUDIES

Brower, Reuben A. *The Poetry of Robert Frost: Constellations of Intention*. New York: Oxford University Press, 1963.

Faggen, Robert. *The Cambridge Introduction to Robert Frost*. New York: Cambridge University Press, 2008.

Kendall, Tim. *The Art of Robert Frost*. New Haven, CT: Yale University Press, 2013.

Orr, David. *The Road Not Taken: Finding America in the Poem Everyone Loves and Almost Everyone Gets Wrong*. New York: Penguin, 2015.

Monteiro, George. *Robert Frost and the New England Renaissance*. Lexington: University of Kentucky Press, 2015.

Pack, Robert. *Belief and Uncertainty in the Poetry of Robert Frost*. Hanover, NH: University Press of New England, 2003.

Poirier, Richard. *Robert Frost: The Work of Knowing*. New York: Oxford University Press, 1977.

Richardson, Mark. *The Ordeal of Robert Frost: The Poet and His Poetics*. Urbana: University of Illinois Press, 1997.

Tharpe, Jac, ed. *Frost: Centennial Essays*. 3 vols. Jackson: University Press of Mississippi, 1974, 1976, 1978.

# INDEX OF TITLES

# INDEX OF FIRST LINES